Populism and Key Concepts in Social and Political Theory

Global Populisms

Series Editors

VOLUME 4

The titles published in this series are listed at *brill.com/gpop*

Populism and Key Concepts in Social and Political Theory

Edited by

Carlos de la Torre and Oscar Mazzoleni

BRILL

LEIDEN | BOSTON

Cover illustration: "Transeunte", 1995. Copyright by Marcelo Aguirre. This painting won the Marco Price of the Monterrey Museum of Contemporary Art in 1995.

Library of Congress Cataloging-in-Publication Data

Names: Torre, Carlos de la, editor. |
Mazzoleni, Oscar, editor.
Title: Populism and key concepts in social and political theory / edited by
Carlos de la Torre and Oscar Mazzoleni.
Description: Leiden ; Boston : Brill, [2023] | Series: Global populisms,
2666-2280 ; volume 4 | Includes index.
Identifiers: LCCN 2023022426 (print) | LCCN 2023022427 (ebook) |
ISBN 9789004512252 (hardback) | ISBN 9789004679016 (ebook)
Subjects: LCSH: Populism. | Political science–Philosophy. | Social
sciences–Philosophy.
Classification: LCC JC423 .P5864 2023 (print) | LCC JC423 (ebook) | DDC
320.56/62–dc23/eng/20230609
LC record available at https://lccn.loc.gov/2023022426
LC ebook record available at https://lccn.loc.gov/2023022427

Typeface for the Latin, Greek, and Cyrillic scripts: "Brill". See and download: brill.com/brill-typeface.

ISSN 2666-2280
ISBN 978-90-04-51225-2 (hardback)
ISBN 978-90-04-67901-6 (e-book)

This book is printed on acid-free paper and produced in a sustainable manner.

In the increasingly crowded field of populism studies, Carlos de la Torre and Oscar Mazzoleni have designed a collection that offers an innovative approach to its subject matter. Instead of the usual populism in this country or that or chapters that focus on parties, the contributions in this collection focus on core social and political concepts such as citizenship, sovereignty, gender, accountability, leadership. The resulting anthology is compact and cohesive. It enables us to see that populism is a concept that cannot be understood independently of its relation to other analytic frames. Scholars of populism will find this collection essential to developing a broader understanding of a form of politics which is now becoming global in its reach.

MABEL BEREZIN, Distinguished Professor of Sociology and Director of Institute for European Studies, Cornell University

This book reacts against a literature on populism that has grown exponentially and is closely interrelated but has gradually become unable to relay to the broader contemporary debates in political science and political sociology, which, however, affect the interpretive relevance of the concept of populism. It does so from multiple perspectives showing how scholarship on such diverse issues as gender, elites, leadership, class, parties, and emotions provides needed context and analytical usefulness to the study of populism. The book then significantly broadens the relevance of populism as an emerging topic needed to understand the contemporary features of classic debates, such as those of the roots of political mobilisation and citizenship. At the same time, it redefines, actualises and expands these debates.

CARLO RUZZA, Senior Professor of Political Sociology at the University of Trento, School of International Studies

This new book edited by top populism experts Carlos de la Torre and Oscar Mazzoleni provides a fresh conceptual look at populism. Key authors in the fields promote a necessary interdisciplinary dialogue that makes populism part of a wider discussion in the Social Sciences. They move beyond insular and self-referential discussions in populism scholarship and connect it to broader conceptual global debates about the politics of the present. This excellent book is a must read for all those interested in past and present challenges to democracy.

FEDERICO FINCHELSTEIN, Professor of History at the New School for Social Research and Eugene Lang College

Contents

PART 3
Actors

Notes on Contributors

Cecilia Biancalana

is a non-tenured assistant professor at the Department of Culture, Politics and Society of the University of Turin. Her research focuses on political ecology, party change, populism, and the relationship between Internet and politics.

Carlos de la Torre

is professor and director of the Center for Larin American Studies at the University of Florida. He has a Ph.D. in Sociology from the New School for Social Research. He is the author of several manuscripts and edited volumes on populism. His most recent books are *Global Populisms* with Treethep Srisanga, (Routledge Press, 2021); *Populisms: A Quick Immersion*, (Tibidabo editions, 2019), and *Populist Seduction in Latin America*, (Ohio University Press, second edition 2010). He is the editor of *The Routledge Handbook of Global Populism*, (Routledge Press, 2019), *The Promises and Perils of Populism: Global Perspectives*, (University Press of Kentucky, 2015) and with Cynthia Arnson, *Latin American Populism of the Twenty First Century*, (Johns Hopkins University Press and Woodrow Wilson Center Press, 2013).

Paula Diehl

is Professor for Political Theory, History of Ideas and Political Culture at the University of Kiel. She is the founding director of the International Populism Network at the University of Kiel. Prof. Diehl received her Ph.D. in political science from the Humboldt University. She was guest professor, among others, at Washington University (St. Louis), Sciences Po (Paris), École des Hautes Études, and Institute for Advanced Studies (Bologna). Diehl's current research projects are dedicated to populism, political representation, and to the concept of the political imaginary.

Reinhard Heinisch

has been Professor of Comparative Austrian Political Science and Department Chair at the University of Salzburg since 2010. His research focuses on radical populism, democracy, and political parties and has appeared in journals such as *Journal of Common Market Studies, Party Politics, European Journal of Political Research, West European Politics, Democratization,* and *Political Studies.* His book publications in English include *Understanding Populist Party Organization* (Palgrave 2016); T*he People and the Nation* (Routledge 2020), Political Populism. A Handbook, (Nomos 2021), and *Politicizing Islam* *in Austria* (Rutgers University Press, forthcoming). His research has been supported by grants from the European Union (Marie Curie, Horizon 2020) and the Swiss and Austrian Science Funds. He remains an associate member of the European Studies Center at the University of Pittsburgh and a regular visiting lecturer at Renmin University of China in Beijing.

Klaudia Koxha

is a Ph.D. candidate at the Salzburg Centre of European Union Studies Doctoral College since 2020 and a visiting scholar at the American University, School of International Service in Washington, District of Columbia. She writes her thesis on "Populism, political parties, and European integration in the Western Balkans." She obtained her Bachelor's Degree in Political Science from the University of Tirana and her Master's Degree in Political Science from the University of Salzburg. During the past years she has contributed to research projects as a research assistant and is co-editor of the forthcoming book "Diverse Voices on Populism – New Accounts from the European 'Periphery'" (Nomos Publishing House).

Alfio Mastropaolo

is emeritus professor of political science at the University of Turin. In 2012 published *Is Democracy a Lost Cause? Paradoxes of an Imperfect Invention*, Colchester, ECPR Press. His last book is *Fare la guerra con altri mezzi. Sociologia storica del governo democratico*, Bologna, Il Mulino, 2023.

Oscar Mazzoleni

is a professor in political science and political sociology at the University of Lausanne. He has a degree in Sociology and Ph.D. in History. He was Visiting Professor and Fellow in various universities including Columbia, Cornell, University of Sorbonne I and Science-Po Paris. His research has been published in international journals such as *Government and Opposition*, *Party Politics*, *Political Studies*, *Comparative European Politics*, and *European Politics and Society*. He is co-editor of *Political Populism. Handbook on Concepts, Questions and Strategies of Research* (Nomos, 2021) and *Sovereignism and Populism: Citizens, Voters and Parties in Western European Democracies* (Routledge, 2021). He is the principal investigator of a four-year international project on populism and conspiracy funded by the national research agencies of Switzerland and Austria.

Enrique Peruzzotti
Ph.D. in Sociology, New School for Social Research is the Chair of the Department of political science and international studies at Torcuato Di Tella University in Buenos Aires and researcher of CONICET. His research interests are in the area of democratization, with a regional focus on Latin America. More specifically, his work analyses transitions to democracy, the strengthening of existing political regimes via social accountability politics processes of democratic innovation, as well as on the challenges that contemporary expressions of populism pose to existing polities. He has published in numerous venues, including *Global Governance, Citizenship Studies, Journal of Democracy, Human Rights Quarterly, Chinese Political Science Review, Journal of Latin American Studies* and *Constellations: An International Journal of Critical and Democratic Theory*.

Kenneth M. Roberts
is the Richard J. Schwartz Professor of Government at Cornell University and a Faculty Fellow of the Democratic Threats and Resilience initiative at Cornell's Mario Einaudi Center for International Studies. His research explores the intersection of political parties, social movements, and populism, with special emphasis on crises of democratic representation in Latin America and beyond. His publications include *Changing Course in Latin America: Party Systems in the Neoliberal Era* (Cambridge University Press), and the recent co-edited volume *Democratic Resilience: Can the United States Withstand Rising Polarization?* (Cambridge University Press). His current research explores polarization and democracy in contemporary Latin American politics.

Luis Roniger
is a comparative political sociologist, Reynolds Professor Emeritus of Latin American Studies, Politics and International Affairs at Wake Forest University, and Associate Professor Emeritus of Sociology and Latin American Studies at the Hebrew University of Jerusalem. He has written pioneer studies on clientelism, political exile and transnational politics. Roniger has published 24 books and over 200 academic journal articles and book chapters; and he serves in editorial boards of academic journals published in Argentina, Colombia, Mexico, Spain, the United Kingdom, Israel, and the United States.

Introduction: Toward Populism as a Dialogical Perspective

Oscar Mazzoleni and Carlos de la Torre

This collective volume aims to create a dialogue between populism and some key concepts in social and political science. While the literature on populism is very rich and diverse, a widespread trend in the current scholarship is the effort to consolidate it as an insular academic sub-field. Populism is a notion that has been adopted by almost all humanities and social sciences. In some disciplines, especially in political science and political sociology, there is a desire to consolidate as a kind of "populist scholarship". Although it does not narrowly form a "paradigm" in the sense of Thomas Kuhn (1970), the populist sub-field has gathered a growing community of scholars sharing concepts and research questions to address the challenges facing contemporary democracies. There are some advantages to building an academic sub-field as such, but the shortcomings are also worth exploring. This book asserts that it is time to move beyond the sub-field and enhance the capacity of populist scholarship to cultivate a dialogue with consolidated traditions in social and political sciences.

1 A Populist Sub-field

In the last decades, an increasing number of global phenomena have been considered through the lens of populism. More and more research on populism is being published in specialized journals and book series, and many recent handbooks on the topic are available (e.g. Rovira Kaltwasser et al. 2017; de la Torre 2019b; Heinisch, Holtz-Bacha and Mazzoleni 2021; Oswald 2021). Thus, the time has come to recognize that, in academic fields, populism is not just a theoretical concept or a label used to describe political reality. The growing importance of this literature in social and political sciences has encouraged the institutionalization of a sub-field usually labelled as "populist scholarship". In academia, populism is more and more a self-referential mood shared by a growing group of scholars and is becoming a global academic sub-field in which theoretical reflections and empirical analysis are shared. Of course, populist scholarship is not just the product of the vast number of academic productions but also the outcome of ongoing controversies surrounding

 | DOI:10.1163/9789004679016_002

populism – namely, the debate over populism as an ideology, political style, political strategy, or political logic, all of which contributes to forming a kind of common ground among scholars. The main consequence of this development is the feeling that populism represents a distinct social and political phenomenon and should be studied as such and not necessarily in connection with other theoretical legacies.

This evolution should not be a surprise. Similar experiences usually occur when a new community of researchers seeks academic legitimacy. For instance, in sociology, successful scholarly community building occurred around different topics, such as the economy, culture, and politics, among others, and in political science between electoral studies, political parties, public policies, and, above all, international relations.

The institutionalization of populist scholarship entails some advantages relating to common conceptual issues and research topics. Firstly, it allows scholars to create communities and improve in-depth reflections, discussions, and analyses. The more the legitimate literature is circumscribed, the more the sub-field allows specific places for publication (e.g. journals on populism), and the more scholars can see their own reflection and conduct their own research while building their academic careers. Secondly, the sub-field strengthens the possibilities of interdisciplinary dialogue between scholars interested in populism in disciplines like sociology, political science, communication sciences, history, economics, and geography. To some extent, populism entails a cross-disciplinary language for some key issues (e.g. the "people" and the "elite"). Thirdly, a populist sub-field helps boost international exchanges among scholars specializing in different world regions and legacies. Thus, it might correct the ethnocentrism of scholars who otherwise do not consider conceptual debates originating in the Global South. In this sense, populist scholarship is not just a series of national sub-fields but virtually an international and transnational sub-field.

However, the institutionalization of populist scholarship also has some shortcomings. The first is what one might call the supremacy paradox. In the sub-field, it is often taken for granted that populism allows a heuristic superiority in understanding social and political challenges, despite ongoing internal disagreements over what populism is. Because it is not easy to accept the use of a concept supported by scholars who do not use a common definition, many scholars tend to be sceptical about its usefulness for academic research. The historian Enzo Traverso (2019, 16), for example, contends that the concept of populism is an "empty shell, which can be filled by the most disparate political contents". This does not mean that he refuses to use the term, however, as in the same volume he describes Trump as a "populist politician" (ibid., 20).

Other scholars consider populism to be the expression of specific ideological orientations and argue that either right-wing or left-wing populism is the real form of populism. The Argentinian political theorists Paula Biglieri and Luciana Cadahia (2021) build on Ernesto Laclau's theory to cast left-wing populism as "just populism" because they argue it is emancipatory, plebeian, republican, egalitarian, and intrinsically emancipatory. According to them, right-wing populism is better understood as fascism because right-wing populists construct the people as one, dissolving the population's heterogeneity into the fantasy of an unitary community. The rejection of the analytical utility of the concept of populism and the artificial classification of "proper and authentic populism" as either right-wing or left-wing showcase the inherently controversial nature of the term.

Other scholars (e.g. Alfio Mastropaolo in his contribution to this volume) maintain that populism is a reactionary rejection of the Enlightenment and challenges the utility of the notion of left-wing populism. We contend that conceptual debates on populism might not disappear because populism is part of our political and social vocabulary. It is what some German scholars consider "a basic concept deployed in the public languages in which political controversy is conducted" (Ritcher 2005, 227). As such, it does not carry a single indisputable meaning, and a variety of conflicting constituencies passionately struggle to make their definitions "authoritative and compelling" (Baehr 2008, 12).

A second and relevant shortcoming of the populist sub-field is the illusion that improvements in theory and research might be achieved within populist scholarship alone. Quoting only articles and books specializing in populism enhances the belief that populist research has a self-reliant heuristic capacity and that the only interesting knowledge is provided by scholars working within these paradigms. However, the concept of populism is always in conversation with classic concepts, such as the people, gender, elites, leadership, class, parties, emotions, etc. While scholars assume that populist parties and leaders might challenge societies, discourses, ideologies, and political systems in the "real" world, most of them surprisingly overlook how populism addresses concepts and theories traditionally discussed in social and political science. Working in a distinct community where scholars cite and debate each other could deprive them of engagement with some other critical debates in the realms of social and political science.

2 The Aim of This Book

The perspective adopted in this volume aims to move beyond an insulating approach. The different chapters focus on some of the key concepts in the social and political sciences. We explore how the concepts of "citizenship", "gender", "class", "sovereignty", "cleavages", "leadership", "mobilization", "parties", and "accountability" were used by scholars of populism in relation to how classical and current theorists developed them. The different chapters explore the concepts' genealogies, their uses in populist studies, and implications for broader conceptual and theoretical debates. The chapters follow a double movement: They address the question of how populism challenges established concepts and theories in social and political science and simultaneously focus on what the category of populism can learn from key conceptual discussions in social and political science. The volume in sum explores what populism tells us about the heuristic advantages and limitations of concepts like "citizenship", "gender", "class", "sovereignty", "cleavages", "leadership", "mobilization", "parties", and "accountability".

The book develops what we term a dialogical perspective between classical and current social and political theory and the conceptual and theoretical understandings of populism. The book is inspired in the history of populist scholarship and on some innovative authors' interactions with social and political theories – above all, the dominant traditions of their times. For instance, the Italian-Argentinian scholar Gino Germani (1971; 1978) engaged the most important paradigms of his time: structural functionalism, modernization theory, and mass society. He not only applied these theories to Latin America but also contributed to the development of theoretically informed comparisons between two variants of authoritarianism: Italian fascism and Argentinian national populism. In his earlier work, Ernesto Laclau (1977) engages with Marxist theory, especially Althusserian post-structuralism. He uses the notion of populism to show that, in addition to class struggles, the population could be split into two antagonistic camps: the people (the underdog) vs. the power bloc. Although he abandoned Marxism in his later work, Laclau (2005) built on his earlier work to argue that populism is a political logic that constructs the people in antagonistic confrontation with the elite. Margaret Canovan (1981) developed a typology of populism following Wittgenstein's notion of family resemblance (Anselmi 2018, 23–29). Cas Mudde (2004) built on Freeden's notions of ideology, Kurt Weyland (2001) on theories of the relative autonomy of politics from the economy and society, and Ostiguy (2017) and Moffitt (2016) on performance theories.

The authors of this book are scholars from different generations and have studied populism in Europe, the US, and Latin America from distinct perspectives. This makes it possible to focus on experiences in both the Global North and South. Some of our contributors focus on key scholars of Latin American populism, like Gino Germani, Ernesto Laclau, and Guillermo O'Donnell, to show the global relevance of their contributions to the study of accountability, leadership, and the relationship between populism and democracy. At the same time, this volume recognizes that populism is an inherently contested category that is used to make theoretical and normative arguments about the nature of democracy, citizenship, national belonging, and the role of political actors. Our contributors combine different concepts or develop their own. For instance, Reinhard Heinisch and Klaudia Koxha use an ideational definition in their chapter, Kenneth M. Roberts builds on Laclau's theory, and others provide their own definitions. Thus, the objective of this volume is not to provide a new universal definition applicable to all geographical and historical contexts.

3 The Chapters

Since it is impossible to address a vast range of concepts in a single book, the editors chose to focus in depth on the historical uses of citizenship, gender, class, cleavages, sovereignty, accountability, participation, leadership, and political party. Luis Roniger engages with the wide debate over citizenship in sociology and political science. His chapter illustrates the different historical patterns of how the state includes those previously excluded by recognizing different demands in terms of citizenship. In Europe, there was a sequence of entitlements to civil, political, and social rights, and in Latin America, political and social rights have had priority over civil rights. Some Latin Americanist scholars argue that there are specific models of populist citizenship (Spanakos 2008; Rein 2013). These are based on the active participation of people in politics beyond elections, and on the individual's right and capacity to spend in the market.

Roniger argues that populism is not a particular type of entitlement to rights but rather reshapes citizenship. "It recalibrates strategies of representation and participation, granting salience to participatory mass mobilization, albeit through state regulation and leadership ameliorating the autonomy of civil society". Roniger shows how populist leaders and movements move the concept of citizenship "beyond the domain of electoral formalities". Populists use emotions and reason to mobilize their social base and create senses of belonging and identity between leaders and followers and among supporters.

Populists "often succeed in reformulating people's lifeworld and markers of certainty". By mobilizing followers beyond electoral moments and by linking political membership, identities, and access to markets, populists reshape liberal and participatory conceptions of citizenship. Populist mass mobilization often constrains the autonomy of organizations of civil society because access to resources depends on loyalty to the leader and the party.

Roniger argues that populists, while claiming to defend national interests, have projected transnational and international strategies of legitimation. The Democracy in Europe Movement 2025 (DiEM25) was an attempt to construct a transnational leftist project "to 'democratize' Europe against Brussels's unaccountable elites". Hugo Chávez conceived of his Bolivarian Revolution as a Latin American and even a global event. His project sought to unite Latin American nations against US imperialism, neoliberalism, and limited bourgeois democracies. Bolivarianism halted free trade agreements. Chávez and other left-wing populists of the twenty-first century increased citizens' expectations of the expansion of rights, and when they could not deliver, they faced massive strikes and marches. Populist understandings of citizenship challenge liberal and republican models by emphasizing participatory mass mobilization, "albeit through state regulation and leadership ameliorating the autonomy of civil society". Populists rely "on performance, embedding claims of citizens' legitimacy in highly affective bonds, and ideally developing a mutual connection and devotion towards leaders supposedly working for the well-being and dignity of the people, while citizens respond with an affective cult of the leader's persona".

Paula Diehl explores theoretically the relationships between gender and populism focusing on debates within the gendered democratic imagination that imagined the masses as feminine and irrational, whereas the citizen and the leader were masculine and rational. Despite excellent historical and social scientific studies, the theoretical relationship between populism and gender continues to be underdeveloped (Navarro 1977; Kampwirth 2010; Abi-Hassan 2017). In her chapter in the *Oxford handbook on populism*, Sahar Abi-Hassan writes that because populism is explained by relying on the moral distinction between "the pure people" and "the corrupt elite", gender is an almost unnecessary or even an irrelevant category for the construction of the people (Abi-Hassan 2017, 428). Instead, Diehl shows the need to include gender seriously and not as an add-up variable in populist studies.

Followers, for example, are gendered by the anti-populist camp as irrational and dangerous and contrasted with the rational male citizen. She also shows how leaders and followers use gender images to cast elites as effeminate and how male populist leaders are represented as extraordinary figures.

Diehl argues that populism promises emancipation: "The 'feminized', passive, and easily manipulated crowd should become an active and sovereign people in order to reverse power relations". It promises to transform the feminized and leader-dependent crowd into "the people as sovereign, inscribed in the male tradition of democratic empowerment". The leader is the one who helps the people change their gender to become male (the promise of sovereignty) and, at the same time, reaffirms the traditional "female" attributes of the guided crowd.

The relationship between gender and populism is more complex than sometimes explained in the literature. Are macho populist leaders, for example, "more attractive to people with a more traditional and machismo culture", as Mudde and Rovira Kaltwasser (2017, 77) assert? What does one make of leaders like Donald Trump, who emerged in cultures that these scholars characterize as more gender-emancipated? Diehl argues that while populism promises universality and equality, it also "affirms gender (class and race) hierarchy and exclusion". On the one hand, populism reproduces the gendered democratic political imaginary and historical traditions based on masculine constructions of the people, the leader, and the emasculation of elites and rivals as feminine. Yet, it is an outcome of the performative efforts of populist actors. In some right-wing populism cases, it is a response to the crises of representation performed as a crisis of masculinity and the articulation of bipolar gender roles, hegemonic masculinity, and sometimes misogyny and sexism. Diehl writes: "[D]espite all efforts to overcome gender-traditional roles and masculine-dominant politics, left-wing populism is still struggling to frame gender in different terms. [...] [They tend to] reinforce female stereotypes of motherhood, emotionality, and 'sensibility', as opposed to the masculine authority, rationality, and aggressive competition".

Kenneth M. Roberts's chapter focuses on the key concept of social class. In the past, this concept used to be at the heart of populism debates. Throughout his academic career that started in the 1950s, Gino Germani argued that fascism and national populism differed because of their class bases. Whereas fascism was supported by a downwardly mobile middle class that attained substitute satisfaction with nationalism and racism, the social base of Perón's movement was the new working class that attained rights to collective bargaining, redistribution of income, and social mobility. Germani's critics use Marxism to argue that populism in Latin America was multiclass movements consisting of the industrial bourgeoisie, the middle class, and the working class (Ianni 1975). Philip Oxhorn (1998) links populism to class formations where most of the population makes a living in the informal sector of the economy and only a few have formal employment with benefits. Surprisingly, class analysis has almost disappeared from most recent populist studies, which focus instead on ideologies (Mudde 2004), political strategies (Weyland 2001), performances (Moffitt 2016; Ostiguy 2017), and populism's formal logic (Laclau 2005).

Roberts develops Laclau's theory to highlight the complexities of historically and geographically situated cases. He shows the crucial roles that social class and the political economy play in distinguishing between right- and left-wing variants. He builds on Weberian and Marxist understandings of class to argue that, even though populism is not a class project, a wide range of class formations and subject positions have given rise to different types of populism. Moreover, he shows that social heterogeneity, fragmentation, and crises of representation are incubators of populism. In Latin America, due to social fragmentation, populism first emerged in the 1930s and 1940s with leaders like Juan Perón in Argentina. It returned with the social dislocations produced by neoliberalism in right-wing variants like Alberto Fujimori in Peru in the 1990s or as a left-wing alternative to neoliberalism with Hugo Chávez and other populists on the left at the turn of the new century. In Europe and the US, populism is the product of weakened class formations that have led to diffuse inequalities, social heterogeneity, political fragmentation, and fluid alignments.

The types of populism vary in whether "the people" are built as an *ethnos* or a *plebeius*. The latter does not correspond to the Marxist notion of a class subject but fits better into the Weberian view of non-privileged social strata defined not only by property, occupation, and income but also by education, power, and prestige. Roberts argues that populism is not the reflection of a particular class but linked to class formations. In both the Global North and South, capitalist development has weakened class cleavages without eliminating social classes while increasing inequalities. Under these conditions, appeals to the people replace classic class discourses of social democrat or communist parties. He concludes by writing that because populism "is most likely to thrive in societal contexts where diffuse inequalities are neither structured by a central class divide, nor organized and represented politically as a class cleavage", populism may prove to have sustained longevity.

Alfio Mastropaolo reconstructs Lipset and Rokkan's classical theory of cleavages. He shows how their theory came in response to a particular historical moment in Western democracies and transcended dominant Parsonian approaches to modernization. He explains the limits of Lipset and Rokkan's conceptualization of cleavages and develops a novel interpretation of populism. Mastropaolo writes that a "cleavage is a point of reference, which a political enterprise can exploit and stabilize" and is made up of "shared experiences, symbols, and political action". He argues that populism corresponds to a cleavage forgotten by Lipset and Rokkan: the one between the *Ancien Régime* and modernity, between the reactionaries nostalgic for the former and modern politics. Left-wing populism does not fit into Mastropaolo's vision because it promises emancipation. If populism is a member of a reactionary family tradition, fascism is its sibling.

Mastropaolo shows that, despite familiarities, these two reactionary ideologies and movements differ in terms of three fundamental characteristics: the use of violence and paramilitarism, the obsession with Bolshevism, and whether elections are used to rise to power legitimately. Unfortunately, Mastropaolo's original interpretation does not analyze non-European variants of fascism and, hence, excludes how formerly fascist sympathizers like Juan Perón in Argentina adapted fascism to democratic times (Finchelstein 2017). The historian Loris Zanatta (2008) offers an alternative argument about the reactionary nature of populists by focusing on their anti-modern notion of community. He argues that populism aims to reinstate antiquated notions of the people understood as an organic and holistic community. Populism dismisses individuation, pluralism, and the rejection of tradition that comes with modernity and the Enlightenment. It is a secular religion with a prophet, a doctrine, cults, and liturgies.

Culturalist perspectives like those of Mastropaolo or Zanatta offer interesting interpretive clues but are of limited use for comparative analysis. According to Zanatta's overarching depiction of populism as a holistic reaction to the Enlightenment and modernity, there are no differences between its right- and left-wing variants. Mastropaolo does not see how class is articulated in right-wing populism. He does not analyze how some left populists reacted to the processes of individuation, pluralism, and autonomy that came with modernization and the unfulfilled promises of the Enlightenment by promising a return to an imaginary and golden past. In Bolivia, Evo Morales imagined a precapitalist time of harmonious relationships between humans and nature without class exploitation or gender inequalities. Similarly, Hugo Chávez aimed to recreate Bolivarianism as an imaginary golden age in the past, an age that never existed, in which Bolívar and other liberators conquered South America in the name of freedom (de la Torre 2010, 148–160; Neuman 2022). However, Mastropaolo is right in arguing that a fundamental difference between populism on the right and the left is that the former politicizes race and racism, while the latter does not.

The relationships between populism and sovereignty are explored by Reinhard Heinisch and Klaudia Koxha. They explain the genealogy of sovereignty in the history of political thought and show that this concept "possesses a collective dimension that is directed both outwards (national sovereignty) and inwards (popular sovereignty)" and argue that sovereignism describes how populists instrumentalize sovereignty. This notion has three dimensions: popular, national, and economic. The first refers to how elites have usurped power from the people. National sovereignism in right-wing populism refers to the distinction between their own people and the cultural others, and left-wing populism focuses on groups, classes, or movements of people that can act transnationally for a common purpose. Economic sovereignism refers to the idea that economic policies should primarily benefit their own people's wealth. Whereas the right stigmatizes the foreign worker as usurpers of jobs for nationals, the left focuses on the state's role in addressing structural inequalities. However, some right-wing populists reject neoliberalism and instead propose welfare chauvinism.

The authors argue that populists offer a promise of change: Instead of producing uncertainty, they vow to return to something familiar, idealized as a glorious past. They promise to restore "popular sovereignty by acting in the present to return to a status quo ante in the future, i.e. to a time and place before elites supposedly usurped power as the central emotional hook". However, the right is not alone in promising a return to the glory days of yore. As argued before, Hugo Chávez promised the return of the Bolivarian utopia of Latin American unity and Evo Morales the return to a glorious pre-Hispanic past (de la Torre 2010; Lindholm and Zúquete 2010). Heinisch and Koxha write that "the concept of sovereignty may take on different meanings or at least contextual hues. Populism studies are illuminating in this respect as they trace populism's capacity to adapt sovereignist claims to cater to particular contexts".

Enrique Peruzzotti explores different uses and understandings of the concept of accountability in the liberal and populist understandings of democratization. His chapter contrasts two interpretations of accountability. The liberal approach focuses on horizontal and vertical mechanisms. The former "refer to intrastate exchanges among accountability agencies while vertical ones involve the control of an external actor over the state, be it the electorate, the media, or civil society". The populist approach argues that the horizontal dimension of state accountability and the institutions that structure accountability (e.g. parties, parliament, and the public sphere) must be dismantled because they encroach on the will of the people. Populist accountability aims to eliminate the horizontal institutions and replace them with multiple presidential elections and plebiscites as the sole vertical mechanism of accountability. Unlike the liberals, who aim to improve the quality of democracy by making the principle of limited government effective, populists seek to establish a constitutional order "that would bring to life the idea of 'unlimited elected government'".

Against liberal models, populists argue that existing institutions protect the domination of elites who constrain the power of the people. They assert that democratization comes from the constituent power of the people that is prioritized over the legal and constitutional order. In practice, they strengthen the power of the elected executive as the figure that incarnates popular aspirations. "Elections are to serve the principle of identification" transforming the institutional mechanisms of liberal democracies into plebiscitary certification. Contrary to the argument of those who consider it the path to radical democratization, populism in power leads to a reduction of the institutional mechanisms that constrain the unlimited power of the executive and replace horizontal accountability with multiple elections. As long as elections are free and competitive, populists remain in the democratic camp; when elections do not count, populism becomes a dictatorship. Elaborating on Guillermo O'Donnell's contrast between liberal and delegative democracies, Peruzzotti shows how the lack of it leads to processes of hybridization and, eventually, to what O'Donnell (2011) describes as the "slow death of democracy". Peruzzotti argues that populist critiques of malfunctioning electoral representation are correct. He also suggests that liberal approaches focused exclusively on controlling governmental abuses of power and authority are insufficient. He concludes by advocating that horizontal and vertical models of accountability should be integrated.

Cecilia Biancalana surveys the political science literature on populism and participation and shows that the concept of participation is crucial to understanding how the people's sovereignty must be restored and how the people reclaim their own voice in politics. She distinguishes between expressive dimensions of participation, which give a sense of collective belonging and identity, and instrumental types of participation. Biancalana differentiates the supply side of participation from the demand side and the impacts of populism on the political system. Finally, she distinguishes between right- and left-wing types of populism. Her survey of the literature shows that Mudde's argument that right-wing populism in Europe does not promote participation does not hold. Populists increase participation, and parties like the Five Star Movement and Podemos, which claim to be beyond left and right, implemented an online participatory mechanism. Even though the participation of common citizens has increased, the type of participation promoted by populism is plebiscitary as the rank and file often approve of the decisions already taken by the leadership. Similarly, in Latin America, left-wing populist parties have promoted top-down participation.

Scholars of US populism have focused on the innovative participatory mechanisms created by the People's Party and other populist movements (Grattan

2016). The legacy of populism in the US from the People's Party to the Tea Party, despite profound ideological differences, lies in their promotion of grassroots democracy. Until Trump became president, populism was on the margins of US politics, and scholars did not have to deal with it in power. By contrast, in Latin America, populists rose to power much earlier, with Perón establishing the first populist regime in Argentina. Latin American scholars have argued that populist movements and parties promoted the participation of citizens beyond the election. Mass demonstrations, rallies, and other forms of collective gathering imbued in common people the sensations of being actors and not passive observers of politics. Yet Latin Americanists had a less optimistic assessment of populist participation in democratization.

Germani (1971) uses the concept of heteronomous mobilization to refer to top-down mass participation on behalf of undemocratic leaders like Perón. Left-wing populists like Hugo Chávez implemented institutions for participatory democracy at the local level. Citizens responded by joining these institutions in large numbers. Grassroots populist participation ultimately depended on the limits imposed by the charismatic leader. Common people used the spaces opened by populist challenges to elites to articulate their claims and were successful as long as their demands recognized the absolute authority of the leader. Focusing on the demands of populism, Biancalana also illustrates that citizens demanded more participation and engagement in politics beyond elections, and they increased their participation in elections and other forms of political participation. Biancalana concludes by arguing that populist participation promotes a pseudo or plebiscitary kind of participation, or what Germani called heteronomous mobilization. Yet populism also shapes collective identities against the establishment or in defence of the people's identity from a threatening other, thus triggering citizens' participation in politics.

Carlos de la Torre's chapter focuses on the role of the leader in the scholarship of populism. Whereas many scholars contend that the notion of populist leadership based on a charismatic leader is crucial, others argue that the definition of populism should not necessarily include it. The point is key because it also relates to historically contextual legacies. While it is difficult to understand Latin American populism and some experiences in Eastern and Southern Europe, where leaders have dominated the political arena for decades without focusing on strong or charismatic leadership, the emphasis on Northern European populism in the past few decades has been more on party organization, ideology, and communication. De la Torre distinguishes between light and full-blown populists. Light populists politicize issues that other parties and leaders do not address, personalize politics at the cost of platforms, and remain within the boundaries of constitutional democracies.

Full-blown populists seek to bring about regime change by altering the constitutional rules of the game. When populism emerges in conditions where all institutions of democracy have lost legitimacy, civil society is in disarray, and the media is weak, they often provoke regime change. Strong civil societies, an autonomous media, and public, and resilient institutions might block undemocratic populist moves to concentrate power and change the constitutional rules of the game.

De la Torre argues that populist scholarship gains from seriously engaging with some classic and contemporary theories of leadership. His chapter underlines some key points: 1) Building on Max Weber, he argues that leadership is not a position but a social relation between the leader and the followers where myths, ceremonies, the body, and collective emotions play crucial roles. 2) Strong leadership is not a proxy for a charismatic leader. Not all authoritative leaders are necessarily "transformational" in the sense of MacGregor Burns (1978) that they would have a transubstantiating effect on the leader and the led. 3) Charismatic leaders are not necessarily populist, as some favoured autonomous institutions and did not build a personalist party. 4) In line with Nadia Urbinati, de la Torre contends that for populist movements or parties to move from the margins of the political system to the centre, they need a leader.

Oscar Mazzoleni challenges the self-referential understanding of what a populist party is. For scholars focusing on ideologies, the answer is simple and lies in their ideology, but can populism be reduced to just an ideology? What does one make of most parties characterized as such by external observers while refusing the label because of its stigma? Moving away from these approaches, Mazzoleni challenges the naturalist prejudice and essentialist labelling of some parties as populists. According to an essentialist epistemological perspective, the researcher can differentiate populist from non-populist parties. Essentialist scholars assume that parties are homogenous and that there is a shared essence of this type of party, regardless of geographic or historical context. However, it is problematic to clearly demarcate a party as populist. Firstly, and with very few exceptions, it is a label of external observers and not a self-definition. Secondly, it is often used in political cultures where this word implies irrationality and demagoguery and is seen as a danger or threat to liberal constitutional democracy. Thirdly, it is quite difficult to clearly differentiate between populist and non-populist parties, as the latter occasionally use populist tropes to attack elites and appeal to the general will.

Mazzoleni's alternative to essentialism is a Weberian approach based on the constructions of ideal types. He writes that "concepts and theories should be considered as ideal types (i.e. approximate attempts to capture the complexity of reality)". He analyzes "parties as associations with ideological supply" but which are also “shaped by different organizational patterns with factional logics and characterized by individuals and groups with different interests and strategies and, consequently, different styles of communication”. Thus, in the intellectual process that scholars use to classify political parties as populist, he analytically distinguishes four moments: defining populism, defining political parties, selecting, and labelling populist parties.

The first step is to consistently define populism as a provisional ideal type. In the second step, one must recognize that populism and party are not the same. An ideal-typical, party-based populist perspective can fruitfully engage with party politics literature. For instance, populist parties can be constructed as charismatic parties. The third step is to look at how populist traits are shared in geographical and historically located party systems. Instead of an essence, populism is a gradation. Finally, it seems better not to label single political parties as “populist” but rather as facets of the political party provisionally labelled as populist. Mazzoleni writes that “[t]his means that discourse, ideology, and style are seen as crucial to party selection, depending on how the party ideal type is defined. Only with an empirical investigation would it be possible to know how and to what extent each party corresponds to this ideal type”. He concludes by noting that “[t]he notion of populism cannot travel in time and space without considering the contextual dimensions shaping its meaning and relevance”.

4 Between Reductionism and Complexity

The dialogical perspective developed in this volume pushes scholars to take more serious account of the limitations of a self-referential use of the concept of populism, as well as the illusion of insular superiority, to understand the complexity of the social and political challenges facing democracy. The dialogue with “external” legacies helps scholars enrich their own approaches but also to be more aware of the necessity of an internal dialogue in terms of both conceptualization and context-oriented knowledge.

Our contributors focus on the complexities of populism. They see it as a gradation, distinguish movements and parties seeking power from populists in office, and often differentiate between types – right and left, light and full-blown – and locate populisms in different historical and geographical contexts. Roniger illustrates the peculiarities of populist views of citizenship that prioritize mobilization, often at the cost of autonomy. Diehl shows how populism partakes in the gendered democratic imagination of the virile people and effeminate elites and of the passive feminized masses that a leader will allegedly transform into autonomous virile citizens. Roberts illustrates how populism forces us to analyze different class formations and the importance of class to distinguish types of populism. Peruzzotti argues that populists favour a particular type of democracy based on constant elections and plebiscites at the cost of the institutional fabric of horizontal accountability.

In Latin America, Asia, Africa, in some Southern and Eastern European nations, and recently in the US with Trump, populisms are leader-centric. Charisma must be studied as a social process where followers recognize a leader who presents him- or herself as extraordinary. In the Global South, parties use informal clientelist networks to exchange votes for services, and many are more personalist and leader-centric than ideological. Moreover, populists promise the people redemption by a charismatic figure and construct politics as antagonistic confrontations with the oligarchy. Western Europe illustrates that right-wing populist parties are not always charismatic, as they have a complex and formalized organization that persists after the departure of the "charismatic" founder (Heinisch and Mazzoleni 2016). As Mastropaolo and Roberts show, cleavages are crucial to understanding populism. Yet they differ in whether populism is a new type of cleavage based on the reactionary rejection of the Enlightenment, or whether it is linked to class formations and experiences. Focusing on the classical notion of sovereignty allows Heinisch and Koxha to analyze the different populist promises to restore economic, national, and political sovereignism.

Several chapters in this volume differentiate between right-wing and left-wing variants. Roberts distinguishes populism when they build the people as an ethnos from constructs as a *plebeius*. Both flaunt the low and desecrate the culture of elites constructed as the high. Yet they differ because right-wing populists construct the people by focusing on particularistic cultural identities associated with nativism, ethno-nationalism, and/or religious nationalism against cosmopolitan, multicultural, and universalist identities. Left-wing populists construct the people in opposition to pro-market and propertied elites. Their counterparts on the right politicize emotions of fear regarding pollution and contamination with the alien ethnic, racial, or cultural other. Left-wing populists politicize resentment regarding socio-economic exclusion, promise to improve democracy, and do not use racist tropes to mobilize electors. Left-wing and right-wing populists create different types of cleavages around socio-economic distinction or ethnic-cultural differences that could last a long time. Alfio Mastropaolo argues that right-wing populism like fascism are products of what he labels as a forgotten cleavage: the reactionary responses to the Enlightenment and modernity. These movements differ in the fact that fascists used violence and paramilitarism to deal with enemies and were a response to the Russian revolution and fears of Bolshevism.

Accepting the complexity of populism allows dialogues to be had with broader concepts in the social and political sciences but also highlights the opportunity for plural approaches to populism. This volume argues that controversies about the definition of populism allow opening debates with broader theoretical issues connected to concept formation. Instead of dreaming about a perfect and concise definition that captures the essence of populism and could travel unproblematically across time and space while reducing populism to one of its components, we propose to accept that populism is a murky and contested concept in epistemological, political, and academic debates.

Following recent critiques of reductionist theories (Arato and Cohen 2021; Diehl and Weber 2022), one might argue that a complex and non-reductionist concept needs to be constructed as an ideal type focused on ideology, organization, and style of communication, or a combination of all these traits. Ideal types make it possible to differentiate between populisms while acknowledging their complexities. Focusing on populist challenges, one could claim that populism promises the further democratization of society. However, populists in power have, at best, included at the cost of limiting contestation and pluralism. Left-wing and right-wing populism are different, and they are both present in the Global North and South. When challenging power, in office, and as regimes, populists present different characteristics.

Our book is the result of several workshops where we discussed the characteristics of this project and drafts of the different chapters. Paula Diehl, Kenneth M. Roberts, Carlos de la Torre, Luis Roniger, and Oscar Mazzoleni met at the 39th International Congress of the Latin American Studies Association, 26–29 May 2021. The other contributors gathered in person or virtually for the international workshop entitled "Populism as a Challenge to Key Concepts in Political and Social Theory", held at the University of Lausanne on 5 and 6 November 2021. Enrique Peruzzotti graciously joined the project later on. We are also grateful to Cecilia Biancalana for coordinating the project and to Laurent Bernhard and Annika Werner for commenting on and suggesting improvements to previous versions of the chapters.

References

Abi-Hassan, S. (2017) Populism and gender. In: Rovira Kaltwasser, C., Taggart, P., Ochoia Espejo, P. and Ostiguy, P. (eds.) *The Oxford handbook of populism*. Oxford: Oxford University Press, 426–445.

Anselmi, M. (2018) *Populism: An introduction*. London-New York: Routledge.

Arato, A. and Cohen, J. (2021) *Populism and civil society: The challenge to constitutional democracy*. Oxford: Oxford University Press.

Baehr, P. (2008) *Caesarism, charisma and fate: Historical sources and modern resonances in the work of Max Weber*. New Brunswick: Transaction Press.

Biglieri, P. and Cadahia, L. (2021) *Seven essays on populism*. Cambridge: Polity Press.

Canovan, M. (1981) *Populism*. New York: Harcourt Brace Jovanovich.

de la Torre, C. (2010) *Populist seduction in Latin America*. Athens: Ohio University Press.

de la Torre, C. (ed.) (2019) *The Routledge international handbook of global populism*. London-New York: Routledge.

Diehl, P. and Weber, T. (2022) Populism: Complex concepts and innovative methods. *Polity*, 54(3).

Finchelstein, F. (2017) *From fascism to populism in history*. Oakland: University of California Press.

Germani, G. (1971) *Política y sociedad en una época de transición*. Buenos Aires: Editorial Paidos.

Germani, G. (1978) *Authoritarianism, fascism, and national populism*. New Brunswick: Transaction Press.

Grattan, L. (2016) *Populism's power*. Oxford: Oxford University Press.

Heinisch, R. and Mazzoleni, O. (2016) *Understanding populist party organisation: The radical right in Western Europe*. London: Palgrave Macmillan.

Heinisch, R., Holtz-Bacha, C. and Mazzoleni, O. (eds.) (2021) *Political populism: Handbook on concepts, questions and strategies of research*. Baden-Baden: Nomos.

Ianni, O. (1975) *La formación del estado populista en América Latina*. Mexico City: Editorial ERA.

Kampwirth, K. (2010) Introduction. In: Kampwirth, K. (eds.) *Gender and populism in Latin America: Passionate politics*. University Park: University of Pennsylvania Press, 1–24.

Kuhn, T. (1970) *The structure of scientific revolutions*. Chicago: University of Chicago Press.

Laclau, E. (1977) *Politics and ideology in Marxist theory*. London: Verso.

Laclau, E. (2005) *On populist reason*. London: Verso.

Lindholm, C. and Zúquete, J. P. (2010) *The struggle for the world: Liberation movements for the 21st century*. Palo Alto: Stanford University Press.

MacGregor Burns, G. (1978) *Leadership*. New York: Open Road Integrated Media.

Moffitt, B. (2016) *The global rise of populism: Performance, political style, representation*. Stanford: Stanford University Press.

Mudde, C. (2004) The populist zeitgeist. *Government and Opposition*, 39(4), 541–563.

Mudde, C. and Rovira Kaltwasser, C. (2017) *Populism: A very short introduction*. New York: Oxford University Press.

Navarro, M. (1977) The case of Eva Perón. *Signs*, *3*(1), 229–240.

Neuman, W. (2022) *Things are so bad that they can't get worse: Inside the collapse of Venezuela*. New York: St. Martin's Press.

O'Donnell, G. (2011) Nuevas reflexiones acerca de la democracia delegativa. In: O'Donnell, G., Iazzetta, O. and Quiroga, H. (eds.) *Democracia delegativa*. Buenos Aires: Prometeo, 19–35.

Ostiguy, P. (2017) Populism: A socio-cultural approach. In: Rovira Kaltwasser, C., Taggart, P., Ochoia Espejo, P. and Ostiguy, P. (eds.) *The Oxford handbook of populism*. Oxford: Oxford University Press, 73–97.

Oswald, M. (ed.) (2021) *The Palgrave handbook of populism*. Cham: Palgrave.

Oxhorn, P. (1998) The social foundation of Latin America's current populism: Problems of popular class formation and collective action. *Journal of Historical Sociology*, *11*(2), 212–246.

Rein, R. (2013) From Juan Perón to Hugo Chávez: Populism reconsidered. In: Sznajder, M., Roniger, L. and Forment, C. (eds.) *Shifting frontiers of citizenship: The Latin American experience*. Leiden-Boston: Brill, 289–313.

Ritcher, M. (2005) A family of political concepts: Tyranny, despotism, Bonapartism, Caesarism, dictatorship, 1750–1917. *European Journal of Political Theory*, *4*(3), 221–248.

Rovira Kaltwasser, C., Taggart, P., Ochoia Espejo, P. and Ostiguy, P. (eds.) (2017) *The Oxford handbook of populism*. Oxford: Oxford University Press.

Spanakos, A. P. (2008) New wine, old bottles, flamboyant sommelier: Chávez, citizenship, and populism. *New Political Science*, *30*(4), 521–544.

Traverso, E. (2019) *The new faces of fascism: Populism and the far right*. London: Verso.

Weyland, K. (2001) Clarifying a contested concept. *Comparative Politics*, *34*(1), 1–22.

Zanatta, L. (2008) El populismo, entre la religión y la política: Sobre las raíces históricas del antiliberalismo en América Latina. *Estudios interdisciplinarios de América Latina y el Caribe*, *19*(2), 29–45.

PART 1

Society and Citizens

CHAPTER 1

Populism and Citizenship: Do Populisms Shape a Sui Generis Type of Citizenship?

Luis Roniger

1 Citizenship as Part of a Populist Equation

To large extent, research has discussed populism in the framework of theories of democracy, pointing particularly to the centrality of the category of "the people" as a discursive construct articulated by a certain style of political leadership. This is understandable as populism thrives in the shadow of the shortcomings of modern democracies. As stressed by Cristóval Rovira Kaltwasser (2015) and Carlos de la Torre (2017), democratic failings and crises open the way for varied forms of "populist ruptures", facilitating the construction of the category of "the people" and manifestations of populist performance. Sometimes these scenarios are democratizing, but often they produce an "authoritarian temptation" by leaders who, while mobilizing supporters, impose top-down controls over society. Gino Germani, a pioneer of this research domain, considered that, due to that tendency, "national populism" resembled fascism (Germani 1978, ch. 3; Anselmi 2018, 11–14; Serra 2019). Andrew Arato and Jean Cohen stressed that the authoritarian tendency turns populism into a "modern form of political theology". In this scenario, populist leaders and their supporters – one part of the population – claim to stand for the whole people and embody the general will (Arato 2015; Arato and Cohen 2019). In her analysis, Nadia Urbinati captured this process of substitution of the whole with one of its parts (Urbinati 2019).

This chapter suggests highlighting the analytical angle of citizenship in the populist equation. Populism develops within the parameters of modern constitutional democracies, at the centre of which lies the concept of citizenship. Analyzing populism against the hindsight of the social and political literature on citizenship, particularly on how modern democracies balance tensions inherent in citizen models as against practices, it becomes intelligible how populist leaders gain prominence once alternative leaderships fail to address those issues in satisfactory ways. In this regard, the chapter discusses the literature on citizenship, and then identifies several domains in which populism challenges customary conceptions of citizenship, primarily liberal yet also

 | DOI:10.1163/9789004679016_003

other participatory conceptions, and what hindsight the literature on citizenship offers to studies of populism, and vice versa.

2 Citizenship: Historical Development and Models

Historically constructed, the concept of citizenship has crystallized in modern societies as the core principle of membership that determines civil, political, socio-economic, and, more recently, cultural rights, bundled with certain obligations. It can be thought as a status and as a bundle of practices (Bendix 1964; Turner 1993). Citizenship defines people's political membership and determines correlated rights and duties, while setting barriers to access from beyond the national borders. As a status, it demarcates sets of full-fledged citizens enjoying rights and duties from those permanent residents and non-citizens or aliens lacking some or most entitlements (while not necessarily being exempt from duties, such as taxation).

Citizenship is contextual. It relates to varied ways of connecting individuals and groups to states and nations. The ways in which national identities and state loyalties are constructed affect how citizenship is conceived and how rights and duties are installed. People often cite Thomas Marshall's analysis (1950) of the cumulative development of rights from legal, civil rights, such as habeas corpus, property and access to a jury system; to a second wave of political rights such as the franchise and the secret ballot, reflected in the institutionalization of political parties and parliaments; and to a third wave of social rights and welfare state policies that have been recognized by the twentieth century (and one should add a fourth wave of recognition of cultural and environmental rights).

That seminal work, grounded in the historical sequence of expansion of rights in Britain, has been widely discussed and criticized, yet many considered it to be rather universal. However, it fails to fit the sequences of development of citizenship in other societies, especially those of the Global South. For example, reflecting on the historical development of citizenship in Brazil, historian José Murilo de Carvalho observed that the sequence of civil rights followed by political rights and then social and economic rights fails to represent the Brazilian experience. In his own words, "when we speak of an English citizen or a North American or Brazilian citizen, we don't speak of the same thing". Carvalho identified a series of long-lasting obstacles to the attainment of full citizenship in Brazil: a prolonged system of slave labour; a lopsided land tenure and the hierarchical dependency of the rural masses; the inner split of working classes between radicalized sectors rejecting the power structure and those sectors unionized under the aegis of the state and closely associated to power.

All these determined that most Brazilian citizens attained their rights in a dependent way, through paternalist and populist policies. As an elitist-hierarchical society for very long, the Brazilian state recognized and granted social rights while still curtailing the enactment of political rights. Social and economic rights were granted to prevent and control alternative avenues of mass mobilization. Such a distinct pattern of development of citizenship shaped an excessive valourization of executive power over checks and balances; expectations of paternalism; politics oriented to entice the government to concede rights rather than of citizens gaining entitlements through activism; impatience with the slow functioning of democratic institutions; a corporatist vision of collective interests; and the proliferation of clientelist networks colonizing the formal structure of the state, still prevalent until a few decades ago (Murilo de Carvalho 2001; Domingues 2013; see also Hilgers 2012).

Beyond their specific configuration across the globe, however, in all modern states citizenship has been intimately associated with processes of nation building and supported by the international system. All modern states have used institutions and a plethora of symbols and ceremonies to shape credible visions of citizenship linked to home territories, collective identities, and historical narratives. In the words of Ralf Dahrendorf, "not the least advantage of the nation-state was that it generalized the ancient idea of citizenship" (2008, 30).

By structuring citizenship, modern states have defined what set of individuals living in a territory bear a collective public identity and share certain rights and duties, denied to aliens and stateless persons. Whoever is recognized as a citizen, i.e. a full-fledged member either by birth or naturalization, enjoys access to certain rights and shares duties, while other individuals are excluded. Beyond specifics, citizenship provides access to possible means of livelihood, a share of the collective resources of a country, and a public persona typified in passports. Among the obligations expected from citizens in modern states have been taxation, military, or public service, and implicitly social reproduction through family formation.

Citizen rights and entitlements have developed in expansive ways, yet even today citizenship remains finite and limited, as it still recreates criteria of inclusion and exclusion within states and vis-à-vis those beyond the territorial or identitarian borders of a state (Gosewinkel 2001; Ellis et al. 2006). Global citizenship and flexible citizenship remain uncertain projects for the future, despite much talk about them, while regional citizenship has met only partial success in certain regions and historical moments (Featherstone et al. 1995).[1] Also worth remarking is that the boundaries and criteria of citizenship are fluid and often change under the impact of socio-economic protest and cultural trends, and as social or political movements challenge the ways in which the frontiers of citizenship are enacted (Sznajder, Roniger and Forment 2013).

Citizenship is not just a status carrying entitlements and obligations. It is also a practice, and here we come closer to the question of whether populism develops a sui generis type of citizenship. Historically, normative models of citizenship have stressed the equality of members of a political community as makers of the law – the "Greek model" – and as equal bearers of duties and beneficiaries of freedoms under the law – typically, the "Roman model" (Bellamy 2008). Already in antiquity, these models set the basis for defining basic institutional frameworks and rules of citizenship and the correlated modes of participation and representation in the body politic. These normative models have evolved and changed multiple times, a trend already perceived in antiquity when the active citizen participation typical of Greek city-states became diluted as citizenship expanded within the boundaries of a vast empire, as was the case of Rome. Nonetheless, a varied balance of participation and representation would remain key to citizenship as practice, subject to the impact of changing times and the expansion or contraction of various rights and duties.

Addressing these models, social and political theories of citizenship emerged, being the major ones the republican, the liberal and the communitarian. In normative terms, liberal approaches have predicated citizen representation and limited, optional political participation. They have emphasized the centrality of market forces, limited government as regulator, the heterogeneity of interests, and conceived citizens as bearers of formal rights making rational choices through procedural mechanisms (e.g. elections and legislative representation) for reaching collective decisions out of the multiplicity of forces in civil society. From this perspective, citizens exercise their main role as controllers of the state, so that the latter would not abuse its power. Contrastingly, republican and communitarian approaches have stressed a more active dimension of participation by citizens in the political process. Republican and neo-republican approaches have prioritized the effective and autonomous participation of citizens in politics and government as the foundation of modern constitutional regimes, with rights as a correlate of public duties. Communitarian approaches have placed more emphasis on the collective needs of a community even to the point of overriding individual rights

1 On flexible citizenship, see Ong 1999; on regional citizenship, see Pace 2006 and Roniger 2011.

in the name of the general will, with extreme implications for rank-and-file citizens when the body politic is dominated by Jacobin tendencies (Schama 1989, 678–792; Eisenstadt 2007).

Conceptually distinguished, in practice the boundaries between the models often blend. For instance, in *Liberal beginnings*, Andreas Kalyvas and Ira Katznelson highlighted that while Anglophone political theory has tended to contrast republicanism and liberal individualism, in fact the leading thinkers of modern liberalism tried to understand the conditions required for the exercise of freedom in a viable republic. Grounding themselves in the "republican language of virtue, corruption, patriotism, and political ethics", they also transcended classical republicanism, as "they stressed individual interests, freedoms and rights, government by consent, the contingent sources of political activity, a wish to protect citizens from potentially predatory rulers, and scepticism toward organized political authority" (Kalyvas and Katznelson 2008, 7). While Thomas Hobbes thought of individuals as delegating all power to the state in order to secure a stable and ordered environment, the main vision of John Locke (1980) and other anti-absolutist thinkers was to recognize the institutional order as the core mechanism for ensuring citizen rights and freedoms, envisioning the state as guaranteeing such institutional order and the limits to arbitrary power. According to this view, citizens have the capacity of self-organization, shaping the normative order of society that the state would ensure thereafter.

The great revolutions shaped the themes of equality, participation, and social justice as bases of legitimation, and after periods of violence and abuse of power, they established procedural legitimation as basic to the political process. The modern constitutional democracies that crystallized in the following centuries created institutional mechanisms of responsive representation that combined liberal and republican emphases as they recognized rights, established the separation of powers, prescribed checks and balances deemed to regulate discretion in terms of abstract norms, and justified and informed citizens of governmental decisions by power holders that eventually could be scrutinized by citizens and their representatives. Equally important – although downplayed in many works – was the concern of some early modern constitutional democracy theorists – e.g. the North American founding fathers – with the role of the state in protecting honest working people from parasitic elites like "crafty and indolent bankers" and those willing to retain aristocratic or oligarchic pretensions (Shklar 1991).

Modern constitutional democracies have faced the constant rise of protest movements lifting the banners of the sovereign people and prompting the incorporation of protest symbols and demands into formally recognized rights.

A process of expansion and contraction of the political realm thus became ingrained in constitutional democracies, which address inner tensions regarding the relative weight of representation and participation, or in other words, the modes of interaction between the "sovereign" and its "representatives". Correlated with it, there have been various cycles of breakdown of democracies and several waves of populism, for instance, in Latin America where early and classical populist leaders have been followed by both neoliberal and radical populists (Roniger 2013; de la Torre 2019, esp. parts III, V, VI).

The late-twentieth-century transitions from authoritarianism and the processes of liberalization recentred the centrality of debates on civil society, depicting empowered citizens deliberating, shaping public opinion, and promoting their affairs autonomously in defence of justifiable demands (Cohen and Arato 1992; Avritzer 2002). On their part, communitarian approaches have similarly underlined the social nature of citizens and their participation as a basic right for promoting the common good, albeit with a greater emphasis on the aggregative nature of the common good and with the state seen more positively as the site able to lead change toward attaining the common good represented by ideals such as equality and social justice (Lister and Pia 2012).

The effects of globalization, cyclical market crises, neoliberal deregulation, and weakening support for covering the costs of public goods have produced more isolated and passive citizens, producing a model of what Bryan S. Turner (2013) defined as "consumer citizenship". In turn, the shortcomings of representative arrangements opened the way for massive anti-systemic protests and a cyclical rise of populism in many societies worldwide. Another major driving force for the rise in global populism in recent decades, particularly yet not only in Europe, has been the backlash to mass migration perceived as undermining the state's control of access to citizenship and thus threatening the sense of collective identity of society. Carlos de la Torre has characterized such reaction as "the populist politicization of inequalities and differences" (de la Torre 2019, 145–215).

These major transformations have prompted a burgeoning literature on populism, closely connected to major theoretical problems and controversies in the social and political sciences, particularly concerning the future of democratic citizenship, the relations between states, markets, and civil societies, and the challenges of mass migration, diversity, and multiculturalism in the format of contemporary states. Hereafter, I analyze four aspects that call attention to the interface and analytical importance of integrating studies of populism and citizenship. This analysis indicates how populism challenges both liberal and participatory conceptualizations of citizenship, and how the study of populism may benefit by dialoguing with citizenship studies.

3 Strategies of Representation and Participation

Citizenship regimes are defined by the intersection of citizens' rights and duties and the modes of interest mediation. This opens the way for an ever-shifting negotiation and balance between representation and participation. Populism is no exception, as it recalibrates key strategies of representation and participation. In this regard, it is common to see populist leaders predicating the active participation of people in politics, yet in a partisan and antagonistic manner by pursuing a "politics of anti-politics" in their search for building a mass following and legitimizing their hold on power. Both when aiming to gain power and when reaching the government, populism stresses people's mobilization and participation in a political movement and coalition working against entrenched and self-serving elites, against "the establishment", or writ large, against external and internal enemies (Spanakos 2008; Rein 2013). In their stead, populists lift the discursive banner of defending the general will, the unity and integrity of society, which would replace particularistic interests and mechanisms for reaching decisions out of the diversity of civil society and the multiplicity of individual choices.

Many populist movements usually go against the liberal models that stress the role of individual citizens as rational human beings making collective decisions just through procedural, electoral mechanisms. While retaining elections as a major mechanism – and even reinforcing their plebiscitarian functions as in recall elections – many populists manufacture them as a major performative means of keeping an active and recurrent mobilization of a majoritarian support. Thus, rather than merely choosing candidates to represent them, supporters are portrayed ideally as politically engaged citizens, working through various channels as "protagonists of their own history".

Paula Diehl has analyzed populism's mechanisms affecting democratic representation. She indicates that in democracies, representatives must maintain a balance between authorization and accountability, so that while entitled to make decisions on behalf of citizens ("their constituency"), they should remain accountable to them. According to Diehl (2019), populism operates a dual twist in the balance between these principles. Populism demands more popular power and claims to empower citizens, while simultaneously promoting strong leadership. In addition, it projects a "mimetic" relationship between the leader and her supporters, with the former expecting and the latter expected to bestow an almost unconditional trust in the leader's wisdom. This mitigates and may even suppress democratic accountability, thus increasing the likelihood for authoritarian or totalitarian power.

Populist leaders thus reduce the key element of democratic accountability, but they cannot eliminate it. For once, they often rise to power by launching discursive attacks on traditional elites and parties for failing to fulfil citizens' expectations of access to resources or social justice, or for being unable to be proper guardians of the boundaries of the nation, e.g. as in recent decades in Europe, where populist politicians predicated distrust of those who failed to prevent migrants from entering the national territory, thus threatening the collective identity or values of society. Contrastingly, at least symbolically, populists stress their responsiveness to popular hopes, interests, and expectations. When they reframe constitutional charters, populist leaders even proclaim and reinforce the formal principles of accountability.

In addition, populists cannot dare to eliminate democratic accountability since their persona is constructed and complemented by various mediating structures of political mobilization and the enthusiastic support of a leader and her project/rule. The idea of non-mediated access between the masses and the leaders is just a chimera. Populism sustains itself through mediating structures of representation that not only impose top-down controls upon followers, but also require a recognition of bottom-up demands to continue to be effective. The most successful populist leaders claim to deepen democratic accountability, strengthening it through a more active political participation. Through varied means, from clientelist networks to the empowerment of those participating in grassroots activities and organizations, they create both a sense of belonging, despite what often is a rather corporative submission to the leadership.

These trends relate to the large corpus of social and political writing and debates on the idea and practice of civil society and the transformation of public spheres in modern constitutional democracies. The concept of civil society alludes to the existence of organized public life and free associations beyond the tutelage of the state yet oriented toward the public sphere and looking to influence public policies. In this sense, the pluralism of a multiple and diverse associational life – ranging from voluntary associations and social movements to intermediary institutions such as local councils – can influence the state from within, for instance, through representative and regulatory institutions or autonomous courts, bringing executive power to reckon a broader social accountability (Fraser 1992; Seligman 1992). From an analytical perspective and beyond the concrete range of arenas and social sectors involved, the notion of civil society has been used to refer to the interlinking arena where private interests meet public concerns, and both are mutually structured in a public sphere with its own rules. Under certain circumstances, these relationships have been institutionalized in the form of entitlements and obligations. Their impact has been increasingly mediated by alphabetization, technological innovations, and the changing format of the media and social media.

Beyond the variability of civil society across historical and cultural settings, the concept has reflected a basic configuration in which society stands apart from the state, develops a certain autonomy – "as the site of alternative hegemonies", in Gramscian terms – and becomes increasingly assertive of such autonomy at both the individual and associative levels. That is, the concept envisages the existence of public spheres that are not fully structured from the top down by those in power, but become increasingly open to dissent, public debate, and the weight of public opinion (Keane 1988; Taylor 1990). It thus requires agents "involved both in private dealings and in debating and acting out different versions of the public interests" (Pérez-Díaz 1993, 57). This is a basic component for the sustainability of modern constitutional liberal democracies organized around legal constraints on the exercise of public authority and public deliberation and scrutiny around policymaking in increasingly complex societies. Civil society can be strengthened through the existence of effective and accountable state structures. What is at stake is a configuration of the public sphere, in which civil society does not necessarily stand in a zero-sum game vis-à-vis the state, but still sustains the legal constrains of the state and forces public accountability (Held 1987).

A vital civil society may sustain and be reinforced by a viable constitutional democracy, through institutions that may prevent the concentration of power. While populism may have a democratizing effect in pre-existing elitist and authoritarian regimes, for instance, by being a corrective for problems of exclusion and marginalization, it may also lead to what Steven Levitsky and James Loxton (2019) have called "competitive authoritarianism". Its intense use of mass mobilization as a major means of deepening the majoritarian-participatory axis may operate to concentrate lopsided power in the mediating organizations. In that case, populism may eliminate checks and balances typical of liberal democratic models and reinforce executive predominance, eventually undermining the autonomy of supposedly independent regulatory bodies, the courts, and the media. When such actions combine with the delegitimation and demonization of any independent voice and opposition, the authoritarian physiognomy of populism becomes full-fledged, hampering the real exercise of an autonomous civil society and the sustainability of democratic citizenship (Weyland 2019). Following crises, such citizenship regimes may witness a declining sense of participation, systemic alienation, and a loss of trust in the system, while the polarized discourse and the mechanisms of control of the populist machinery remain in force, thus vacating the ability of citizens to exercise their dual function of being autonomous and exercising their influence on state power holders.

4 The Interface of Market Access, Political Membership, and Public Identities

Analyzing the key category of "the people" that stands at the centre of populist discourse, Ernesto Laclau stressed that it is constructed by bringing together empty and free-floating signifiers that can be interpreted expansively in multiple ways. Through its nebulous character, this quality enables a rather inclusive articulation of many sectors and social classes, while remaining at the same time exclusionary of those defined as the enemy, the "anti-people" (Laclau 2005).

Likewise, some theorists have claimed that populism constitutes a "thin ideology", as it claims to stay away from clear-cut ideologies. In that line, Michael Freeden indicated that

> it not only falls short of comprehensiveness but short of nuanced specificity in what it *does* offer. Vagueness and indeterminacy may be good vote-catchers, but the result is at best a phantom ideology, a specter that can be draped over pressing and intricate socio-political issues in order to blur and to conceal.
>
> 2017, 10–11

Nonetheless, populism is clear enough when it comes to endorse the role of the state vis-à-vis citizens, and about its role as controlling or liberating the workings of market economy.

Populism structures particular connections between market access, political membership, and public identities. It stresses aspects of public identity just as much as it concomitantly defines access to resources, social justice, and redistribution policies. Discursively, it makes concrete policy part of a general statement about society's collective identity and sense of direction at large. In addition to structuring the political process and policymaking, populism claims those decisions are entwined with the broader premises of social order. It thus moves the terms of debate on citizen exclusion and inclusion from a mere question of inequalities and mediated access to resources into the symbolic realm of redefining the boundaries of the citizens' body politic in terms of a "collective purpose" (Yilmaz and Morieson 2022).

Whatever the varied mode of articulating the economy, varied populisms share a push back on any assumption of state neutrality in shaping the contours of citizenship. They stress aspects of collective identity as much as they predicate a more inclusive system, for instance, stressing social justice and better management and redistribution of national resources, at least for those sharing the leader's sense of collective direction and purpose. As such, by demanding support, providing benefits and actively legitimizing and de-legitimizing the boundaries of allowed participation, populism redefines the sense of citizenship.

In many cases, populism amplifies the use of clientelist access to material and symbolic resources through patron-client exchanges, redistributive programs, and corporatist structures (Oxhorn 1998, esp. 223–226; de la Torre 2010, 20). For instance, progressive populist governments have exploited clientelist relations at the service of political rallying. Grassroots sectors linked politically received continuous rewards from state budgets, which particularly contributed to structuring mass mobilization. Consequently, through massive redistribution programs with highly politicized criteria, the progressive populist governments patronized the popular mobilization of grassroots movements for legitimation purposes (Roberts 2007, esp. 11–13; Weyland 2009, esp. 151–159).

Populist leaders and movements address major concerns of citizens. Whether they are strongly redistributive or not, they seem to be effective in rechannelling social and economic concerns by combining these with a restructuring of public identities. Where populist leaders make their full impact is when they succeed in channelling citizens' concerns while embedding them within general themes of collective goals. It is not by chance that many populist leaders often phrase their programs and concrete policies – whether expanding market liberalization or supporting social justice and redistribution of resources – in terms of a general will and a politics of identity. Such politics articulates diverse social interests – and thus may build multi-class and multi-sectorial coalitions.

What merits equal emphasis is that populist leaders not only reflect the world view and policy priorities of citizens, but rather shape those world views and policy priorities through their performative wisdom and ability. Populist leaders, movements and parties tend to affect what Claude Lefort (1988) and Shmuel N. Eisenstadt (2009) defined as "markers of certainty" and Jürgen Habermas (1987) identified as "lifeworld". These various concepts refer to the self-evident outlooks, unstated perceptions and given practices that people come to accept and experience together when living in a particular time and place. It is my claim that populist leaders ground themselves on existing implicit meanings[2] and expectations (mainly of those excluded or who feel marginalized by the existing citizenship regime, aka the "old system"), while they aim and often succeed in reformulating people's lifeworld and markers of certainty. They do so by connecting their agendas and concrete policies within strategies of reconstruction of public identities.

2 On implicit meanings, see also Schwartz 1994 and Douglas 2002.

A major aspect of such a mode of operation is the projection of wider claims about reconnecting society with "its own sense of purpose". More than once, populist leaderships aim at rejuvenating a sense of collective purpose by triggering and honouring memories and figures of the past, inspiring the living into joining the herculean tasks that they define for the entire society. Extrapolating Anthony Smith's conceptualization of national identities, we may define what populist leaders claim to be doing as "the expression of intimate and powerful relationships between the dead, the living and the unborn" (Smith 1996, 23). It is in this sense that some populist leaderships claim to be revolutionary rather than merely reformist.

In some cases, as in European populism, the intersection of market access, political membership, and public identities has taken the form of defending the primordial character of collective identity against external forces and intruders, such as the migrants arriving to their shores (Ruzza 2019). Likewise, in Turkey, India and Myanmar, civilizational populism has crystalized, claiming to defend collective identity against religious minorities portrayed as embodying values antithetical to the cultural premises of those societies (Yilmaz and Morieson 2022). Exclusive populisms have also emerged in Africa in contexts of ethnic and racial divisiveness (Cheesman 2019). Contrastingly, most cases of populism in Latin America have exhibited an integrative character and lacked overt xenophobic overtones. They have rather focused on endorsing the idea of citizenship as predicating egalitarian access and social justice, while redefining politically the "right to have rights" in partisan terms, claiming to exclude only those opposed to those national goals as expressed by the populist leadership (de la Torre and Peruzzotti 2008; Cartes Montory and Díaz Polanco 2015). Notwithstanding that, even "integrative" populist leaders have fallen for the allure of conspiracy theories, predicating the fight against internal and external enemies, as in the classic case of Juan Domingo Perón and his poisoning discourse on the International Synarchy and its home allies (Roniger and Senkman 2018). That is, it is not unusual for populist leaders, irrespective of their left-wing or right-wing leanings, to project and popularize conspiracy theories, even when these aggrandized by rumours, fake news, and disinformation, as a means of gaining and keeping power.[3]

3 For a broader analysis on conspiracy theories in Latin American cases of populism, see Ablard and Bohoslavsky 2021; Roniger and Senkman 2022, 57–62, 141–169.

5 The Emotional Tonality of Populist Citizenship

The third aspect in which populist citizenship stands out stems from its performative function or, to put it differently, the "politics of emotion" (Åhäll 2018) that populist leaderships often evoke. Populist leaders and movements place great emphasis on the emotional aspects of belonging and participating, moving the concept of citizenship beyond the domain of electoral formalities. Instead, populism often stresses the experiential aspects of citizenship, in which members exhibit non-neutral emotional relationships, ranging from empathy to hatred. Their strategy intertwines emotions and judgement, promoting an emphasis on performance, and granting new salience to participatory mass mobilization, albeit through state regulation and leadership.

Like any other political actors, populist leaders and activists interact with different types of audiences, identify their sentiments, and ultimately aim to attract their support. Populism often holds a promise, as in the US populist movement of the 1880s that led millions of people "to believe fervently that a wholesale overhauling of their society was going to happen in their lifetimes" (Goodwyn 1979, viii). Willing to become the legitimate voice of a society, populists generate deep emotions as they try to galvanize support. Passionate feelings like fear, anger, guilt, and hope generate a common sense of identity among audiences and thus embed legitimacy in highly affective bonds. Adding to Max Weber's analysis of charismatic legitimacy as unique yet ephemeral (Gerth and Mills 1958, 52–55; Kalberg 2021, ch. 2), both anthropologists of emotions (Lewis et al. 2010) and international relations scholars (Franck 1990, 91–95; Adler 2010) have registered the role of emotive expression in research on political legitimization. When studying populist movements from this perspective, research registers the emotional tonality of performing citizenship as central to populist strategies that colour and give affective density to specific claims and policies (Laclau 2005, 111; Weyland 2001; Drezner 2017, esp. 30–39).

Populists' performative styles and affective underpinnings magnify hate and love, fear and euphoria, as their communicative and mobilization bases (see among others Moffitt 2016; Kinnvall 2018; Skonieczny 2018). Populists aim at developing a mutual connection of devotion and sacrifice in the framework of generous and heroic leaders bringing dignity to their followers and the latter responding with an incremental affective cult of the leaders' persona (de la Torre 2007). To this aim, the "Pink Tide" populists adopted a personalist diplomatic style, while meeting with supportive intellectuals, unionists, students, and political elites during presidential tours as a way of transferring their personality cult abroad.

Among other means used to strengthen this almost messianic liaison of mutual commitment, they used inflammatory defiant speeches, nationalist slogans, slang, and mannerisms resounding with local audiences were particularly effective (Capriles 2006; Levitsky and Loxton 2013, esp. 110; Drezner 2017). Conspiracy theories have been also instrumental as manoeuvrers to produce such emotional commitment, particularly when empowered in situations of crisis and former institutional distrust. For instance, Hugo Chávez and the Chavista movements aimed at generating empathy through the dissemination of enshrined images of the leaders' personality abroad and the transmission of a grassroots-led festive visualization of the practices of forceful defiance and cooperation. They attempted and partially managed to disseminate devotional and almost mythical images of leadership claiming a high moral standing abroad. These images may be cherished by supporters and hated by others (Panizza 2005, 22–25; for Europe, see Zúquete 2007).

Populists' success has depended much on the emotional tonality of leadership and the leader's cult as a policy priority, exploiting his/her protagonist role in legitimizing political projects domestically and regionally. In the case of progressive left-wing populism in the Americas, despite occasionally successful overturns by the Kirchners, Ortega, Correa, Morales, and Maduro, who were able to produce such committed relationships with diaspora, ethnic, or political groups outside their countries, they fell well short of Chávez's capacity to perform empathetic resonance with international audiences. In the case of Chávez, his defiant leadership was cherished partly due to his willingness to allocate resources to generate an effective and affective relationship to back up professions of solidarity (Sagarzazu and Thies 2019). Since Chávez's death in 2013, the progressive populist wave has been lacking a similar impetus, despite efforts to eternalize the figure of the deceased leader, even bordering in the idea of reincarnation, as illustrated by the portrayal of images and the speeches pronounced during the anniversaries of "Chávez's immortality".

6 The Transnational Overflow of Citizenship

While claiming to defend the national interest, populist leaderships have increasingly decoupled legitimation from its sole endorsement by citizens within a national territory, projecting also transnational and international strategies of legitimation. Traditionally, works focusing on populism have concentrated on national constituencies and downplayed transnational strategies of commitment and legitimation. It may be argued, however, that the practices of international legitimization have always been central to the power of all kinds of regimes and institutions, and particularly for those leaderships whose effective hold on power and claims of authoritative rule are grounded in popular support (Hurd 2008, 2–3). As populist governments base their right to rule on the claim that they act and speak in the name of "the people", their illiberal deficits often place them at the centre of major debates over their legitimacy in local, regional, and global arenas. Given the polarization they create, the stakes they play for, and the passions they generate, populist leaders and governments are objects of constant international scrutiny, particularly during moments of crisis. Unsurprisingly, populist leaderships have increasingly engaged regional and global publics through public diplomacy, interactive social media, cults of personality, and diaspora gatherings (Moffitt 2016; Chryssogelos 2017; Destradi and Plagemann 2019; Wajner 2021).

In recent decades, such tendency has characterized both Euroalternativism and the left-wing Latin American populism that have sought to legitimize their political projects transnationally. Euroalternativism, particularly the Democracy in Europe Movement 2025 (DiEM25) launched by former Greek Finance Minister Yanis Varoufakis, was an attempt to construct a transnational leftist project to "democratize" Europe against Brussels's unaccountable elites (De Cleen et al. 2019; Fanoulis and Guerra 2020). Likewise, Latin American progressive populisms have also made huge efforts and devoted national resources to cultivate connections with transnational audiences through ceremonial gatherings and celebratory aesthetics, turning to festive mobilization of popular sectors as support basis. Political movements, student associations, ethno-religious groups, and other civil society organizations developed transnational and transcontinental ties and organized joint events, helping to shape a common discourse of "grassroots networking".

Pink Tide populists promoted social activism all through Latin America, moving in parallel to the role assigned for constructing collective commitments as in the "Bolivarian Circles" in Venezuela, the *piqueteros* in Argentina, and the coca growers in Bolivia (Hawkins and Hansen 2006; Roberts 2006, esp. 141–143). Based on mobilizing mass protest and a heterodox political steering by charismatic leaderships, the Pink Tide leaders found common ground with social movements such as the Mexican Zapatistas and the Brazilian MST, the landless peasant movement. To expand their communication among both local and external audiences, Pink Tide leaders created new mass communication channels put to work at the service of their project, contributing to the dissemination of epic content and the mobilization of support. The desire to communicate directly with Latino audiences all through the region was highlighted since 2005 by Telesur, the Latin American television network that aims to compete with the Northern satellite channels from the US and Europe (Zúquete 2008; Dinneen 2012, esp. 45–46). The promoted themes enabled progressive populists to influence public opinion beyond their borders, aimed at reaching a regional sense of commitment, support and political mobilization.

Those transnational connections became evident during international meetings. During the Summit of the Americas, which took place in Mar del Plata in November 2005, Chavista supporters organized a "counter-summit" (*anti-cumbre*), organizing impressive demonstrations of popular support. Among them, a massive march involving popular icons, joined by multiple student associations, workers syndicates, and all kinds of gender, environmental, ethnic, human rights or social organizations from all around Latin America (Saguier 2007). Impassioned speeches by the progressive populist leaders at the final event in the World Cup Stadium emboldened the resolution of tens of thousands attending the event. There, Chávez gave his famous speech calling for the abandonment of the free trade agreement with the United States (the Free Trade Agreement of the Americas, FTAA, or ALCA in Spanish), while a powerful media campaign ("No al ALCA") projected the popular struggle against it in terms of a colossus confrontation between two distinct hemispheric visions.

By dominating like-minded audiences in the region, progressive populist governments succeeded in shaping the political agenda, confronting, and ultimately halting the advance of the free trade agreement (Wajner and Roniger 2019; Roniger 2022, 181–203). With time, several of the social groups whose rights were promoted transnationally in these demonstrations produced a sort of "identity boomerang", which increasingly criticized the gap between discourse and concrete policymaking. Disenchantment with those governments and the regional institutions they (re)assembled grew accordingly. This could be seen by the 2010s in the massive strikes and marches in several of these countries, primarily Venezuela and Nicaragua, where the governments opted to use violence and criminalize protest once they faced internal opposition. In other words, the tension between citizen expectations and systemic failings were reproduced and even exacerbated by the transnational outreach of that populist wave.

7 Concluding Remarks

Research on populism has pointed out that populism thrives in the shadow of the failings of modern constitutional democracies. In this chapter, I have added hindsight stemming from studies of citizenship. Specifically, the chapter assessed how populism challenges certain conceptualizations of citizenship, and what the social and political literature on citizenship brings to the study of populism. Populism reshapes citizenship. It recalibrates strategies of representation and participation, granting salience to participatory mass mobilization, albeit through state regulation and leadership ameliorating the autonomy of civil society. I claimed that populists reduce yet cannot eliminate democratic accountability, and that their mediating structures of representation and participation not only impose top-down controls upon their followings, but also require a recognition of bottom-up demands to continue being effective. It is worth reiterating that the idea of non-mediated access between the masses and populist leaders is just a chimera. As discussed, the intense use of mass mobilization as a means of deepening majoritarian support creates lopsided power structures both within the mediating organizations and at the apex of state leadership.

In addition, populism turns concrete policymaking into part of a general statement about society's sense of identity and direction. It is in the interface of market access, political membership, and public identities that populist leaders, movements or parties make their full impact. This analysis also pointed out that populism relies heavily on performance, embedding claims of citizens' legitimacy in highly affective bonds, and ideally developing a mutual connection and devotion towards leaders supposedly working for the well-being and dignity of the people, while citizens respond with an affective cult of the leader's persona. Finally, this examination registered an increasing reliance on transnational strategies of building and maintaining support, moving from a traditional focus on support within the boundaries of a home territory towards adding a transnational overflow of support and alliances.

As much as populist leaders, movements and parties raise high expectations, they often fail to deliver and beget deceptions. As Benjamín Fernández Bogado, one of the drafters of the 1992 post-authoritarian constitution of Paraguay put it: "[P]opulisms are good interpreters of the winds, but in practice they have shown a lack of capacity to turn the state into a driver of development and of solid institutions preventing the motivation [of power holders] to stay in power simply because 'those preceding them were worse'" (2009, 225). Once clinging to power, populist citizenship regimes often witness a declining sense of participation and increased alienation from the system. If the polarizing discourse and mechanisms of control of the populist machinery remain in force, such system often vacates citizens' ability to exercise the dual function of being autonomous and exercising their influence on state power holders. The arts have also managed to portray with subtlety this dynamic, as exemplified in a text published by Roberto Bolaño close to his death in 2003. In *El gaucho insufrible* (The insufferable gaucho), the renowned Chilean writer brought up the following metaphor to reflect on the effects of Peronism on neighbour Argentine society and politics:

> For Pereda [a fictional character of a lawyer turned gaucho], the great problem of Argentina, of the Argentina of those years, was precisely the problem of the stepmother. We Argentines, he used to say, did not have a mother or our mother was invisible or [perhaps] she abandoned us on the doors of an *inclusa* [a house for orphans and unwanted children]. Stepmothers, on the other hand, we had too many and from all colors, starting with the great Peronist stepmother.
>
> BOLAÑO 2003, 16

While they reach and routinize power, many populist leaders and movements engage continuously in recreating the specific connection they have established between political membership, public identities, and market access. The maintenance and reproduction of a sense of collective direction and meaning is operated in populism through the reactivation of mechanisms of control and dependency, channelling participatory mobilization at the expense of representation and citizen autonomy. As they enter such stage of development, populist leaders and governments face a dynamic that other types of citizenship have also evinced; namely, a loss of trust in political ideas and practices (Berlin 1982, 26). On its part, populist leaderships and their performative machinery resent citizen resistance and disenchantment and may generate the scenario that Roberto Bolaño captured in his narrative. Namely, a sense of living as minors under the whims of a "stepmother" structure of power that can provide needs while autonomous agency is relinquished. Facing such problems and contestation, many of the tensions and crises affecting any democratic system are recreated within populist citizenship. These dynamics promise to continue haunting populist governments that, like any other modern constitutional democracy, have placed the status and practice of citizenship at their normative and performative core.

References

Ablard, J. D. and Bohoslavsky, E. (2021) Rumors, "pescado podrido" and disinformation in interwar Argentina. *Journal of Social History*, *55*(1), 65–84.

Adler, E. (2010) Damned if you do, damned if you don't: Performative power and the strategy of conventional and nuclear defusing. *Security Studies*, *19*(2), 199–229.

Åhäll, L. (2018) Affect as methodology: Feminism and the politics of emotion. *International Political Sociology, 12*(1), 36–52.

Anselmi, M. (2018) *Populism: An introduction.* London-New York: Routledge.

Arato, A. (2015) Political theology and populism. In: de la Torre (ed.) *The promise and perils of populism: Global perspectives.* Louisville: University Press of Kentucky, 31–58.

Arato, A. and Cohen, J. L. (2019) Civil society, populism and religion. In: de la Torre (ed.) *Routledge handbook of global populism.* London-New York: Routledge, 98–112.

Avritzer, L. (2002) *Democracy and the public sphere in Latin America.* Princeton: Princeton University Press.

Bellamy, R. (2008) *Citizenship: A very short introduction.* Oxford: Oxford University Press.

Bendix, R. (1964) *Nation building and citizenship.* Berkeley: University of California Press.

Berlin, I. (1982) Political ideas in the twentieth century. In Berlin, I., *Four essays on liberty.* Oxford: Oxford University Press, 55–93.

Bolaño, R. (2003) *El gaucho insufrible.* Barcelona: Anagrama.

Capriles, C. (2006) La enciclopedia del chavismo o hacia una teología del populismo. *Revista Venezolana de Ciencia Política, 29*, 73–92.

Cartes Montory, A. and Díaz Polanco, P. (eds.) (2015) *Ciudadanía, temas y debates.* Santiago de Chile: Centro de Estudios Bicentenario.

Cheesman, N. (2019) Populism in Africa and the potential for "ethnically blind" politics. In: de la Torre, C. (ed.) *Routledge handbook of global populism.* London-New York: Routledge, 362–366.

Chryssogelos, A. (2017) Populism in foreign policy. In *Oxford research encyclopedia of politics.* Oxford: Oxford University Press.

Cohen, J. L. and Arato, A. (1992) *Civil society and political theory.* Cambridge, MA: MIT Press.

Dahrendorf, R. (2008) *The modern social conflict: An essay in the politics of liberty.* Berkeley: University of California Press.

De Cleen, B., Moffitt, B., Panayotu, P. and Stavrakakis, Y. (2019) The potentials and difficulties of transnational populism: The case of the Democracy in Europe Movement 2025 (DiEM2025). *Political Studies, 68*(1),146–166.

de la Torre, C. (2007) The resurgence of radical populism in Latin America. *Constellations 14*(3), 384–397.

de la Torre, C. (2010) *Populist seduction in Latin America.* Athens: Ohio University Press.

de la Torre, C. (2017) Trump's populism: Lessons from Latin America. *Postcolonial Studies, 20*(2), 187–198.

de la Torre, C. (ed.) (2019) *Routledge handbook of global populism.* London-New York: Routledge.

de la Torre, C. and Peruzzotti, E. (eds.) (2008) *El retorno del pueblo. Populismo y nuevas democracias en América Latina.* Quito: Flacso Ecuador.

Destradi, S. and Plagemann, J. (2019) Populism and international relations: (Un)predictability, personalisation, and the reinforcement of existing trends in world politics. *Review of International Studies, 45*(5), 711–730.

Diehl, P. (2019) Twisting representation. In: de la Torre, C. (ed.) *Routledge handbook of global populism.* London-New York: Routledge, 129–143.

Dinneen, M. (2012) The Chávez government and the battle over the media in Venezuela. *Asian Journal of Latin American Studies, 25*(2), 27–53.

Domingues, J. M. (2013) Democracy, freedom and domination: A theoretical discussion with special reference to Brazil via India. In: Sznajder, M., Roniger, L. and Forment, C. A. (eds.) *Shifting frontiers of citizenship: Latin American perspectives.* Leiden: Brill, 83–97.

Douglas, M. (2002) *Implicit meanings.* London: Routledge.

Drezner, D. (2017) The angry populist as foreign policy leader: Real change or just hot air. *Fletcher Forum of World Affairs, 41*(2), 23–43.

Eisenstadt, S. N. (2007) *Las grandes revoluciones y las civilizaciones de la modernidad.* Madrid: Centro de Estudios Políticos y Constitucionales.

Eisenstadt, S. N. (2009) The reconstitution of the realm of the political in modern societies. In: Giri, A. K. (ed.) *The modern prince and the modern sage.* London: Sage, 3–24.

Ellis, S., Hálfdanarson, G. and Isaacs, A. K. (eds.) (2006) *Citizenship in historical perspective.* Pisa: Pisa University Press.

Fanoulis, E. and Guerra, S. (2020) Veridiction and leadership in transnational populism: The case of DiEM25. *Politics and Governance, 8*(1), 217–225.

Featherstone, M., Lash, S. and Robertson, R. (eds.) (1995) *Global modernities.* London: Sage.

Fernández Bogado, B. (2009) *¿Y ahora qué? Itinerario de la eterna desilusión política en América Latina.* Fernando de la Mora: Editorial Libre.

Franck, T. M. (1990) *The power of legitimacy among nations.* Oxford: Oxford University Press.

Fraser, N. (1992) Rethinking the public sphere. In: Calhoun, C. (ed.) *Habermas and the public sphere.* Cambridge, MA: MIT Press, 109–142.

Freeden, M. (2017) After the Brexit referendum: Revisiting populism as an ideology. *Journal of Political Ideologies, 22*(1), 1–11.

Germani, G. (1978) *Authoritarianism, fascism and national populism.* New York: Transaction.

Gerth, H. H. and Mills, C. W. (eds.) (1958) *From Max Weber: Essays in sociology.* Oxford: Oxford University Press.

Goodwyn, L. (1979) *The populist movement: A short history of the agrarian revolt in America.* Oxford: Oxford University Press.

Gosewinkel, D. (2001) Citizenship: Historical development. In: Smelser, N. J. and Baltes, P. B. (eds.) *International encyclopedia of behavioral and social sciences*. Amsterdam: Elsevier, 1852–1857.

Habermas, J. (1987) *The theory of communicative action*. Boston: Beacon Press.

Hawkins, K. A. and Hansen, D. R. (2006) Dependent civil society: The Círculos Bolivarianos in Venezuela. *Latin American Research Review, 41*(1), 102–132.

Held, D. (1987) *Models of democracy*. Stanford: Stanford University Press.

Hilgers, T. (ed.) (2012) *Clientelism in everyday Latin American politics*. New York: Palgrave Macmillan.

Hurd, I. (2008) *After anarchy: Legitimacy and power in the United Nations Security Council*. Princeton: Princeton University Press.

Kalberg, S. (2021) *Max Weber's sociology of civilizations*. London-New York: Routledge.

Kalyvas, A. and Katznelson, I. (2008) *Liberal beginnings: Making a republic for the moderns*. Cambridge: Cambridge University Press.

Keane, J. (1988) *Democracy and civil society: On the predicaments of European socialism, the prospects for democracy, and the problem of controlling social and political power*. London: Verso.

Kinnvall, C. (2018) Ontological insecurities and postcolonial imaginaries: The emotional appeal of populism. *Humanity & Society, 42*(4), 523–543.

Laclau, E. (2005) *On populist reason*. London: Verso.

Lefort, C. (1988) *Democracy and political theory*. Minneapolis: University of Minnesota Press.

Levitsky, S. and Loxton, J. (2013) Populism and competitive authoritarianism in the Andes. *Democratization, 20*(1), 107–136.

Levitsky, S. and Loxton, J. (2019) Populism and competitive authoritarianism in Latin America. In: de la Torre, C. (ed.) *Routledge handbook of global populism*. London-New York: Routledge, 334–350.

Lewis, M., Haviland-Jones, J. and Barrett, L. (eds.) (2010) *Handbook of emotions*. New York: Guilford Press.

Lister, M. and Pia, E. (2012) *Citizenship in contemporary Europe*. Edinburgh: Edinburgh Scholarship.

Locke, J. (1980) *Ensayo sobre el gobierno civil*. Madrid: Aguilar.

Marshall, T. (1950) *Citizenship and social class, and other essays*. Cambridge: Cambridge University Press.

Moffitt, B. (2016) *The global rise of populism: Performance, political style, and representation*. Stanford: Stanford University Press.

Murilo de Carvalho, J. (2001) *Cidadania no Brasil, o longo camino*. São Paulo: Civilização Brasileira.

Ong, A. (1999) *Flexible citizenship: The cultural logics of transnationality*. Durham-London: Duke University Press.

Oxhorn, P. (1998) The social foundations of Latin American's recurrent populism: Problems of class formation and collective action. *Journal of Historical Sociology, 11*(2), 212–246.

Pace, M. (2006) *Politics of regional identity.* London-New York: Routledge.

Panizza, F. (ed.) (2005) *Populism and the mirror of democracy.* London: Verso.

Pérez-Díaz, V. M. (1993) *The return of civil society.* Cambridge, MA: Harvard University Press.

Rein, R. (2013) From Juan Perón to Hugo Chávez and back: Populism reconsidered. In: Sznajder, M., Roniger, L. and Forment, C. A. (eds.) *Shifting frontiers of citizenship: Latin American perspectives.* Leiden: Brill, 289–309.

Roberts, K. M. (2006) Populism, political conflict, and grass-roots organization in Latin America. *Comparative Politics, 38*(2), 127–148.

Roberts, K. M. (2007) Latin American's populist revival. *SAIS Review of International Affairs, 27*(1), 3–15.

Roniger, L. (2011) *Transnational politics in Central America.* Gainesville: University Press of Florida.

Roniger, L. (2013) Modern populism in Latin America. In: Vinson, B. et al. (eds.) *Oxford bibliographies online.* Oxford: Oxford University Press.

Roniger, L. (2022) *Transnational perspectives on Latin America: The entwined histories of a multi-state region.* Oxford: Oxford University Press.

Roniger, L. and Senkman, L. (2018) Conspirationism, synarchism and the long shadow of Perón in Argentina. *Journal of Modern Jewish Studies, 17*(4), 434–454.

Roniger, L. and Senkman, L. (2022) *Conspiracy theories and Latin American history: Lurking in the shadows.* London-New York: Routledge.

Rovira Kaltwasser, C. (2015) Explaining the emergence of populism in Europe and the Americas. In: de la Torre, C. (ed.) *The promise and perils of populism: Global perspectives.* Louisville: University Press of Kentucky, 189–227.

Ruzza, C. (2019) Populism, migration, and xenophobia in Europe. In: de la Torre, C. (ed.) *Routledge handbook of global populism.* London-New York: Routledge, 201–215.

Sagarzazu, I. and Thies, C. G. (2019) The foreign policy rhetoric of populism: Chávez, oil and anti-imperialism. *Political Science Quarterly, 72*(1), 205–214.

Saguier, M. (2007) The hemispheric social alliance and the free trade area of the Americas process: The challenges and opportunities of transnational coalitions against neo-liberalism. *Globalizations, 4*(2), 251–265.

Schama, S. (1989) *Citizens: A chronicle of the French Revolution.* New York: Alfred Knopf.

Schwartz, S. B. (ed.) (1994) *Implicit understandings.* Cambridge: Cambridge University Press.

Seligman, A. (1992) *The idea of civil society.* New York: Free Press.

Serra, P. (2019) Populismo, democrazia e limite del potere político. *Questione Giustizia, 1*, 55–66.

Shklar, J. (1991) *American citizenship: The quest for inclusion.* Cambridge, MA: Harvard University Press.

Skonieczny, A. (2018) Emotions and political narratives: Populism, Trump and trade. *Politics and Governance*, 6(4), 62–72.

Smith, A. D. (1996) Commemorating the dead, inspiring the living: Maps, memories and moralities in the recreation of national identities. Paper presented at the ECRS conference on collective identities, Paris.

Spanakos, A. P. (2008) New wine, old bottles, flamboyant sommelier: Chávez, citizenship, and populism. *New Political Science*, *30*(4), 521–544.

Sznajder, M., Roniger, L. and Forment, C. A. (eds.) (2013) *Shifting frontiers of citizenship: Latin American perspectives.* Leiden: Brill.

Taylor, C. (1990) Modes of civil society. *Public Culture*, *3*(1), 95–118.

Turner, B. S. (2013) Four models of citizenship: From authoritarianism to consumer citizenship. In: Sznajder, M., Roniger, L. and Forment, C. A. (eds.) *Shifting frontiers of citizenship: Latin American perspectives.* Leiden: Brill, 55–81.

Turner, B. S. (ed.) (1993) *Citizenship and social theory*. London: Sage.

Urbinati, N. (2019) Antiestablishment and the substitution of the whole with one of its parts. In: de la Torre, C. (ed.) *Routledge handbook of global populism.* London-New York: Routledge, 77–97.

Wajner, D. (2021). Exploring the Foreign Policies of Populist Governments: (Latin) America First. *Journal of International Relations and Development*, *24*(1): 651–680.

Wajner, D. and Roniger, L. (2019) Transnational identity politics in the Americas: Reshaping "Nuestramérica" as Chavismo's regional legitimation strategy. *Latin American Research Review*, *54*(2), 458–475.

Weyland, K. (2001) Clarifying a contested concept: Populism in the study of Latin American politics. *Comparative politics*, *34*(1), 1–22.

Weyland, K. (2009) The rise of Latin America's two lefts: Insights from rentier state theory. *Comparative Politics*, *41*(2), 145–164.

Weyland, K. (2019) Populism and authoritarianism. In: de la Torre, C. (ed.) *Routledge handbook of global populism.* London-New York: Routledge, 319–333.

Yilmaz, Ihsan and Nicholas Morieson (2022). Civilizational Populism: Definition, Literature, Theory, and Practice. *Religions* 13: 1026–1051.

Zúquete, J. P. (2007) *Missionary politics in contemporary Europe.* Syracuse: Syracuse University Press.

Zúquete, J. P. (2008) The missionary politics of Hugo Chávez. *Latin American Politics and Society*, *50*(1), 91–121.

CHAPTER 2

Gender Contradictions in the Democratic Imaginary: The Populist Response

Paula Diehl

> We need to rediscover our manhood. Only when we take back our manhood will we become manful. And only when we become manful, will we be able to defend ourselves. And we must be able to defend ourselves.
>
> BJÖRN HÖCKE, Alternative for Germany

•••

> The Amazon is a virgin that every sex maniac from abroad wants to violate. Brazil cannot become the paradise of gay tourism. If you want to have sex with a woman here, feel free to do so. But this should not become the paradise of the gay world.
>
> JAIR BOLSONARO, President of Brazil

1 Introduction

Although populism has become one of the major topics in political science, its relationship to gender is still underdeveloped. The question of a specific populist approach to gender remains unanswered. There are strong reasons to assume that the gender approach taken by populism depends on the cultural context and on the strong ideology added to it (Mudde and Rovira Kaltwasser 2015). Generally, gender research focuses on very different subjects such as social policy, distribution of power, political discourse, or leadership. Yet does a coherent picture emerge from these? Is it possible to detect a specific populist relationship to gender that is valid for all populist variations? In this Chapter I will explore the following hypothesis: There may be a specific

 | DOI:10.1163/9789004679016_004

relationship between populism and gender that can be found in the populist response to existing contradictions within modern democracy.

From this perspective, the problems found in the relationship between populism and gender can be traced back to the political imaginary and the history of modern democracy. If populism is always possible because "modern democratic politics is premised upon claims about the history of popular sovereignty", making the history of modern populism and the history of modern popular sovereignty coterminous, as Duncan Kelly (2017) states, reflecting on this history in terms of gender can tap into a new vein for understanding the phenomenon of populism and its relationship to democracy. Exploring populist responses to the contradictions of the modern democratic imaginary can contribute to an understanding of the specific approach to gender taken by populism in general and right-wing populism in particular.

The goal of this chapter is to enrich the approach to gender in populism research by taking the contradictions of the democratic imaginary and its history into consideration. It develops this argument by describing the gender challenges and ambivalences of the modern democratic imaginary. In what follows, the limits of the gender approach in inclusionary populism and its promises of gender equality are tested. Importantly, even in cases where populist policy is committed to gender inclusion, symbolism and discourse seem to rely on traditional gender models. As will be shown, populist constructions of the people and the leader as well as their relationship are deeply embedded in a democratic imaginary shaped by traditional gender relations.

By contemplating the constitutive ambiguity of populism (Mény and Surel 2002), this chapter briefly depicts the populist relationship to democracy and adds a second layer of reading by taking the gendered imagination of democracy into account. Special attention will be given to the tradition that contributes to shaping the modern democratic imaginary. At this point, the evaluation of populist constructions of the people and the leader shows to what extent populism presents a common lineage attached to traditional gender relations in modern democracy. This is particularly visible when it comes to the populist narrative of the betrayed people (Taguieff 2007; Diehl 2018) and to the promise of popular empowerment (Laclau 2005). Two oppositions emerge here: First, the people (as a single actor) is depicted as the "male" sovereign while the "female" elite is rejected. Second, the crowd is characterized as feminized while its transformation into the sovereign people presupposes a gender transformation connected to the emancipation promise.

Having said that, I do not assume that society is unchangeable. On the contrary, political culture and social norms are always the subject of dispute and struggle. As such, gender roles, relations, and imagination are contested subjects of populist politics and are also objects of their performative interferences. Gender stereotypes have become increasingly porous and gender norms more and more diverse. Nevertheless, this same gender diversity is generating strong reactions from anti-democratic movements, which link authoritarian far-right ideologies with gender anxiety, echoing the crisis of masculinity described by George Mosse at the beginning of the twentieth century (1996a; 1996b). In the twenty-first century, gender discourse has become a catalyst for right-wing populism and extremism. The chapter concludes with a reflection on the impact of right-wing populism on gender relations and its costs for democratic norms.

2 Gender in Populism Research

A few years ago, scholars in the field started paying more attention to the gender dimension of populism (Kampwirth 2010b; Abi-Hassan 2017; Dingler, Lefkofridi and Marent 2017).[1] However, most of these works do not focus on populism as a general phenomenon, but on its specific form as right-wing populism (among others: Spierings et al. 2015; Abi-Hassan 2017; Kötting, Bitzan and Pető 2017; Coffé 2018; Dietze and Roth 2020; Donà 2020).

Research on right-wing populism shows key elements related to gender: It is masculinist and homophobic, propagates gender relationships based on the "heterosexual matrix" (Butler 1993, 239), cultivates family ideals from the nineteenth century, and reinforces authoritarian relationships between the leader and the people as well as between the *pater familias* and his wife and children. Some scholars claim that there is an intrinsic relationship between right-wing populism and gender since an awareness of unequal gender relations is declared the enemy of right-wing populist movements. Gender has become "a meta-language for negotiating different conditions of inequality and power in the context of current struggles over hegemony, and over resources forged by neoliberalism" (Dietze and Roth 2020, 8). Right-wing populists react to that and are obsessed with gender, connecting it to "ethno-sexism". They "question, oppose, and ambitiously fight feminists, non-traditional ways of life, and gender studies, perceiving them as obstacles to demographic goals" (ibid., 13). Right-wing ideologies use gender "in an intersecting way to create the 'other'

1 Carlos de la Torre reminded me that Latin American scholars were already paying attention to the gender aspect of populism before it became a topic of populism studies in Europe and North America (Navarro 1977; Finchelstein 2010, 142). For an intersectional perspective, see de la Torre (2010, 88–92).

and at the same time to create the 'we' or 'the people' in different European countries" (Mayer, Šori and Sauer 2016, 86).

However, the dependency of right-wing populism on the affirmation of masculinism, which is traced and highlighted by gender scholars, seems to be much more connected with right-wing ideologies than with populism. In inclusionary populism, for example, the elements described above are missing. Sometimes, the contrary is the case: Left-wing populist parties like the United Socialist Party of Venezuela explicitly advocate for equality of the sexes and recognition of marginalized groups, even if they do not embrace LGBT causes (Corrales 2015, 55), while Podemos in Spain is committed to transgender and homosexual rights and is very critical of the masculinist political style (Caravantes 2019). These findings make the question of a specific relationship between populism and gender more complicated.

3 The Interplay between Populism and Gender: Testing the Limits of Inclusionary Populism

If scholars agree on a specific attitude of right-wing populism regarding gender issues, the picture becomes more ambivalent when it comes to inclusionary populism. In Latin America, populism from the 1930s to the 1960s and left-wing populism in the 1990s seem to play an inclusionary role concerning women. Populist policies were responsible for extending electoral rights to women and for opening up public jobs and education opportunities for them. According to Latin America specialists, there are two ways in which the populists of the early wave related to women: They promoted the expansion of women's political rights and provided them with "new social services", as Lola Luna states (quoted in Kampwirth 2010a, 4). In Argentina, for example, women obtained the right to vote in 1947, during Juan Domingo Perón's government. In Brazil, depending on state legislation, educated women had had the right to vote since the nineteenth century, but it was only during Getúlio Vargas's government that this right was incorporated in the constitution regardless of women's education level. These findings confirm the hypothesis of inclusionary populism in Latin America (Mudde and Rovira Kaltwasser 2013), even though the case of Perón, unlike that of Vargas, seems to include many aspects of fascism (Finchelstein 2019).

Looking at the early examples in Latin America, populism seems to be a democratizing and including force for gender relations, but things become more complicated if one looks behind the policies mentioned above. Women's traditional roles as mothers and wives first and foremost were not challenged but rather confirmed by populism. The most complex use of traditional women's roles and politics of inclusion can be observed in the case of Evita. Maria Eva Duarte Perón and her husband, Juan Domingo Perón, related to the people in a traditional family structure: While Juan Domingo impersonated the father of the nation and symbolized authority, Evita was the mother, incarnating charity and love. However, this did not prevent her becoming "the second most powerful political figure in Argentina" in her time (Navarro 1977, 229). Symbolically, Eva Perón played an intermediary role between the people and the leader, but institutionally, too, she organized the contact between politicians and trade union representatives and her husband. By 1946 "all contact with Perón was channelled through his wife", who became his personal representative in the Ministry of Labour (ibid., 237).

How did Evita acquire this power? First, there is a metamorphosis of her status through her marriage (ibid., 235). Being married "honoured" her, elevating her social position. If she was an actress with a dubious reputation before, becoming a wife gave her the social acceptance that she needed, confirming the gender hierarchy. Second, and unexpectedly, she did not try to hide her modest background, but made use of her low-class origins to relate to the people and to invoke the life experience of the *descamisados*, the "shirtless" poor people defended by Juan Domingo Perón. By intersecting class and gender, Evita responded to populist symbolic revindications without questioning the traditional female role. In addition, she used luxury and glamour to generate fantasies and identification with her image as the radio and film star that she was before coming to politics. This is an important element linking populism to media culture and helps explain how apparently contradictory performances, such as claiming to be one of the people while at the same time displaying ostentatious luxury, could be perceived as coherent by her audience.

Comparing the populist approach to gender incorporated by Evita to twentieth-century inclusionary populism, it seems that the role of women in Latin American left-wing populism has gone through an emancipation process. In Venezuela, Chávez incorporated demands and organizations of feminist movements in his social policies. "Although we could find no evidence that Chávez has ever used the term 'gender,' he has backed up such initiatives implicitly or explicitly" by signing institutional agreements or making references to women's rights in his speeches. Yet these emancipatory feminist achievements were attributed to Chávez's personal engagement (Espina and Rokowski 2010, 192).

Although Chávez's social policies and populist discourse contributed to an increase in women's rights and recognition, at the same time, political confrontation and struggle were represented in militaristic and masculinist terms while "popular women" were addressed through a discourse of "revolutionary motherhood" (ibid., 194). This becomes quite clear in a TV interview: "Yes, I am a feminist. I think that machismo, and I was 'machista', I think that the woman is important to save the movement. Capitalism is 'machista', wars are 'machista' the macho's dominance over the world. [...] I think we need the woman's spirit."[2] While Evita's traditional image can be traced back to the female role of her time and is disconnected from feminist revindications, the feminist struggle within Chávez's populism is more intriguing since it was based on the initiative of feminist groups but framed in traditional gender roles, focusing on the imagination of women as mothers.

However, some authors are more optimistic about left-wing populism embracing feminist positions and highlight the increase in female representatives: "[D]uring the presidency of Néstor Kirchner (2003–2007), women began to occupy decision-making roles, such as the Ministries of Economy and Production, of Defense, and of Social Development." In the same way, they interpret the election of Cristina Fernández de Kirchner to the presidency as "the most recent achievement in the struggle for gender equality" (Abi-Hassan 2017, 434). However, addressing the traditional association of leadership with masculinity, Abi-Hassan writes: "[T]he style of populist female leaders is also a reflection of the contradiction between social traditional values and public life." Looking at right-wing populist leaders as Abi-Hassan does, this contradiction takes on more vivid colours, but it does not mean that it disappears when it comes to left-wing populist female leaders. Moreover, Cristina Fernández de Kirchner saw herself in the same tradition as Evita. After her husband, Néstor Kirchner, the former president of Argentina, died, she promised to wear black for a year, which she did. This was not only a symbol of personal grief, but also a political sign of her complementary bond with the former leader. Although Cristina was already president when her husband died, the couple had constructed an image of gender complementarity. The year of mourning seems to accomplish a *rite de passage*, in which Kirchner took a crucial step towards a new gender definition of her own leadership.

Faced with the cases of Eva Perón and Cristina de Kirchner, one could argue that the gender question involved here is not concerned with populism, but with the specific cultural background in Latin America. Yet, this hypothesis can be easily contested since it presupposes a homogeneous political culture in a large continent and during different historical contexts. The answer to

2 "Sí, yo soy feminista. Yo creo que el machismo, y yo fui machista, yo creo que la mujer hace falta para salvar este movimiento. El capitalismo es machista, las guerras son machistas, el dominio del macho sobre el mundo. [...] Creo que hace falta el espíritu de la mujer."

these assumptions is twofold: First, Argentina in the first half of the twentieth century is very different from Venezuela in the first half of the twenty-first century. Equating both would be culturally and historically mistaken. Second, the ambivalent relationship between left-wing populism and gender can be observed in other examples around the globe. The difficulties of inclusionary populism in transcending traditional gender roles remain despite any potential feminist revindications, as Chávez's case shows.

In Spain, Podemos reveals "a friction between feminist and pluralist elements and the reproduction of a dominant masculine party culture" (Caravantes 2019, 466). Whereas Chávez's commitment to feminism avoided casting gender discrimination issues in these terms and never questioned the masculine frame of power or leader's performances, members of Podemos explicitly attack dominant masculine party culture and "stress the need to move away from [...] the exercising of power that accentuates hierarchy, confrontation, and imposition"; instead, the party advocates for leadership "based on dialogue, collaboration, and inclusiveness. Podemos just frames 'new' politics through the transformation of the gender order" (ibid., 468). The party not only promotes inclusionary populism but questions the masculine paradigm of power. However, despite this explicit criticism and its commitment to a gender transformation of politics, Podemos still reproduces the masculine models that the party rejects.

Podemos's internal organization, strategy, and leadership style reveal patriarchal structures, although the party is committed to representing the diversity of the people. Podemos's competitive discourse is one of these elements: "The duty of a revolutionary is to win", Pablo Iglesias stated (quoted by Caravantes 2019, 474). Caravantes regards this attitude as one that reinforces masculinist structures, privileging the dominance of the stronger over the weaker. In addition, the party reproduces hierarchy based on intellectual authority and the dominance of experts and cannot escape from the populist centrality of a charismatic leader that reinforces male authority. These issues are debated critically by the party, but the answer found by many of its members is highly problematic: They advocate for the "feminization of politics" and have even employed the term in electoral campaigns. Some leaders of Podemos defended the use of the term because it defines "women's style, tone, and attitude" or as "a distinctive capacity of motherly care" suitable for politics (ibid., 473). In so doing, they reiterate traditional gender stereotypes, even if "femininity" is considered positively. Here the imagination of femaleness characterized by softness, sensibility, and care reaffirms the power and aggressivity attributed to masculinity, thereby contributing to traditional gender imagination.

It appears that, despite all efforts to overcome gender-traditional roles and masculine-dominant politics, left-wing populism is still struggling to frame gender in different terms. The examples above reinforce female stereotypes of motherhood, emotionality, and "sensibility", as opposed to the masculine authority, rationality, and aggressive competition. I argue that there is, indeed, a specific relationship of populism to gender that can be detected in the construction of the leader and of the people and also in the presentation of their relationship. Yet these constructions cannot be dissociated from the democratic imaginary or from the relationship between populism and democracy. In the following two sections I examine the relationship between populism and democracy and present a reading of the Western democratic tradition by considering its gender aspects in depicting the people, the citizens, and the political representatives. Despite the democratic promise of equality, democratic imagination is embedded in socially hierarchical gender, class, and race constructions that contradict the principle of equality (Diehl 2019). Populism just incorporates and reacts to these contradictions.

4 A Gender Reading of Democratic History and Populism

Before locating populism's response to gender contradictions in democracy, it is necessary to briefly introduce the notion of the political imaginary. The political imaginary can be described as a dimension of social and individual life that makes constructions of political reality possible. It includes, on the one hand, the repertoire of images, discourse, symbols, and emotions and, on the other, the imagination and patterns of perception shared by a collectivity. In this sense, the imaginary encompasses the imaginative and creative capacities of human beings (Diehl 2019). Cornelius Castoriadis characterizes it as a crucial dimension and source of social life. It is the singular and collective capacity to create forms, presentations, and self-presentations of society.

> From this perspective, the imaginary is conceived of as a productive source of meaning, able to hold members of society together. It is the instituting capacity of society in the full sense of the word, since it enables the creation of the social. At the same time, the imaginary is a social construction itself, since it refers to society as an institutionalized world.
>
> DIEHL 2019, 414

More importantly, the political imaginary is not unchangeable, but a product of human beings and their history. This is important for understanding the contradictions of the democratic imaginary.

The relationship between populism and democracy is characterized by the affirmation of the people as sovereign, and by the rejection of the elite and established institutions connected to them (Mény and Surel 2002; Mudde 2004). Following Mudde's minimal approach to populism, Sahar Abi-Hassan states that one of the consequences of the populist moral distinction between "the pure people" and "the corrupt elite" is that it makes gender an almost unnecessary, or even irrelevant, category for the construction of the people (Abi-Hassan 2017, 428). Abi-Hassan is right regarding the explicit construction of the people as a collective identity. Indeed, the people in populism serves as a symbolic glue, helping to overcome differences between groups and individuals, but this is only on the surface. When the political imaginary is taken into consideration, gender becomes much more relevant.

The historical perspective helps explain how the revolutions of the eighteenth century contribute to the shaping of the democratic imaginary, including its gender implications. In the French Revolution, in particular, the imagination of political actors such as the leader, the people, the citizen, and, of course, the elite has become extremely gendered. While political actors with positive connotations (leader, people, and citizen) were, and still are, imagined as male, the imagination of the elite as corrupt, or of the crowd as infantilized and manipulable are still clearly associated with femininity. Considering the gendered aspect of the democratic imaginary can help to explain how populism – including its variations along the ideological spectrum – deals with gendered patterns of perception for the role of the leader, the people, the citizen, "the common man", the crowd, and the elites involved in the populist narrative.

After the revolutions of the eighteenth century, the emerging forms of modern democracy developed a gender-dichotomized imagination of collectivities and political subjects, which shaped the democratic imaginary and continues to echo in the contradictions denounced especially by feminist movements. Modern democracy makes a promise of universality and equality but, at the same time, affirms gender (class and race) hierarchy and exclusion (Diehl 2019). Furthermore, the Western democratic imaginary develops and promotes gender fantasies about the elites, the citizens, the people, the crowd, and the political leaders. These contradictions derive from the hegemonic imagination of a male, white, and educated citizen (Fraser 1987) that serves as a prototype for the idealization of the democratic actor affecting political representation until today (Celis 2008; Childs 2004; Lombardo and Meier 2014).

In revolutionary France, the male citizen opposed the feminized aristocrat (Landes 2006, 73). By the end of the eighteenth and the beginning of the nineteenth centuries, another gender opposition came to the fore: The masculine people that act as a political subject is opposed to the feminized crowd described by Le Bon (1897) and Freud (2018 [1922]). On this basis, populism can be understood as a complex response to these gender oppositions in modern democracy and as their manifestations in the imagination of the people, the leader, and their relationship. Populism makes a promise of emancipation: The silent majority (Taggart 2000, 93; Canovan 2005) should become the sovereign people and "take back control" – to quote the Brexit slogan. Yet if the background of the democratic imaginary is considered, this promise reveals several gender implications: The "feminized", passive, and easily manipulated crowd should become an active and sovereign people in order to reverse power relations.

In what follows I will examine the gender aspect of the modern political imaginary by considering three gender arrangements replicating the opposition between female and male. The first arrangement concerns the imagination of the people as a male political subject in opposition to the feminized elite. The second arrangement is depicted by the opposition between the feminine crowd (passive, seducible, passionate, and manipulable) and the masculine people (active and sovereign). The third gender arrangement concerns the relation between the masculinized leader and the oscillating (male) sovereign/feminized crowd status of the people. This arrangement is particularly important for understanding populism and the way it twists political representation (Diehl 2018). If the gender of the leader is based on the imagination of male leadership and stresses political activity as a male one, the status of the people switches between the feminized and leader-dependent crowd, on the one hand, and, on the other, the people as sovereign, inscribed in the male tradition of democratic empowerment. As I show elsewhere, the populist twist consists in radicalizing the tension between vertical leadership and the promise of a horizontal relationship between the leader and the people in a democratic setting.

4.1 *The Male People and the Feminine Elite*

The first arrangement is depicted by the imagination of the male citizen opposed to the feminized aristocrat. With the emergence of the idea of popular sovereignty, gendered fantasies of the people have come to the fore, shaping the democratic imagination of citizenship and political activity. Jean-Jacques Rousseau described the citizen as a public person, distinct from the private person. If the private person is concerned with his private interests, needs, and pleasures, the citizen is defined by his commitment to the common good. Only the citizen can participate in the *volonté générale* and integrate the sovereign. In *Émile*, Rousseau was very clear about the sex of the citizens – the notion of gender applies here but, historically, Rousseau was concerned with the biological character of it. In the chapter "Sophie ou la femme" ("Sophie or the woman"), Rousseau depicts the role of women and men as follows:

> La femme n'existe que par rapport à l'homme, elle est faite pour lui plaire et lui obéir ; ainsi l'a voulu la nature. Les devoirs relatifs aux deux sexes ne sont pas les mêmes: la femme, plus que l'homme, a le devoir d'être fidèle, et d'être jugée telle. Soutenir l'égalité des sexes n'est qu'une vaine déclamation.[3]
>
> ROUSSEAU 1919, 196

For Rousseau, men are capable of public judgement and have a duty to exercise it. This is an integral part of being a citizen. Women, by contrast, were still dependent on their morality/customs (*mœurs*), passions, tastes, pleasures, and goodness (Rousseau 1919, 199). Influenced by Rousseau, the French Revolution shapes the relationship between men and women based on the separation of the political and the private. With the creation of citizenship in the eighteenth century, "masculinity marked the line where citizenship ended and the condition of civil emasculation – effeminacy – began" (Leonard and Tronto 2007, 37). As a consequence, effeminacy became "the antithesis of both good citizenship and a well-ordered gender identity" (ibid., 37). Characteristics attributed to women determined the line between public life and the private sphere. Moreover, "effeminacy denoted a political weakness, an unwillingness to assume the proper public, manly, role" (ibid., 38).

Before the French Revolution, effeminacy had already been used to delegitimize political opponents and, above all, the aristocracy. "Revolutionary rhetoric was distinctly anti-aristocratic, and it was developed in the first place as an instrument of attack on the old society" (Hunt 1984, 50). Characterizing the male body as effeminate was one of the most powerful tools of delegitimization (De Baecque 1997; Landes 2006). The revolutionary imagination created a sharp gender dichotomy between the aristocracy, associating it with femininity, and the bourgeois members of the *tiers-état*, who were cast in masculine

---

3 Woman only exists in relationship to man. She is made to please him and to obey him. This is nature's will. The duties relating to the two sexes are not the same: the woman, more than the man, has the duty to be faithful, and to be judged as such. To advocate equality of the sexes is only a vain declamation (author's translation).

terms. Since women were conceived as being incapable of taking rational decisions or commanding, by depicting aristocrats as feminized, French revolutionaries dismissed their political role and privileges in *ancien* society. After the revolution, women, who had fought in the barricades, were not integrated as political actors. On the contrary, they experienced increasing exclusion from the public sphere (Reichardt and Kohl 2008, 155), as the bourgeois gender dichotomy was simply consolidated.

Populism comes back to gendered imagination discrediting the elites by building the opposition between the feminine elite and the masculine "common man" (Canovan 1981, 232; Mudde 2004, 560). This rhetoric is interesting, since it is not the construction of the people as a crowd, which comes to the fore, but the concentration on the "common man" as a single actor, a prototype of all men in the people. This imagined "common man" is sometimes vulgar, sometimes rough, and always connected to a presumed popular taste. Populist leaders mimic this prototype. Populist leaders perform their belonging to the people in a superposition of gender and class, even if not all populist leaders are vulgar or use sexist appeals like Trump or Bolsonaro. Hugo Chávez, for example, was very careful in performing the low-class man (Diehl 2017). Mixing elements of class and gender in the performance helps the leader to make the most important populist claims plausible: that he is one of the people and that he is the one who can guide the people. For women, mirroring the "common man" is far more difficult.

4.2 *The Masculine People and the Feminine Crowd*

Revolutionary experiences help shape the second gender arrangement in the modern democratic imaginary: the opposition between the male sovereign people and the female crowd. As was mentioned above, the idea of popular sovereignty coined by Rousseau imagines the people as a collective political actor associated with masculinity. If in the *Ancien Régime* the king was the source of absolute sovereignty, as Bodin and Bossuet stated, with the revolution, sovereignty was supposed to migrate to the people. This was a decisive step towards democratic emancipation, but, at the same time, the translation of sovereignty in terms of masculinity contributes to consolidating gender hierarchies in the same political imaginary that promoted emancipation and equality in democracy (Diehl 2019). In revolutionary symbolism, only the passive roles of allegories were attributed to women. Women never incorporate active citizens or the people but stand for the principles of the revolution like equality, justice, fraternity, or freedom, emphasizing their abstract character (Landes 2006, 5). In contrast, the democratic tradition stressed the active role of the male citizens and their unity as a people, as already proposed by Rousseau.

In the nineteenth century though, the democratic imaginary developed a strong gendered imagination of the people as an emotional feminine crowd while the leader is supposed to be the masculine figure of guidance and domination. The imagination of the feminine crowd was first articulated by Gustave Le Bon and was perpetuated by many observers of modern society, among others, by Sigmund Freud. For Le Bon, "[c]rowds are everywhere distinguished by feminine characteristics" and "Latin crowds are the most" (1897, 38). Already in his introductory remarks, Le Bon explains why the crowd needs to be regarded as feminine: "It will be remarked that among the special characteristics of crowds there are several – such as impulsiveness, irritability, incapacity to reason, the absence of judgement and of the critical spirit, the exaggeration of the sentiments, and others besides – which are almost always observed in beings belonging to inferior forms of evolution – in women, savages, and children, for instance" (ibid., 31).

It is quite evident that, at the end of the nineteenth century, femininity was still connected to emotionality and weakness and could not characterize politically mature human beings. Almost three decades later, Freud took up Le Bon's idea and developed a far more nuanced view without describing the crowd as feminized. Instead, he focused on the mechanisms that generate and dissolve the crowd and gave particular emphasis to its relation to the leader. Crowds are highly emotional. Once in the crowd, individuals react differently. "A group is impulsive, changeable and irritable. It is led almost exclusively by the unconscious" (Freud 1999, 83). "The most remarkable and also the most important result of the formation of a group is the 'exaltation or intensification of emotion' produced in every member of it" (ibid., 91).[4] However, this resonates with gender roles in the nineteenth and twentieth centuries. Women were, and sometimes still are, regarded as emotional, vulnerable and more susceptible to manipulation than men. Their exclusion from political life and their legal dependency on their husbands, fathers, and brothers were present in many countries even after World War II.

The imagination of the people as sovereign is in direct opposition to the manipulable crowd. The transformation of the crowd into a people is the core of the populist promise. The work of populism and populist leaders is to awaken the "passive" "silent majority" and politicize them in order to build

4 The quotations are based on the German edition from 1999 and complemented by James Strachey's English translation (Freud 2018 [1922]).

a collective subject that can revindicate legitimate power (Laclau 2005). As the third arrangement shows, this is a complex process that is deeply dependent on the leader.

4.3 *The Masculinized Leader and the Oscillating Gender Status of the People*

The relationship between the leader and the people in populism is very intriguing and based on a twist of representation (Diehl 2018). In populism the leader occupies a double position: He/she is one of the people and, at the same time, one above the people. Therefore, the gender arrangement implicated in populism is highly complex and ambivalent. The status of the people oscillates between two positions vis-à-vis the leader: a) as guided by the leader and b) as a sovereign. Moreover, populism creates a symbiotic relationship between the leader and the people based on this oscillation.

The imagination of the crowd as feminine and of the leader as masculine plays a crucial role in this oscillation. As has been shown before, Le Bon's imagination of the crowd was strongly associated with femininity. There are two conflations in the assumption of male leadership and female crowd. First, feminine behaviour is presupposed to be emotional and irrational, preventing the crowd from making their own political decisions. Le Bon and Freud see the crowd as a highly emotional group. Second, good political leadership is based on rationality and associated with virility. Becoming a political actor means becoming male. Today, this imagination is strongly contested by emancipatory movements. However, it is still available for symbolic use in politics, such as in populism. Not all populists adopt this imagination in the same manner, but the quotations of Jair Bolsonaro and Björn Höcke at the beginning of this chapter show that they are still effective at least for significant groups who vote for Bolsonaro and for Alternative for Germany.

Populist leaders aim to mirror the people. Their performances are substantial elements in the populist construction of the people as a political subject. This, however, presupposes two assumptions: The first assumption is about who the people *is* (singular). Populism has first to imagine the people before the leader can mirror the people. This imagination is closely linked to the second assumption: the idea of an active political subject. In the history of modern democracy, the ideal political subject (individual and collective) was mostly conceived as male, white, and educated (Fraser 1987). In many regards, this ideal is called into question by populism, since populism positions itself against the elites – mostly including the educated parts of society. In some contexts of left-wing populism, white hegemony is contested as well. This is the case in Bolivia and, to some extent, in Venezuela, where the indigenous groups are portrayed as the exploited in the colonial and capitalist context. However, the point is that populism necessarily mobilizes a male ideal to reinforce the idea of the strong and unified people against the elite. But gender imagination can never be analyzed in isolation. The populist response to the contradictions of the democratic imaginary must consider the intersectional perspective, since masculinist ideals can counterbalance class and be added to whiteness (right-wing populism) or opposed to it (Latin American cases).

Obviously, things become more complicated if the populism promise of emancipation is read through the gender lens. While the leader is mostly inscribed in a masculine imagination, the people can occupy a male position as the sovereign or a female position as a crowd. On the one hand, the people *is* imagined as one single political actor and follows the traditional imagination of the active male citizen. Here the people and the leader stay in a horizontal relationship to each other. On the other hand, the people as the feminine crowd needs the leader's guidance, building a clear vertical relationship to him. This situation is capitalized on by the populist twist (see Diehl 2018). This contradictory double position towards the leader makes the construction of the people unstable and can only be held because populism makes a promise: The betrayed people, as a crowd, is to become the popular sovereign.

5 The Populist Promise and the Gender Transformation of the People

Populism reacts to the three gender arrangements in the history of democracy in a very specific way. Its major promise is to bring power back to the people: "Take back control" (UKIP), "Transfer the power to the people" (Trump). It is a promise of emancipation which puts popular sovereignty in the centre, reinforces the empowerment of the "common man", deplores the corrupt elite, and imagines a special relationship between the leader and the people. Together with the leader, the people can fight to win back power. Looking closer, it is possible to detect the gender implications this carries.

The first implication is the reinforcement of the male imagination of the people as a "common man", cast as a hard-working man excluded by the elites, and therefore as their antithesis. Unlike the hard-working people, the elite does not know what it is like to fight for everyday survival. It is used to luxury and superfluous things and its manners are often regarded as feminized. At this point, gender and class are intricate. The same move occurs in the idealization of the leader. If, since the beginning of modern democracy, the leader is imagined as white and educated, populism modifies this modern ideal by introducing popular roots instead of education. Attributes concerning race and ethnicity vary depending on the ideology added to populism and the specific cultural context. In right-wing populism, the leader mirrors the idealization of the culturally, ethnically, and sometimes even racially homogenous people, excluding the others. In left-wing populism, the idealization of the people is inclusive and the line between in and out is absent (Mudde and Rovira Kaltwasser 2013).

The second implication concerns the distinction between the feminine crowd and the masculine people and the transformation of the first into the second. Populism promises to transform the unorganized crowd into the sovereign people. Looking at the gender connotation of the crowd described above, this can be read as a promise to reverse the gender of the people, seen as a "passive", "manipulable", and "feminine" majority. In the populism promise, the "immature" crowd goes through a process of emancipation to become the masculine popular sovereign. Although cultural and social transformations in Western societies have pluralized gender roles, populism operates in a meta narrative, which is still shaped by the binary gender imagination (heterosexual matrix), as feminist analyses of Podemos have shown. The passive, emotional, and guided woman on the one hand and the active, rational man on the other are stereotypes, but they are still available as symbolic resources for populist narratives. The passage from one gender to the other can be cast as the political achievement of emancipation.

It is not a coincidence that Ernesto Laclau dedicated two chapters of *On populist reason* (2005) to the discussion of the role of the "crowd" and the "suggestion", paying special attention to Le Bon, Tarde, and Freud. Of course, his reading of these authors takes the discourse perspective and is connected to his theory of populism. Laclau's goal is to correct two assumptions made by Le Bon: The first is that

> the dividing line between rational forms of social organization and mass phenomena coincides, to a large extent, with the frontier separating the normal from the pathological. This first assumption is, in turn, embedded in another which is certainly present in Le Bon, but also in most of the literature of his time concerning mass behaviour: the distinction between rationality and irrationality would largely overlap with the distinction between the individual and the group. The individual experiences a process of social degradation by becoming part of a group.
>
> LACLAU 2005, 29

Laclau clearly rejects Le Bon's premises, but in so doing, he shows how important they still are today. If one wants to understand how the political imaginary operates, it is not necessary to take ideas, images, and imaginations shared by society and social scientists. Powerful imagination reveals itself when there is a need for their negation.

Yet there is another important point made by Laclau for the understanding of populism. As a specific political logic, populism is capable of naming the people and therefore constituting the political subject by naming it (ibid., 101, 103, 231). This performative work of discourse is the key for the transformation of the silent majority into the popular sovereign. What is missing in this argument is that the transformation promise of populism entails the twisted double relationship between the people and the leader: horizontal, between the people and the leader; and vertical, when the leader is above the crowd. The status of the people oscillates between the crowd and the sovereign. This makes populism profoundly ambivalent and, as I have written elsewhere, is the precondition for the representational twist (Diehl 2018). The consequences were described by Benjamin Arditi:

> Like Rousseau, populists distrust representation as a corruption of the general will and see themselves less as representatives than as simple placeholders or spokespeople for the common man, but unlike Rousseau they also distrust autonomous initiatives that empower citizens and encourage them to act by themselves. This ambivalent oscillation between the glorification of the independent action of the people (they are merely their placeholders) and the instrumental appropriation of that action (they incarnate the people and speak in their name) furnishes populist representation with a convenient permanent alibi.
>
> ARDITI 2005, 82–83

This shows how ambiguous the populist relationship between the leader and the people is. The leader is one of the people and at the same time the one who leads the people (Diehl 2018). The populist imagination ascribes to the leader the attributes associated with masculinity but, at the same time, it promises to transform the crowd into the popular sovereign, suggesting in traditional terms a change of its gender status. This transformation process is deeply dependent on the leader's capacity to make the people conscious of their status as the sovereign. From the gender perspective, the leader is the one who helps the people change their gender to become male (the promise of sovereignty) and at the same time the one who reaffirms traditional "female" attributes of the guided crowd.

Of course, these are specific constructions of femininity and masculinity and, as such, they need to be historically contextualized. The imagination of leader and people is not fixed, but dependent on historical and cultural context. Emancipation and the growing inclusion of women, homosexuals and transgender persons in politics and society is changing the game and softening the binary gender code. In addition, the demands of LGBTQ groups have become an important factor in politics. Although gender stereotypes have lost their force in the twenty-first century, they have not completely disappeared. Instead, these stereotypes are still present in the political imaginary and available for different political purposes.

6 Right-Wing Populism and the Crisis of Masculinity

This is the case when political discourse reacts to the crisis of masculinity facing the softening of traditional roles and pluralization of gender. Right-wing populism reacts to these changes. It is a combination of right-wing extremist ideology and populism, and as such it entails anti-democratic ideologemes. In contrast to other ideological variations, right-wing extremist ideologies provide populism with a clear structure concerning the gender question, since they have a binary imagination of the sexes and reactionary family ideals (Mayer, Šori and Sauer 2016). The mirroring of the low-class "common man" can be connected to these ideals and can include masculinist elements to symbolically emphasize the right-wing gender conception. Sometimes right-wing leaders verbalize the need for more maleness and make the crisis of masculinity (Mosse 1996b) visible. Björn Höcke (Alternative for Germany) expresses the "need" to take back the masculinity of the people. Taking back masculinity can be read as both reacting to the crisis of the heterosexual matrix and becoming an active political subject in opposition to the feminine crowd (as described by Le Bon).

In right-wing populism there is a translation of the crisis of representation into a crisis of masculinity (Sauer forthcoming). It not only echoes democratic contradictions but exacerbates them. Sovereignty is equated to masculinity. The first epigraph to this chapter by Höcke clearly articulates this equation: "Only when we take back our manhood will we become manful. And only when we become manful, will we be able to defend ourselves. And we must be able to defend ourselves." At the same time, the fixation on manhood channels feelings of insecurity and fear into aggression against presumed weak groups and politics of gender emancipation. This phenomenon was first analyzed by scholars focusing on national socialist aesthetics and ideology. Klaus Theweleit describes a specific fear of a vulnerable body and vulnerable masculinity, especially after the experiences of World War I. National socialism reacts to these fears by constructing a "panzer-body", reaffirming an aggressive masculinity (1987). The "ideal which fascism projected so strongly, and which symbolized progress and order (or as fascists put it, virility and discipline), was an aggressive masculinity" (Mosse 1996a, 250).

Right-wing populism presents bipolar gender roles, hegemonic masculinity, and sometimes misogyny and sexism. This is quite clear in the discourse of Donald Trump ("my button is bigger and more powerful than his") and Jair Bolsonaro, as seen in the second epigraph to this chapter. For Birgit Sauer, right-wing populism and extremism implement a specific affective regime that "authorizes" man to exercise violence as a legitimate way of expressing sovereignty (Sauer forthcoming). In the twenty-first century, right-wing populism reacts to gender emancipation, globalization, and multiculturalism with regression. If the imaginary of modern democracy carries contradictions and shadows that can be observed in gender relations and imagination, right-wing populism exacerbates gender and race inequalities, radicalizing these contradictions. The imagination of the feminized elite, of the masculinized leader, and of the "common man" appear now in much more vivid colours.

Sometimes right-wing populist parties find it harder to propagate a binary gender imagination and often opt for contradictory messages when they need to make a compromise. Although Höcke is a powerful leader in Alternative for Germany, the party strategically embraces gay rights when it comes to portraying Muslims as intolerant, anti-Western, and anti-democratic. Similarly, Gert Wilders showed his support for a pro-Donald Trump LGBTQ rally in 2016, after an ISIL supporter shot 49 people in a gay nightclub in Orlando, Florida.

7 Conclusion

This chapter proposes an alternative approach to populism by depicting the historical imagination of the people, the leader, and the citizen and by taking gender into consideration. Reading populism through the lenses of the democratic imaginary and gender helps to understand how populism reacts to gender stereotypes and their transformations in modern democracy. All ideological variations of populism come up against the background of democratic imaginary and its contradictions with regard to gender. They react to this background and make use of it in very different ways. From the attempts to establish emancipatory gender politics in left-wing populism to the exacerbation of male dominance and regression in right-wing populism – including right-wing populists' strategic uses of emancipatory gender promises against minorities – democratic contradictions regarding gender and equality resonate in all these kinds of populism. Is there a specific populist relation to gender? Yes and no. Yes, since populism promises to transform the feminine crowd into the masculine sovereign. In a strict sense, however, the answer should be no because this connection is already generated by the contradictions of the democratic imaginary.

Populism's relationship to gender is complex. On the one hand, populist actors reproduce patterns of the political imaginary and historical traditions, such as the contradictions of democracy regarding gender relations, the gendered imagination of the leader, the people, and the elite. On the other hand, populists' performances, discourses, and images are themselves elements of change of the democratic imaginary and, as such, they can help push emancipatory demands, as in the cases of Podemos and Chávez, or they can challenge democratic achievements, as seen in the cases of Alternative for Germany and Bolsonaro. For gender studies, considering the populist response to these contradictions offers a new way to understand the political struggles within democratic society. It provides a tool for tracing the structural gendered imaginary of democracy, on the one hand, and for observing the different ways populist politicians, movements, and parties respond to the contradictions of democracy, on the other. Although it has only been possible here to indicate the intersectional aspect of the democratic imaginary and political practice, it will be an important task for further research to put intersectionality at the core of populism research. Taking it into account allows greater accuracy in depicting and understanding the promises made by populism.

References

Abi-Hassan, S. (2017) Populism and gender. In: Rovira Kaltwasser, C., Taggart, P., Ochoia Espejo, P. and Ostiguy, P. (eds.) *The Oxford handbook of populism*. Oxford: Oxford University Press, 426–444.

Arditi, B. (2005) Populism as an internal periphery of democratic politics. In: Panizza, P. (ed.) *Populism and the mirror of democracy*. London: Verso, 72–89.

Butler, J. (1993) *Bodies that matter: On the discursive limits of sex*. New York: Routledge.

Canovan, M. (1981) *Populism*. New York and London: Harcourt Brace Jovanovich.

Canovan, M. (2005) *The people*. New York: Polity.

Caravantes, P. (2019) New versus old politics in Podemos: Feminization and masculinized party discourse. *Men and Masculinities*, 22(3), 465–490.

Celis, K. (2008) Gendering representation. In: Goertz, G. and Masur, G. (eds.) *Politics, gender, and concepts: Theory and methodology*. Cambridge: Cambridge University Press, 71–93.

Childs, S. (2004) A feminised style of politics? Women MPs in the House of Commons. *The British Journal of Politics and International Relations*, *6*(1), 3–19.

Coffé, H. (2018) Gender and the radical right. In: Rydgren, J. (ed.): *The Oxford handbook of the radical right*. Oxford: Oxford University Press, 200–211.

Corrales, J. (2015) The politics of LGBT rights in Latin America and the Caribbean: Research agendas. *European Review of Latin American and Caribbean Studies/ Revista Europea de Estudios Latinoamericanos y del Caribe*, *100*, 53–62.

De Baecque, A. (1997) *The body politic. Corporeal metaphor in revolutionary France, 1770–1800*. Stanford: Stanford University Press.

de la Torre, C. (2010) *Populist seduction in Latin America*. Athens: Ohio University Press.

Diehl, P. (2017) The body in populism. In: Holtz-Bacha, C., Heinisch, R. and Mazzoleni, O. (eds.) *Political populism: A handbook*. Baden-Baden, Nomos, 361–373.

Diehl, P. (2018) Twisting representation. In: de la Torre, C. (ed.) *The Routledge international handbook of global populism*. London-New York: Routledge, 129–143.

Diehl, P. (2019) Temporality and the political imaginary in the dynamics of political representation. *Social Epistemology*, *33*(5), 410–421.

Dietze, G. and Roth, J. (eds.) (2020) *Right-wing populism and gender*. Bielefeld: Transcript.

Dingler, S. C., Lefkofridi, Z. and Marent, V. (2017) The gender dimension of populism. In: Holtz-Bacha, C., Heinisch, R. and Mazzoleni, O. (eds.) *Political populism: A handbook*. Baden-Baden, Nomos, 345–360.

Donà, A. (2020) What's gender got to do with populism? *European Journal of Women's Studies*, *27*(3), 285–292.

Espina, G. and Rokowski, C. (2010) Waking women up? Hugo Chávez, populism, and Venezuela's popular women. In: Kampwith, K. (ed.) *Gender and populism in Latin America: Passionate politics*. University Park: Pennsylvania State University Press, 180–201.

Finchelstein, F. (2010) *Transatlantic fascism: Ideology, violence, and the sacred in Argentina and Italy, 1919–1945*. Durham-London: Duke University Press.

Finchelstein, F. (2019) Fascism and populism. In: de la Torre, C. (ed.) *The Routledge international handbook of global populism*. London-New York: Routledge, 307–318.

Fraser, N. (1987) What's critical about critical theory? The case of Habermas and gender. In: Benhabib, S. and Cornell, D. (eds.) *Feminism as critique: On the politics of gender*. Minneapolis: University of Minnesota Press, 31–56.

Freud, S. (1999) *Gesammelte Werke, Vol. VIII*. Frankfurt am Main: Fischer Verlag.

Freud, S. (2018 [1922]) *Group psychology and the analysis of the ego*, trans. J. Straches. Vienna-London: The International Psycho-Analytical Press.

Hunt, L. (1984) *Politics, culture, and class in the French Revolution*. Berkeley: University of California Press.

Kampwirth, K. (2010a) Introduction. In: Kampwirth, K. (ed.) *Gender and populism in Latin America: Passionate politics*. University Park: Pennsylvania State University Press, 1–24.

Kampwirth, K. (ed.) (2010b) *Gender and populism in Latin America: Passionate politics*. University Park: Pennsylvania State University Press.

Kelly, D. (2017) Populism and history of popular sovereignty. In: Rovira Kaltwasser, C., Taggart, P., Ochoia Espejo, P. and Ostiguy, P. (eds.) *The Oxford handbook of populism*. Oxford: Oxford University Press, 511–534.

Köttig, M., Bitzan, R. and Pető, A. (eds.) (2017) *Gender and far right politics in Europe*. London-New York: Palgrave Macmillan.

Laclau, E. (2005) *On populist reason*. London: Verso.

Landes, J. B. (2006) *Visualizing the nation: Gender, representation, and revolution in eighteenth-century France*. Ithaca-London: Cornell University Press.

Le Bon, G. (1897) *The crowd: A study of the popular mind*. London: T. Fisher Unwin.

Leonard, S. T. and Tronto, J. C. (2007) The genders of citizenship. *American Political Science Review, 101*(1), 33–46.

Lombardo, E. and Meier, P. (2014) *The symbolic representation of gender: A discursive approach*. Farnham and Burlington: Ashgate.

Mayer, S., Šori, I. and Sauer, B. (2016) Gendering "the people": Heteronormativity and "ethno-masochism" in populist imaginary. In: Ranieri, M. (ed.): *Populism, media, and education: Challenging discrimination in contemporary digital societies*. London-New York: Routledge, 84–104.

Meny, Y. and Surel, Y. (2002): The constitutive ambiguity of populism. In: Mény, Y. and Surel, Y. (eds.), *Democracy and the populist challenge*. New York: Palgrave Macmillan, 1–21.

Mosse, G. (1996a) Fascist aesthetics and society: Some considerations. *Journal of Contemporary History, 31*(2), 245–252.

Mosse, G. (1996b) *The image of man: The creation of modern masculinity*. Oxford: Oxford University Press.

Mudde, C. (2004) The populist zeitgeist. *Government and Opposition, 39*(4), 541–563.

Mudde, C. and Rovira, C. (2013) Exclusionary vs. inclusionary populism: Comparing contemporary Europe and Latin America. *Government and Opposition, 48*(2), 147–174.

Mudde, C. and Rovira Kaltwasser, C. (2015) Vox populi or vox masculini? Populism and gender in Northern Europe and South America. *Patterns of Prejudice, 49*(1–2), 16–36.

Navarro, M. (1977) The case of Eva Perón. *Signs: Journal of Women in Culture and Society, 3*(1), 229–240.

Reichardt, R. and Kohl, H. (2008) *Visualizing the revolution: Politics and the pictorial arts in late eighteenth-century France*. London: Reaktion Books.

Rousseau, J.-J. (1919) *Émile ou l'éducation*. Paris: Bibliothèque Larousse.

Sauer, B. (forthcoming) Gender as an analytical approach to authoritarian right-wing populism. In: Diehl, P. and Bargetz, B. (eds.) *The complexity of populism: New approaches and methods*. London-New York: Routledge.

Spierings, N., Zaslove, A., Mügge, L. M. and De Lange, S. L. (2015) Gender and populist radical-right politics: An introduction. *Patterns of Prejudice*, *49*(1–2), 3–15.

Taggart, P. (2000) *Populism*. Philadelphia: Open University Press.

Taguieff, P.-A. (2007) *L'illusion populiste. Essai sur les démagogies de l'âge démocratique*. Paris: Flammarion.

Theweleit, K. (1987) *Male fantasies*. Minneapolis: University of Minnesota Press.

CHAPTER 3

Populism and Social Class: Constituting "the People" and Cleaving the Political Field

Kenneth M. Roberts

1 Introduction

Populism is not a class project. That basic sociological reality may be poorly understood, but it is an essential starting point for grasping the political logic of populism, and understanding what it is and is not. Recognizing populism's independence from social class – that is, its compatibility with a wide range of class formations and subject positions – makes it easier to identify the commonalities hidden behind its multiple and varied expressions, as well as the historical contexts that give rise to different sub-types of populism. Indeed, a recognition of this independence is essential for comprehending populism's remarkable political ascendance around the world in recent times. Simply put, populism has found fertile terrain in social and political landscapes marked by the progressive demise or generalized weakness and disarticulation of class-based popular subjects. It thrives where the working class lacks organized and autonomous political expression, or where such expression has been diffused by the pluralization of subject positions, interests, and social identities.

If social heterogeneity and fragmentation are the social incubators of populism, globalized market liberalism – or neoliberalism, for short – has provided its structural underpinnings in recent decades. The latter weakened or dissolved the class-based subjects and sociopolitical cleavages of industrial society, uprooted and unsettled its representative institutions, and pluralized the social field. At the same time, neoliberalism created a tinderbox of market insecurities and material grievances amenable to populist articulation. Modern-day populism, then, in its varied expressions, is the bastard offspring of a globalized, post-industrial market society – in many cases, a Polanyian "double movement" in resistance to the market's inexorable advance (Polanyi 1944). It is also, dialectically speaking, the most formidable contender to neoliberalism's technocratic depoliticization and "hollowing out" of democratic governance (Brown 2015).

This chapter suggests that theories of social class and class cleavages provide a unique vantage point for understanding what is distinctive about populist

 | DOI:10.1163/9789004679016_005

politics – that is, for differentiating populism from other forms of political representation and political struggle.[1] More fundamentally, however, a focus on class provides a theoretical cornerstone for explaining the genesis of populism and its contemporary migration from the political margins of Western democracies to their central fault lines. Theories of social class and class politics, therefore, provide a fruitful lens through which to interpret what Mudde (2004) declared, with considerable foresight, to be the "populist zeitgeist" of the early twenty-first century.

2 Class, Social Heterogeneity, and the Constitution of "the People"

Although populism is a notoriously slippery and contested concept, its analytical core is largely shared by alternative approaches to the study of the phenomenon (Mansbridge and Macedo 2019).[2] Stripped to this analytical core, as theorized most explicitly by Laclau (2005), populism can be defined as the constitution of "the people" as a political subject, in opposition to an elite or establishment power bloc. A populist constitution of the political field necessarily entails a redemptive invocation of popular sovereignty – that is, appeals to empower "the people" against a power elite that has abandoned or betrayed them. This antagonistic structure and emancipatory imaginary place populism in a natural dialogue with Marxist conceptions of class struggle and socialist revolution, but these base-level symmetries mask fundamentally different political logics and constitutive processes. These differences are heavily conditioned by the role of social class, or the lack thereof, in the constitution of emancipatory subjects and antagonistic relations. Indeed, the break with class reductionism is an essential starting point for contemporary theorizing of populist politics (Laclau 1977, 11–12).

1 Careful readers may note that I am not distinguishing populism here from ideologies or belief systems like liberalism, socialism, nationalism or fascism, as I do not conceptualize populism to be a stand-alone belief system. As explained below, my approach understands populism to be a concrete way of structuring and dividing the political field, and it locates the phenomenon ontologically within the domain of political representation rather than that of ideology. So conceived, the logic of populist articulation can coexist with, or be grafted onto, a wide range of quite different belief systems, including nationalism, socialism and fascism, as recognized in Mudde's (2004, 543–544) influential conceptualization of populism as a "thin-centered" ideology.

2 These alternative approaches – often referred to as ideational, strategic, discursive and socio-cultural – are reviewed in the opening sections of two leading recent collections of populism studies: de la Torre (2019) and Rovira Kaltwasser et al. (2017).

Populism is not a class project because its political subject, "the people", 1) is not defined in class terms; 2) need not be constructed or led by class-based social actors; and 3) does not act in pursuit of political goals that serve a given class interest. As such, the antagonistic relationship between "the people" and the power elite is a "non-class contradiction", as formulated by Laclau (1977, 164). The "people", in short, is not a sociological category bounded and defined by structural positioning in the sphere of production, as is the proletariat in the Marxist tradition – the revolutionary subject par excellence. Neither is "the people" a simple alliance of class actors, or, necessarily, the lower strata (or status groups) in a more multidimensional, Weberian conception of social stratification (see Weber 1946). The "people" as a collective is a highly contingent and variable political construct, one forged out of myriad grievances or demands, many of which are not defined in terms of a class position or class identity (or, as Weber called it, a shared "class situation"). As Laclau states, "the people" must be conceived "as a *political* category, not as a *datum* of the social structure" or any specified social group; it is a new, unified political agent, an amalgam constructed out of a "plurality of heterogeneous elements" (Laclau 2005, 224; italics in the original). This subject is necessarily a product of political agency, mobilization, discourse, and struggle in concrete historical settings. It is formed through the discursive articulation and convergence of disparate individuals and social groups who share little in common other than unmet demands and alienation from a power elite – also a political construct – that denies their collective will.

As a collective subject, therefore, "the people" may well include class actors, but it transcends social class, whether the latter is conceived in Marxian or Weberian terms. Depending on the specific historical context, a remarkably wide range of social groups have been targeted or mobilized as core constituencies of socially heterogeneous, typically multi-class populist movements. In the nineteenth century, populist movements sought to mobilize – with varying degrees of success – peasants, small farmers, and rural workers in Russia, France, and the US. In mid-twentieth-century Latin America, during the early stages of industrialization, populist figures like Juan Perón (Argentina), Getulio Vargas (Brazil), Victor Raúl Haya de la Torre (Peru), and Lázaro Cárdenas (Mexico) mobilized urban workers in multi-class movements that also included peasants or rural workers along with sectors of the middle class and even national capitalists opposed to the political dominance of traditional agrarian elites (Conniff 2012). More recently, informal sector workers, the urban and rural poor, and, in Bolivia, coca growers and indigenous communities have swelled the ranks of Latin American populist movements (Madrid 2008). In Europe and the United States, the populist radical right has often garnered substantial support among blue collar workers, small business owners, rural and small town populations, the religious, and the less educated, including those who Kriesi (2008) identified as the "losers of globalization".

As a political construct, therefore, "the people" does not have a predefined class position, and populism is not dependent on any specified class formation in capitalist society. This does not mean, however, that "the people" is devoid of *any* structural positioning; it simply means that it's positioning lies predominantly in the political domain, as it is defined by "the people's" political exclusion or marginality vis-à-vis a power elite that neither respects nor represents their popular will. This marginality is accentuated by "the people's" self-proclaimed cultural and political authenticity. The "people" need not claim any transcendent merits or virtues beyond its assertion of being the true, genuine, and proper – that is, the authentic – *demos* in a given political order (see Ostiguy 2017, 76, 91–92). Sovereign power is naturally and properly vested in this *demos*; populist discourse invariably includes a narrative of victimhood under which this sovereign power is denaturalized, stripped from "the people", and arrogated by an alien, abusive, or inauthentic power elite (see Pappas 2019, 114–116).

Populist movements may construct the *demos* as an *ethnos* or a *plebeius*, depending on whether they make ethno-national cultural identities or commoner status, respectively, a basis for constituting a new collective subject and defining an antagonistic frontier. While an *ethnos* is clearly not a class construct, the latter, plebian construction of the *demos* may loosely correspond to a subject composed of Weber's (1946) lower or non-privileged social strata, as defined not only by property, occupation, and income but also by education, skill levels, power, and prestige. Even this plebian form, however, should not be conflated with the creation of a *class* subject. The latter, for Marx, is comprised of those without property who derive a living by selling their labour power, and act collectively to defend common interests against the propertied classes that exploit them. As Wright (2015, 21–41) points out, Weber largely shared Marx's narrow, economistic understanding of social class rooted in property relations and opportunities for income, even if he downplayed the exploitative character of class relations and their proclivity to generate class conflict. Weber and those who followed him departed from Marx largely by embedding class within a broader theory of social stratification that incorporated non-economic status considerations. Properly speaking, however, neither Weber nor Marx would consider a populist movement composed largely of commoners or the non-privileged to be a *class* subject, though it certainly might claim to represent the authentic "people". And whatever its social composition, such a movement would not identify with or act collectively in the name of a working class embroiled in conflict with its propertied oppressors; neither the populist subject nor the central antagonism is structured by property relations and class interests.

Much the same could be said of the populist subject in Ostiguy's sociocultural approach, which understands populism to be the antagonistic "flaunting" of the cultural "low", along with its obverse, the "celebratory desecration" of the cultural "high" (Ostiguy 2017, 74–76). Although the sociocultural high and low may well be correlated with income and education levels, Ostiguy is explicit in stating that they cannot be reduced to class positions (as conceived in either the Marxian or the Weberian tradition). The hierarchy has more to do "with ways of *being* and *acting* in politics", including such cultural traits as "manners, demeanours, ways of speaking and dressing, vocabulary, and tastes displayed in public". As Ostiguy (2017, 77–78) puts it: "It cannot be stated enough that the 'low' in politics is *not* synonymous with poor people or lower social strata" (Ostiguy 2017, 77–78).

Ultimately, then, the plebes or commoners who swell the ranks of populist movements are non-privileged but highly pluralistic in their social composition and class locations, or class "situations", as Weber would have it. And it is precisely this social ambiguity and pluralism that make them the breeding ground for populist articulations of "the people". Populism flourishes in pluralistic social milieus characterized by social heterogeneity, diffuse inequalities, political fragmentation, and fluid alignments. The essence of populism is to condense that pluralism by cleaving the political field along a binary divide between "the people" and the power elite, thereby forcing diverse social actors to locate themselves along one side or the other of the central fault line. Populism, then, is invariably a process of cleavage formation (see the chapter in the volume by Mastropaolo), and one that is intrinsically polarizing (McCoy and Somer 2019; Roberts 2021): it weakens or dissolves cross-cutting interests and intermediary positions, while mapping them onto an "antagonistic frontier" that is necessarily a fluid political construct (Laclau 2005, 153). But neither the working class nor any other social group is structurally predestined to exercise hegemony within a newly constituted populist subject – a point on which the mature Laclau (2005) departed from the structural Marxist logic that influenced some of his earlier work (Laclau 1977). As Laclau stated in *On populist reason* (2005, 115–116), "there is nothing in the materiality of the particular parts which predetermines one or the other to function as a whole", as "the hegemonic approach breaks decisively" with "the essentialist social logic" of traditional Marxism.

So conceived, populism has no deterministic *social* logic, but it does have an essentialist *political* logic, one which condenses social pluralism and reconstitutes the political field along an antagonistic divide between "the people" and a power elite. Its decisive break with structural Marxism is readily apparent on both of these analytically distinct but interrelated planes: the condensation of the social field, and the bifurcation of the political field. Marx believed that capitalist development itself would progressively condense the social field as peasants, artisans, guilds, and diverse middle sectors were draw into the proletariat by the inexorable tide of industrialization. The dissolution of antiquated and intermediate social positions through a process of proletarianization would thus generate a binary cleaving of the social field between the "modern" classes spawned by capitalism – that is, capitalists and workers. As Marx and Engels stated in the *Communist manifesto*:

> The lower strata of the middle class – the small tradespeople, shopkeepers, and retired tradesmen generally, the handicraftsmen and peasants – all these sink gradually into the proletariat, partly because their diminutive capital does not suffice for the scale on which Modern Industry is carried on, and is swamped in the competition with the large capitalists, partly because their specialised skill is rendered worthless by new methods of production. Thus the proletariat is recruited from all classes of the population.

As a result, "Our epoch, the epoch of the bourgeoisie, possesses [...] this distinct feature: it has simplified class antagonisms. [...] Society as a whole is more and more splitting up into two great hostile camps, into two great classes directly facing each other – Bourgeoisie and Proletariat" (Marx and Engels 1978, 474, 479–480).

Given the structural trade-off between wages and profits, and the expected pauperization of workers over time, Marx understood this class divide to be intrinsically antagonistic and polarizing. It would thus provide a structural foundation for class-based political conflict, and eventual socialist revolution, as capitalism advanced and its contradictions intensified. As other, intermediate classes "decay and finally disappear in the face of Modern Industry", the proletarian movement becomes "the self-conscious, independent movement of the immense majority, in the interest of the immense majority" (Marx and Engels 1978).

Populism, on the other hand, aims to achieve in the political field what Marx expected capitalism to structurally induce in an endogenous manner – that is, social condensation and political bifurcation. Populist mobilization may be a process of cleavage formation, but it is one without fixed or predefined sociological anchors and class subjects. Indeed, populism decouples the cleavage from any particular structural underpinnings. This decoupling is, in large part, a response to the basic challenge of social heterogeneity – or, phrased differently, the failure of endogenous or structurally induced social condensation – that Marx's successors, from Bernstein to Gramsci and Laclau, have grappled with in theorizing the political sociology of modern capitalism. Bernstein (1907; see also Berman 2006), for example, examined the expansion, rather than the contraction and proletarianization, of the middle class and intermediate sectors in Europe; Gramsci (1989) advocated a "historic bloc" to unify distinct subaltern groups in an Italy divided between an industrializing north and a still-agrarian south; and Laclau (1977) sought to explain the rise of multiclass "popular democratic" subjects in contexts of dependent and uneven capitalist development, where the urban and rural poor, middle sectors, and even part of the national bourgeoisie might align themselves with the working class at particular historical junctures. Across these diverse settings – in both the "core" and the "periphery" of the global economy – capitalist development did not simplify or condense the social field into binary camps, and the proletariat did not represent the "immense majority", as Marx had expected. Much less did it develop into a class-conscious revolutionary subject as a result of capitalism's built-in contradictions.

Given this structural reality of social heterogeneity, even the early Laclau (1977, 196) suggested that no class can attempt to assert its hegemony "without articulating the people" in its discourse. The "abstract character" of the latter, populist discourse, moreover, "permits of its presence in the ideology of the most varied of classes" (Laclau 1977, 194). Not surprisingly, then, complex social heterogeneity or pluralism appears as a type of structural precondition for populist mobilization in Laclau's work, as opposed to mobilization along a central line of cleavage with well-defined sociological correlates and political identities (such as class, ethnicity, or religion). This structural precondition, and the resulting absence of a well-defined, politically autonomous and hegemonic social subject helps explain why populist mobilization is so often centred around a charismatic leader with the capacity to articulate the diverse claims or grievances of myriad actors and unify them as a political subject on the same side of a newly constructed antagonistic frontier (Weyland 2017; see also the chapter by de la Torre in this volume). Notably, these structural preconditions have parallels to those identified by Marx (1963) in his classic study of the political crisis in post-1848 France in *The Eighteenth Brumaire of Louis Bonaparte*. In Marx's account, when neither the proletariat nor any other class was capable of asserting political leadership, the standoff set the stage for the rise of an autocratic figure who drew support from diverse sectors of society.

It is important to recognize that Laclau's populist political logic has an institutional precondition as well as a structural one – a precondition that was also foreshadowed in Marx's *Eighteenth Brumaire*. Populism thrives in a political field characterized by a crisis of representation, such that the myriad demands arising from the pluralist social milieu are incapable of being fulfilled by established governing institutions (see Laclau 2005, 74–75, 177). As explained below, these structural and institutional preconditions allow for a remarkably broad range of populist articulations of "the people".

3 Populist Articulations of "the People"

Although populism transcends social class, it is rife with implications for class politics and the politics of inequality more broadly. Indeed, populist movements are often heavily conditioned by their specific assemblage of class interests. Workers, both organized and unorganized, are routinely incorporated within populist movements, and populism usually involves an articulation of grievances related to economic hardships and/or inequalities. If populism mobilizes "the people" in opposition to some sort of power elite, the former nearly always includes those who occupy subaltern status in the society at question. While subalternity is not restricted or reducible to economic forms of social stratification, as the Weberian tradition reminds us, rarely is it orthogonal to them. Even forms of populism that construct "the people" largely in terms of national and cultural identities – typically those characterized as "radical right" – tend to take on a plebeian cast and politicize economic grievances in addition to (or, more likely, in synergy with) cultural resentments (Rydgren 2013). Other forms of populism, more clearly located on the political left, mobilize explicitly against economic inequalities and make economic stratification, or subalternity, integral to their construction of "the people" and the power elite.

But if left and right populisms both appeal to plebes and commoners, they ultimately construct "the people" not only on different poles of antagonism, but along very different antagonistic frontiers and axes of political conflict. As depicted in Figure 3.1, these axes are at least potentially orthogonal (see Kitschelt and McGann 1995; Kriesi 2008; Bornschier 2010; Ostiguy 2017). Left populisms construct "the people" on the statist and redistributive left pole on the conventional economic axis of contestation, in opposition to pro-market positions and staunch defence of propertied interests on the right pole. Right populisms, on the other hand, construct "the people" on a cultural axis of contestation – that is, on the lower pole of an axis where communitarian or particularistic cultural identities associated with nativism, ethno-nationalism, and/or religious nationalism are located, in opposition to more cosmopolitan, multicultural, and universalistic identities or values on the upper pole.

Figure 3.1 includes prominent political leaders (or a movement party, in the case of Spain's Podemos) associated with these different types of populism. As the figure depicts, left populism can incorporate both high and low cultural positions, while the arguably mislabelled populist radical right (PRR) is defined by its low positioning on the cultural axis rather than market fundamentalist positions on the right pole of the economic axis. Indeed, some right-wing populists adopt highly contradictory and unorthodox economic platforms, as seen in Donald Trump's combination of pro-business tax cuts and deregulatory policies with highly nationalistic and statist forms of trade protectionism. Likewise, over time some European PRR parties have shifted from orthodox neoliberal platforms, which reflected their generalized hostility toward existing state institutions (Kitschelt and McGann 1995), to forms of "welfare chauvinism" that defend trade protectionism and national welfare states while restricting the benefits of the latter to nativist (or non-immigrant) populations (Harteveld 2016; De Lange 2017). These welfare chauvinist platforms allowed PRR parties to appeal to working-class constituencies concerned about globalization and multiculturalism on both the economic and cultural dimensions of contestation, demonstrating the intrinsic programmatic flexibility of populist parties (Bornschier 2010).

As this flexibility suggests, populism's plebeian cast can be mapped onto a wide range of socio-economic and cultural divisions, and it can be coupled with a diverse array of economic and social policies. If populism is not defined by its class composition, neither is it defined by its policy content; specific polices may be instrumental to a populist project, enhancing its popular appeal and concretizing pledges to reward "the people", or they can be incidental to its populist political logic, but never are they essential for identifying its populist character. Policy platforms advocating statist, protectionist, and/or redistributive measures are often associated with populism, but policies advancing anti-state market individualism can also be grafted onto populism's political logic. Examples include critiques of the state or the political establishment for taxing "the people's" hard-earned income, transferring said income to alien or "undeserving" sectors of society, or creating a maze of bureaucratic regulations that restrict economic opportunities or individual liberties. Along these lines, Latin American scholarship in the 1990s examined the populist logic of political leaders like Peru's Alberto Fujimori who imposed neoliberal economic reforms in contexts of acute economic crises and profound representational failures (Roberts 1995; Weyland 1996). In so doing, this scholarship

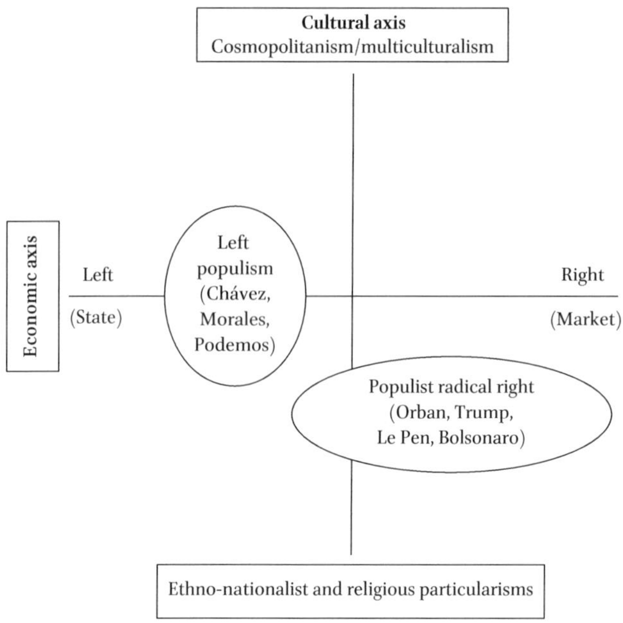

FIGURE 3.1 Economic and cultural axes of contestation

challenged the conventional assumption that populism in Latin America was inextricably tied to a specific era or stage of state-led industrialization. The failure to understand populism's essential political logic, its multidimensional competitive space, and its second-order programmatic malleability lies at the heart of US progressives' befuddlement at the increasingly populist – and plebeian – appeal of Republican conservatism in recent decades, despite the party's (pre-Trump) market fundamentalism and its defence of elite economic interests (see Pierson 2017 for an analysis of Trump's "plutocratic populism").

Even more statist and redistributive left-wing variants of populism, however, do not define "the people" in class terms, and rarely do they organize it as such – with Argentina under Juan Perón being, perhaps, a partial outlier, given early Peronism's intensive organization and mobilization of labour unions within its multi-class base.[3] More typically, left populist movements subsume class within an overarching critique of social and economic inequality that

3 Early Peronism, however, should not be considered a form of left populism, despite its support for labour mobilization and redistributive social policies. The movement advocated a type of "third way" between capitalism and socialism, but it incorporated political currents that spanned the ideological spectrum from the fascist right to the socialist left. On Peronism's labour bases, see Collier and Collier (1991) and McGuire (1997).

allows for a plethora of subject positions and identities, unified by means of "equivalential chains" in the constitution of a populist subject (Laclau 2005, 74–75). Occupy Wall Street's signature slogan "We are the 99%" is a paradigmatic example. Indeed, a populist subject can be stitched together in a pluralized, neoliberal social landscape that has thoroughly deconstructed class subjects while deepening forms of "classless inequality" (Ossowski 1963, 96–110). Conversely, where class-based political subjects are broadly representative and capable of contesting extant inequalities, class cleavages are more likely to organize and structure political contestation, and political space for populist articulations is likely to be constricted. Taken together, these postulates suggest that the recent proliferation and strengthening of populist alternatives – on both the left and right sides of the political spectrum, in diverse national and regional settings – is an unintended sequel to liberalism's global triumph and its political correlate, the disarticulation of the class cleavages and labour-based parties of the industrial era.

4 Neoliberalism and Class Politics: (De)Constructing the Populist Zeitgeist

An understanding of populism's political logic and how its binary structuring of the political field differs from that of Marx can help shed light on the historical contexts in which it has emerged and thrived. Revisiting populism's structural and institutional preconditions, a cross-regional comparative historical perspective suggests the following basic proposition: that major populist eruptions are inversely related to the organizational density and political closure of class cleavages in national party systems. The deductive reasoning for this proposition is that class cleavages and populist cleavages are alternative fault lines or antagonistic frontiers for mobilizing mass constituencies in national political orders; the more fully developed the former, the more constricted is the political space for the latter.

Although the size and strength of working-class movements in industrialized capitalist societies fell well short of Marx's expectations, in most of post-war Western Europe they were still able to structure and align political competition along a central line of cleavage between a labour-based socialist or social democratic party and a conservative party with strong ties to business interests (see Lipset and Rokkan 1967; Bartolini 2000; Mastropaolo in this volume). As depicted in Bartolini and Mair's (1990) three-dimensional conceptualization of social cleavages, strong class cleavages differentiated and sorted voters into rival partisan camps; created mass-based, densely organized party-union blocs; and generated durable collective identities within these blocs anchored in ideology, class solidarity, and programmatic commitments to redistributive policies and social citizenship rights. In so doing they integrated the working classes into democratic politics (Berman 2006) and stabilized national party systems over most of the twentieth century in Western Europe. Although building an electoral majority for social democracy required that the working-class forge alliances with small farmers and/or middle class sectors (see Castles 1978; Przeworski 1985), the centrality of organized labour in civil society and corporatist systems of interest representation, and the ability of labour unions to anchor one side of the party system, meant that neither the structural nor the institutional preconditions for populism were readily available. Deeply entrenched and encompassing class cleavages, therefore, constrained individual voter mobility and closed off the electoral marketplace to major partisan or movement contenders – including populist challengers – located off the central axis of sociopolitical contestation.

By contrast, Latin America offered exceptionally fertile terrain for populist mobilization in the middle of the twentieth century. Following a century of post-independence oligarchic rule and agro-export based development, the onset of mass politics during the early stages of industrialization in Latin America was ushered in by substantial working-class sociopolitical mobilization, but little effective political incorporation by traditional parties dominated by agrarian elites. The urban proletariat, therefore, was often available for political mobilization by parties or movements that challenged oligarchic elites and export-based economies, but delayed industrialization and dependent capitalist development provided a weak structural foundation for class-based social democratic alternatives. The unionized, formal sector working class remained a relatively small percentage of the region's heterogeneous "popular sectors", which typically included large numbers of peasants as well as the urban and rural informal workforce and an expanding urban middle class. As such, socialist and communist parties targeting a well-defined proletarian subject were very small and weak in the region outside of Chile. Nevertheless, populist leaders and movements often succeeded in condensing this social pluralism by constructing a multi-class "people" along an antagonistic frontier that positioned the oligarchy and its international allies against diverse social groups who stood to benefit from an inward-looking, state-directed process of import substitution industrialization (Germani, di Tella and Ianni 1973; Conniff 2012; Collier and Collier 1991; de la Torre 2010). Although the specific social composition of "the people" varied from one country to another – and from one time period to another within the same country – it generally included the urban proletariat, peasants, urban and rural informal workers, sectors of the middle class, and even domestic industrialists who partnered with the state to challenge agrarian elites and promote more nationalistic development policies.

In short, both the structural and institutional preconditions for populism were readily apparent during this era of state-led development in Latin America. Even in a country like Argentina, where Perón dramatically accelerated unionization and made trade unions the organizational backbone of his multiclass "people", populism mobilized a national-popular subject along an oligarchy/populist cleavage that was quite different from European social democracy's more pronounced class-based political identities and cleavage structures. Similarly, although populism and social democracy both supported pro-worker social reforms and redistributive policies, social democracy had a formal ideological doctrine grounded in the socialist tradition and its conception of working-class interests, in contrast to populism's more eclectic and ambiguous commitments to class compromise and a "third way" between capitalism and socialism. Populism, in short, served as a type of Latin American surrogate for social democracy in a context where class cleavages were inchoate or only partially formed.

Although many observers assumed that Latin American populism had run its course with the demise of state-led industrialization and the transition to technocratic neoliberalism in the 1980s and 1990s (Kaufman and Stallings 1991, 31–32), the political logic of populism proved extraordinarily resilient in the region and highly independent of any specific stage or model of capitalist development. Indeed, the structural and institutional preconditions for populism – social heterogeneity and crises of representation – remained chronic features of the sociopolitical landscape across macro-level shifts in political regimes and development models. As economic crises and market-based structural adjustment spread across the region in the 1980s and 1990s, the working class became increasingly informalized, dualistic, and precarious, deepening inequalities while dramatically weakening labour unions and further pluralizing the social field. The net effect was to undermine the party-union representational "hubs" of the state-centric era (Roberts 2002; Collier and Handlin 2009), opening the door for new populist articulations of "the people" against the political establishment (de la Torre and Arnson 2013).

These articulations initially became wedded to neoliberal assaults on the old order (Roberts 1995; Weyland 1996), but following economic stabilization in the mid-1990s they veered sharply to the left under leaders like Hugo Chávez in Venezuela, Evo Morales in Bolivia, and Rafael Correa in Ecuador. In these countries, historic left-leaning or labour-based parties had played major roles in the adoption of neoliberal reforms, causing mainstream party systems to converge programmatically on neoliberal orthodoxy. Lacking an institutionalized voice in the democratic arena, societal discontent with market insecurities and deepening inequalities was channelled into extra-systemic forms of mass social protest. Austerity-induced urban riots in Venezuela, a series of indigenous uprisings in Ecuador, and indigenous-led anti-neoliberal protests in Bolivia placed traditional parties on the defensive (Silva 2009), while opening political space on the left flank for new populist outsiders who articulated societal grievances, denounced neoliberalism, and promised to sweep aside the party establishments that upheld it. Social protest, therefore, set the stage for mass electoral protest and the triumph of populist outsiders who pledged to convoke constituent assemblies and refound national democratic regimes (Roberts 2014).

This post-neoliberal resurgence of populism in Latin America repoliticized the left pole on the economic axis of figure 3.1, breaking the elite-level "Washington Consensus" for globalized market liberalization. The populist movements drew support from diverse subaltern constituencies, especially the urban and rural poor; the role of organized labour was greater in Bolivia than in Venezuela or Ecuador, but even in Bolivia a union of small producers (indigenous coca growers) rather than wage earners provided the organizational core of the movement (Madrid 2008; Simmons 2016; Anria 2018). As such, they mobilized "the people" not in class terms but in terms of those left behind as the state retreated from traditional social protection roles. In so doing they swept aside many of the decaying institutional remnants of the region's first wave of populism. Populism, rather than class-based social democracy, has thus been central to both Latin America's first and second historical phases of mass political incorporation, in the mid-twentieth and the early twenty-first centuries, respectively (Silva and Rossi 2018).

A similar populist logic lay behind the rise of movement-based left populist alternatives in Spain (Podemos) and Greece (Syriza) following the imposition of neoliberal austerity measures during Southern Europe's post-2009 financial crisis (Stavrakakis and Katsambekis 2014; Aslinidis 2017; Portos 2020). As in the aforementioned Latin American cases, mainstream parties in Greece and Spain – including traditional socialist parties – converged in their support of orthodox adjustment policies during the crisis under pressure from European creditor institutions, leading to widespread social protest that was quickly translated into mass electoral protest. New populist rivals, therefore, outflanked mainstream parties to the left, challenging the political establishment while articulating diverse societal demands related to housing, employment, and social services.

In Central and Northern Europe, by contrast, the early twenty-first century populist surge was right-wing in inspiration, and it politicized the lower, ethno-nationalist pole on the cultural axis in figure 3.1 more than the horizontal economic axis. The politicization of the cultural axis had begun earlier, with the rise of a new, more libertarian left associated with European Green parties in the 1980s located near the upper pole on the cultural axis. Left libertarian parties advocated cosmopolitan and post-materialist values associated with the environmental, women's, gay rights, and peace movements (Kitschelt 1988; Inglehart 1989), and they generally supported European integration, multiculturalism, and immigrants' rights. The response of the PRR was to politicize the opposite, lower pole of nativist ethno-nationalism and moral traditionalism (Ignazi 1992; Kitschelt and McGann 1995; Mudde 2007 and 2017; Bornschier 2010; Betz 2017; Norris and Inglehart 2019). PRR parties constructed "the people" in terms of an *ethnos* around national and cultural identities, in a context where the mainstream centre-left and centre-right parties had gravitated towards the cosmopolitan upper pole on the cultural axis.

This politicization of the cultural axis by new left-wing and right-wing alternatives clearly cut across the class cleavage that historically structured left-right contestation on the economic axis. Indeed, it demonstrated that in increasingly complex and socially heterogeneous post-industrial societies – that is, in societies where the proletariat was shrinking, the middle class was expanding and diversifying, and the workforce was becoming better educated, more highly skilled, and more culturally diverse – the plurality of subject positions and identities could not easily be mapped onto a single, materially based axis of political contestation. The orthogonal politicization of cultural identities both capitalized on and accelerated the erosion of the traditional class cleavage by the forces of socio-economic and political modernization, and it helped weaken the hold of social democracy on working-class constituencies (Kitschelt 1994; Berman 2016). As Oesch (2013, 32–36) suggests, although the polarized cultural identities of the libertarian left and the populist right were not determined by material self-interests, neither were they sociologically ungrounded; they reflected, instead, the divergent workplace experiences and social interactions of different occupational and professional roles that inclined some individuals toward a tolerance for diversity and individual autonomy, and others toward an emphasis on cultural homogeneity and traditional authority. Whereas professionals engaged in cultural and social service work were more likely to be found in the left-libertarian sphere, production workers and small business owners were disproportionally represented among supporters of the PRR.

These sociological patterns of cleavage dealignment and realignment were reinforced by institutional changes in the sphere of partisan politics. Over time, programmatic differences between mainstream social democratic and conservative parties had narrowed in Western Europe, as parties largely converged in their support for European integration, economic globalization, and relatively inclusive welfare states within the fiscal and monetary constraints of a currency union. In the process, social democratic parties asserted their autonomy from organized labour and became increasingly catch-all in their social composition, with a growing dependence on the electoral support of the educated middle class and professionals. Parties' roots in society progressively withered as party membership declined and party organizations professionalized and gained access to ample state resources (Katz and Mair 1995). The detachment of traditional parties from their social bases was arguably reinforced by the erosion of national policymaking autonomy – a process that reflected the constraints of market globalization, as well as the assumption of new responsibilities by highly bureaucratic EU institutions with limited democratic accountability. Peter Mair's (2013) depiction of collusive mainstream party cartels ruling a political void captured the spirit of an era primed for a populist backlash against a power elite that appeared increasingly aloof and distant.

The dominant expression of this backlash was an exclusionary ethno-nationalist construction of "the people" that attempted to draw a very different line of cleavage in national political arenas – one that arrayed an elite cosmopolitan "high" against a popular nativist "low", while seeking to defend national political and cultural autonomy from the external pressures of transnational institutions and international immigration. This populist construct emerged both in Eastern Europe, where post-communist party systems were never well structured by class cleavages, and in Western Europe, where class cleavages had a diminished capacity to align and close off the electoral marketplace. In contexts were class-based identities and organizational forms had been weakened, PRR parties offered workers an alternative, more communitarian form of collective identity and political integration within an *ethnos* (Bornschier 2010; Oesch 2013, 35). In some cases, they also shifted away from their initial neoliberal platforms to support more nationalist, protectionist, and welfare chauvinist policies that sought to appeal to working-class and less educated voters at a competitive disadvantage in highly globalized economies (Harteveld 2016; De Lange 2017).

Despite such attempts to appeal to workers on both the cultural and economic axes of contestation, PRR parties should *not* be mistaken for working-class parties. They have neither constructed a new class cleavage in European party systems nor fully displaced social democracy as a partisan expression of working-class interests. As Abou-Chadi, Mitteregger and Mudde (2021) report, PRR parties attract votes from a broad cross-section of society, even if their support is most heavily concentrated among production workers and small business owners. Moreover, most of their supporters have migrated from the traditional right rather than the social democratic left, and the latter have lost more votes to Green parties, the traditional right, and other leftist alternatives than they have to the PRR. Production workers continue to be more likely to vote for social democrats and the traditional right than for PRR parties. As such, rather than constructing a new, binary elite-populist cleavage in European party politics, PRR parties have helped to consolidate a multi-polar two-dimensional competitive field that is structured by cultural and material divides, but prone to shifting partisan identities and voter loyalties.

These divides exist as well in the United States, although the conventional class cleavage was never as fully developed as it was in Western Europe, and two-dimensional competition mapped differently onto a highly polarized two-party system cleaved along racial, ethnic, and religious lines (Mason 2018). The presidential primary system in the US allowed outsider billionaire Donald Trump to channel populist radical right currents within the Republican Party (Skocpol and Williamson 2013; Blum 2020) and capture the presidency in 2016. Trump thoroughly politicized white ethno-nationalist and Christian nationalist identities on the lower pole of the cultural axis by harshly criticizing immigration, pledging to build a wall on the southern border, adopting an anti-abortion stand, and promising to "make America great again". He also relaxed his party's market fundamentalism on the right pole of the economic axis by advocating highly nationalistic and protectionist trade policies, while still supporting pro-business tax cuts and deregulatory policies for the party's traditional elite constituencies.

This unorthodox platform, combined with trenchant criticism of establishment politicians and other elite institutions, allowed Trump to build on and extend a long-term shift of the white American working class toward the Republican Party. The percentage of white working-class voters supporting the Republican presidential candidate increased from 32 per cent in 1992 to 50 per cent in 2000 and 62 per cent in 2016 (Carnes and Lupu 2021, 60). Although Trump's rise owed much to the peculiarities of US political institutions, it nonetheless demonstrated the potential of populist radical right candidates to build multi-class bases of support through a combination of cultural and economic appeals – namely, appeals to white nativism and racial resentments (Parker and Barreto 2013), economic and religious nationalism, and pro-business fiscal and regulatory policies (Pierson 2017).

5 Conclusion

Although populism is not a class project, the study of populism ignores social class at its own peril. Indeed, it is greatly enriched by examining the complex interactions between class formations and populist mobilization. Theories of social class and class cleavages provide analytical cornerstones for understanding populism's distinctive political logic. In so doing, they shed light on the social and political conditions most conducive to the rise of different expressions of populism. To construct "the people" as a political subject, populism must simplify and condense social pluralism by unifying myriad unmet demands on the same side of a central fault line of political antagonism, across from which lies a similarly constructed power elite. Populist leaders and movements, therefore, construct in the political field the type of binary divide that Marx assumed capitalism would generate endogenously, according to its own internal dynamics and class contradictions.

The social heterogeneity that Marx expected capitalism to extinguish is thus a basic precondition for a populist logic of articulation. So also is a crisis or failure of political representation, such that governing institutions are incapable of responding to a plethora of societal demands, and a proliferation of grievances can be equivalentially linked in opposition to a power elite. Given these structural and institutional preconditions, populism is most likely to thrive in societal contexts where diffuse inequalities are neither structured by a central class divide, nor organized and represented politically as a class cleavage. That propitious combination of structural and institutional preconditions has characterized Latin America for much of its modern political history, including the initial onset of mass politics during the early stages of industrialization and the more recent reconstitution of popular subjects in resistance to neoliberal orthodoxy. So also does this combination prevail in contemporary European and US politics, where the erosion of class cleavages under the constraints of societal modernization and market globalization has opened new political space for populist contestation of cultural identities and ethno-nationalist constructions of "the people" as an *ethnos*.

By shedding light on these structural and institutional preconditions, the lens of social class suggests a perhaps unsettling conclusion: Mudde's (2004) "populist zeitgeist" may well prove to be of *longue durée*. If that is the case, it not only behoves scholars of populism to pay attention to class dynamics; it also behoves scholars of social class to broaden their horizons and incorporate insights from populism studies into their own research. Doing so may help them better understand what takes the place of class politics when class-based cleavages and political subjects cannot be readily constituted.

References

Abou-Chadi, T., Mitteregger, R., Mudde, C. and Friedrich-Ebert-Stiftung, F. E. S. (2021) *Left behind by the working class? Social democracy's electoral crisis and the rise of the radical right*. Berlin: Friedrich-Ebert-Stiftung.

Anria, S. (2018) *When movements become parties: The Bolivian MAS in comparative perspective*. New York: Cambridge University Press.

Aslinidis, P. (2017) Populism and social movements. In: Rovira Kaltwasser, C., Taggart, P., Ochoia Espejo, P. and Ostiguy, P. (eds.) *The Oxford handbook of populism*. Oxford: Oxford University Press, 305–325.

Bartolini, S. (2000) *The political mobilization of the European left, 1860–1980: The class cleavage*. Cambridge: Cambridge University Press.

Bartolini, S. and Mair, P. (1990) *Identity, competition, and electoral availability: The stabilisation of European electorates 1885–1985*. Cambridge: Cambridge University Press.

Berman, S. (2006) *Social democracy and the making of Europe's twentieth century*. New York: Cambridge University Press.

Berman, S. (2016) The lost left. *Journal of Democracy* 27(4), 69–76.

Bernstein, E. (1907) *Evolutionary socialism*. New York: Independent Labour Party.

Betz, H.-G. (2017) The new politics of resentment: Radical right-wing populist parties in Western Europe. In: Mudde, C. (ed.) *The populist radical right: A reader*. London-New York: Routledge, 338–351.

Blum, R. M. (2020) *How the Tea Party captured the GOP: Insurgent factions in American politics*. Chicago: University of Chicago Press.

Bornschier, S. (2010) *Cleavage politics and the populist right: The new cultural conflict in Western Europe*. Philadelphia: Temple University Press.

Brown, W. (2015) *Undoing the demos: Neoliberalism's stealth revolution*. Brooklyn: Zone Books.

Carnes, N. and Lupu, N. (2021) The white working class vote and the 2016 election. *Perspectives on Politics*, 19(1), 55–72.

Castles, F. (1978) *The social-democratic image of society*. London: Routledge and Kegan Paul.

Collier, R. B. and Collier, D. (1991) *Shaping the political arena: Critical junctures, the labor movement, and regime dynamics in Latin America*. Princeton: Princeton University Press.

Collier, R. B. and Handlin, S. (eds.) 2009. *Popular participation and interest regimes in Latin America: From union–party hubs to associational networks*. University Park: Pennsylvania State University Press.

Conniff, M. L. (2012) *Populism in Latin America*. Tuscaloosa: University of Alabama Press.

De Lange, S. L. (2017) A new winning formula? The programmatic appeal of the radical right. In: Mudde, C. (ed.) *The populist radical right: A reader.* London-New York: Routledge, 83–102.

de la Torre, C. (2010) *Populist seduction in Latin America.* Athens: Ohio University Press.

de la Torre, C. (ed.) (2019) *Routledge handbook of global populism.* London-New York: Routledge.

de la Torre, C. and Arnson, C. (eds.) (2013) *Latin America populism in the twenty-first century.* Washington, DC: Woodrow Wilson Center Press.

Germani, G., di Tella, T. S. and Ianni, O. (1973) *Populismo y contradicciones de clase en Latinoamérica.* Mexico City: Ediciones Era S.A.

Gramsci, A. (1989) *Selections from the Prison Notebooks*, Q. Hoare and G. N. Smith (eds.). New York: International Publishers.

Harteveld, E. (2016) Winning the "losers" but losing the "winners"? The electoral consequences of the radical right moving to the economic left. *Electoral Studies, 44*, 225–234.

Ignazi, P. (1992) The silent counter-revolution: Hypotheses on the emergence of extreme right-wing parties in Europe. *European Journal of Political Research, 22*(1), 3–34.

Inglehart, R. (1989) *Culture shift in advanced industrial society.* Princeton: Princeton University Press.

Katz, R. S. and Mair, P. (1995) Changing models of party organization and party democracy: The emergence of the cartel party. *Party politics, 1*(1), 5–28.

Kaufman, R. R. and Stallings, B. (1991) The political economy of Latin American populism. In: Dornbusch, R. and Edwards, S. (eds.) *The macroeconomics of populism in Latin America.* Chicago: University of Chicago Press, 15–34.

Kitschelt, H. (1988) The rise of left-libertarian parties in Western democracies: Explaining innovation in competitive party systems. *World Politics, 40*(2), 194–234.

Kitschelt, H. (1994) *The transformation of European social democracy.* New York: Cambridge University Press.

Kitschelt, H. and McGann, A. J. (1995) *The radical right in Western Europe: A comparative analysis.* Ann Arbor: University of Michigan Press.

Kriesi, H. (2008) Contexts of party mobilization. In: Kriesi, H., Grande, E., Lachat, R., Dolezal, M., Bornschier, S. and Frey, T. (eds.) *West European politics in the age of globalization.* New York: Cambridge University Press, 23–52.

Laclau, E. (1977) *Politics and ideology in Marxist theory.* London: New Left Books.

Laclau, E. (2005) *On populist reason.* London: Verso.

Lipset, S. M. and Rokkan, S. (1967) Cleavage structures, party systems, and voter alignments: An introduction. In: Lipset, S. M. and Rokkan, S. (eds.) *Party systems and voter alignments: Cross-national perspectives.* New York: Free Press, 1–64.

Madrid, R. L. (2008) The rise of ethnopopulism in Latin America. *World Politics*, *60*(3), 475–508.

Mair, P. (2013) *Ruling the void: The hollowing of Western democracy.* London: Verso.

Mansbridge, J. and Macedo, S. (2019) Populism and democratic theory. *Annual Review of Law and Social Science*, *15*, 59–77.

Marx, K. (1963) *The Eighteenth Brumaire of Louis Bonaparte.* New York: International Publishers.

Marx, K. and Engels, F. (1978) Manifesto of the Communist Party. In: Tucker, R. C. (ed.) *The Marx–Engels reader.* New York: W. W. Norton, 469–500.

Mason, L. (2018) *Uncivil agreement: How politics became our identity.* Chicago: University of Chicago Press.

McCoy, J. and Somer, M. (eds.) (2019) *Polarizing polities: A global threat to democracies.* Los Angeles: Sage.

McGuire, J. W. (1997) *Peronism without Perón: Unions, parties, and democracy in Argentina.* Stanford: Stanford University Press.

Mudde, C. (2004) The populist zeitgeist. *Government and Opposition*, *39*(3), 541–563.

Mudde, C. (2007) *Populist radical right parties in Europe.* New York: Cambridge University Press.

Mudde, C. (ed.) (2017) *The populist radical right: A reader.* London-New York: Routledge.

Norris, P. and Inglehart, R. (2019) *Cultural backlash: Trump, Brexit, and authoritarian populism.* New York: Cambridge University Press.

Oesch, D. (2013) The class basis of the cleavage between the New Left and the radical right: An analysis for Austria, Denmark, Norway and Switzerland. In: Rydgren, J. (ed.) *Class politics and the radical right.* London-New York: Routledge, 31–51.

Ossowski, S. (1963) *Class structure in the social consciousness.* New York: Free Press.

Ostiguy, P. (2017) Populism: A socio-cultural approach. In: Rovira Kaltwasser, C., Taggart, P., Ochoia Espejo, P. and Ostiguy, P. (eds.) *The Oxford handbook of populism.* Oxford: Oxford University Press, 73–97.

Pappas, T. S. (2019) *Populism and liberal democracy.* Oxford: Oxford University Press.

Parker, C. S. and Barreto, M. A. (2013) *Change they can't believe in: The Tea Party and reactionary politics in America.* Princeton: Princeton University Press.

Pierson, P. (2017) American hybrid: Donald Trump and the strange merger of populism and plutocracy. *British Journal of* Sociology, *68*(S1), 105–119.

Polanyi, K. (1944) *The great transformation: The political and economic origins of our time.* New York: Farrar and Rinehart.

Portos, M. (2020) *Grievances and public protest: Political mobilisation in Spain in the age of austerity.* London: Palgrave Macmillan.

Przeworski, A. (1985) *Capitalism and social democracy.* New York: Cambridge University Press.

Roberts, K. M. (1995) Neoliberalism and the transformation of populism in Latin America: The Peruvian Case. *World Politics*, *48*(1), 82–116.

Roberts, K. M. (2002) Social inequalities without class cleavages in Latin America's neoliberal era. *Studies in Comparative International Development*, *36*(4), 3–33.

Roberts, K. M. (2014) *Changing course in Latin America: Party systems in the neoliberal era.* New York: Cambridge University Press.

Roberts, K. M. (2021) Populism and polarization in comparative perspective: Constitutive, spatial, and institutional dimensions. *Government and Opposition*, online first.

Rovira Kaltwasser, C., Taggart, P., Ochoia Espejo, P. and Ostiguy, P. (eds.) (2017) *The Oxford handbook of populism.* Oxford: Oxford University Press.

Rydgren, J. (ed.) (2013) *Class politics and the radical right.* London-New York: Routledge.

Silva, E. (2009) *Challenging neoliberalism in Latin America.* New York: Cambridge University Press.

Silva, E. and Rossi, F. (eds.) (2018) *Reshaping the political arena in Latin America: From resisting neoliberalism to the second incorporation.* Pittsburgh: University of Pittsburgh Press.

Simmons, E. S. (2016) *Meaningful resistance: Market reforms and the roots of social protest in Latin America.* New York: Cambridge University Press.

Skocpol, T. and Williamson, V. (2013) *The Tea Party and the remaking of Republican conservatism.* Oxford: Oxford University Press.

Stavrakakis, Y. and Katsambekis, G. (2014) Left-wing populism in the European periphery: The case of SYRIZA. *Journal of Political Ideologies*, *19*(2), 119–142.

Weber, M. (1946) Class, status, party. In: Gerth, H. H. and Mills, C. W. (eds.) *From Max Weber: Essays in sociology.* New York: Oxford University Press, 180–195.

Weyland, K. (1996) Neoliberalism and neopopulism in Latin America: Unexpected affinities. *Studies in Comparative International Development*, *31*(3), 3–31.

Weyland, K. (2017) Populism: A political-strategic approach. In: Rovira Kaltwasser, C., Taggart, P., Ochoia Espejo, P. and Ostiguy, P. (eds.) *The Oxford handbook of populism.* Oxford: Oxford University Press, 48–72.

Wright, E. O. (2015) *Understanding class.* London: Verso.

PART 2

Structures and Processes

CHAPTER 4

Cleavage Theory and Populism: Rediscovering a Forgotten Cleavage?

Alfio Mastropaolo

1 Revisiting Cleavage Theory

Populism is a highly controversial phenomenon. Over the past quarter century, it has been the focus of a gargantuan research effort. Yet scholars are still striving for consensus concerning its perimeters and its precise nature. Is it a Western, European, Latin American, or planetary phenomenon? Is it a contemporary or a more ancient phenomenon? Is it a "subtle" ideology, a political style, a rhetoric, or something else? In this chapter, we examine populism in relation to one of the best-known theoretical frameworks in political science: the theory of cleavages. Populism is clearly a phenomenon that the original cleavages perspective did not contemplate. Is cleavage theory of any help to understand it? Might populism represent an opportunity to confirm the validity of the theory?

Within the field of political science, a key turning point was marked by Seymour Martin Lipset and Stein Rokkan's long editorial introduction to a 1967 volume on party systems (Lipset and Rokkan 1967). The framework proposed therein has ever since been viewed as the most powerful tool available for comparing European political systems and explaining their diversity. Comparison of the different systems' historical trajectories, within what the authors viewed as a unitary, overarching European history, seemed more fruitful than the analyses based on abstract categories such as modernization, crisis, or sequences favoured by the comparatists of the preceding period. This constitutes somewhat of a paradox: while Lipset and Rokkan's chapter paid homage to Talcott Parsons's abstract and evolutionist theory, their model relied on historical recognition of the conflicts that had shaken up the history of Europe. In any case, the authors' tribute to Parsons justified them in drawing on his two fundamental axes of social division, the territorial axis and the functional axis, which represent their key coordinates for mapping party systems.

Evoking Parsonsian theory served to legitimize an original drawing together of functionalist sociology and the sociology of conflict, which in the 1960s was still dominated by Marxism. In Lipset and Rokkan's view, the class struggle was

 | DOI:10.1163/9789004679016_006

not the only salient type of conflict. European political systems were also configured around other conflicts: these were more or less the same throughout the continent, yet structured differently from country to country. Each nation had its own history and its own peculiar set of conditions for the expression of protest and the representation of interests. Key variables underpinning diversity among the various states included: 1) national traditions in the sphere of decision-making; 2) the customary channels for expressing and mobilizing protest; 3) the opportunities, payoffs, and costs of alliances; 4) the possibilities, implications, and limitations of majority rule, and therefore the rules governing elections.

According to Lipset and Rokkan, the decisive factor in structuring party systems has been a set of "critical junctures", that is to say, key crises and major opportunities for accelerated, radical change. Under certain circumstances, society underwent transformation, and new political arrangements developed. To date, there have been four such main junctures in European history: the Protestant Reformation and the Counter-Reformation of the sixteenth and seventeenth centuries; the national and democratic revolutions that followed in the wake of 1789; the Industrial Revolution; and, finally, the Russian Revolution of 1917. The upshot has been the formation of four basic fault lines. The first is that dividing nation-building elites from the populations of peripheral regions. The second is that between nation builders and the Church, with the education system as the primary bone of contention. A third line of conflict pits cities against rural areas. Finally, a fourth line separates entrepreneurs and landowners on the one hand from the workforce on the other. Not only do these cleavages interact with one other, but the timing of their appearance also plays a crucial part. They all developed to a large extent before the introduction of universal suffrage. Such are the ingredients with which Lipset and Rokkan produced their theory concerning the formation of party systems and developed their fascinating political map.

From this point onwards, our discussion will progress through four stages. First, we revisit the theory of cleavages itself and explore how it may be usefully enhanced in light of the theory of representation. Second, we discuss attempts to date to relate cleavage theory and populism: one such effort attributes populism to the cleavage between the winners and losers of the globalization process; another associates populism with the cleavage between the people and elites, in regimes based on popular sovereignty. Third, we venture to air an alternative hypothesis: What if populism were linked to the cleavage between modernity and the tradition of the *Ancien Régime*, that is to say, the reactionary far-right? The fourth and final stage in our analysis homes in on the so-called left-wing populists: Do they not perhaps represent the subordinated social groups that have replaced the traditional working class, now atomized by the effects of post-industrial societies and globalization?

2 Starting from Lipset and Rokkan

The seminal work penned by Lipset and Rokkan has enlightened two generations of scholars. Their essay's core premise has also been a source of illumination: to those who might have forgotten, the authors pointed out that while European political systems were different, the countries of Western Europe had all shared the same history. This is not to say that their piece was free of flaws or that it has not suffered the assault of time. It introduced a volume that came out in 1967. At that time, there was no "peer review" process, meaning that publication procedures were speedier; nevertheless, we may assume that it had been written at least 12 months prior. The year 1966 was a relatively propitious moment for European politics. The theory presented in the introduction reflected a political landscape that was peaceful in the main. The authors set out to observe "the genesis of the system of contrasts and cleavages within the national community" (Lipset and Rokkan 1967, 1). This system of contrasts had stabilized and become predictable over the long term. The conflicts du jour were often extremely heated, but over time they had shaped relatively stable social groups and specific collective identities.

While a few prophets, or pessimists, had begun to notice clouds gathering, or possibly moving in from the far side of the Atlantic, the social sciences were generally oblivious to the possibility of imminent new conflicts in Europe. They did not know what was soon to befall democratic regimes: potentially, new critical junctures. Aside from this blind spot, it is not disrespectful to observe that Lipset and Rokkan's theory displayed a number of other weaknesses from the outset. For example, attributing the divide between socialist and communist parties to quarrels between state builders and the Church is not a terribly robust explanation. Neither is the accompanying interpretation of the fascist movement wholly convincing; fascism was plausibly something more than a protest against "the leaders of the new large bureaucracies of industry and government, those who control the various sectors of the communications industry, the heads of mass organizations, the leaders in some countries of once weak or low-status minority ethnic or religious groups, and the like" (Lipset and Rokkan 1967, 23). In relation to fascism and communism, it may have been the authors' biases that led them to view both as forms of irrational protest.

The second weakness of the political map drawn by Lipset and Rokkan is the fact that it is heavily conditioned by the time at which it was drawn.

The authors took into account the parties that were active in the second half of the 1960s: i.e. liberal, conservative, confessional, socialist, and communist parties. There were also some smaller formations, such as regional parties. Now, the map only detected the cleavages underlying these parties and ignored cleavages that had not given rise to any party, or that had given rise to parties that had not been successful, or had failed, or that Lipset and Rokkan viewed as marginal, such as the post-fascist parties present in some places.

A third shortcoming is that times change. They change in many ways. The causes of conflict have been changing and the parties have evolved accordingly. Lipset and Rokkan bear no responsibility for this defect. Following the stabilization of the party systems in the 1960s, as flagged by Kirchheimer with the concept of a "catch-all" party (Kirchheimer 1969), change began to truly manifest itself in the 1970s. The parties active at that time were likely persuaded that they had established a monopoly over representation and that no newcomer could seriously challenge them. But subsequently, during the final decades of the second millennium, European party systems changed somewhat radically. New regional parties appeared, reflecting the mobilization of "stateless nations", environmental parties entered the pictured, followed by the parties that are now commonly referred to as "populist".

Going in search of the cleavages from which the new parties have emerged has therefore become a highly fashionable sport. Regarding the parties that formed on the territories of supposed stateless nations, this has not been a difficult task: Lipset and Rokkan had already offered sufficient guidance. In relation to the environmental parties, the most frequently adopted solution has been to invoke the dilemma theorized by Ronald Inglehart (1977) between post-materialist and materialist values. Advanced modernity aroused new specific values, so there was no need to investigate whether environmental parties had deeper roots. However, the issue became more complex when populist parties appeared upon the scene.

Political science and the social sciences are also evolving. Again, Lipset and Rokkan bear no responsibility for this. Concerning how cleavages are formed, aside from the contribution of critical junctures, they did not have much to say. A key contribution in this regard has been offered by Stefano Bartolini and Peter Mair. These authors emphasized the organizational action of the political parties themselves; it was the parties that gave rise to the cleavages. According to this view, there are socio-structural conditions such as classes, religious beliefs, ethnic or territorial affiliations, and so on, on which collective identities are based. Nevertheless, organizational action plays a crucial role in stabilizing identities and mobilizing them politically (Bartolini and Mair 1990;

Bartolini 2000). This point of view may be usefully refined by drawing on the constructivist sociology of representation.

A great theorist of democracy, J. A. Schumpeter, argued that there are "genuine group-wise volitions", but that these "do not as a rule assert themselves directly". Such volitions require spokespersons to organize them, that is to say, political parties (Schumpeter 1942, 285). Closer to the present, Bernard Manin went a step further, arguing that in "audience democracy", what we might term supply-side politics has become pre-eminent. And yet he applied this theory to post-class politics (Manin 1997). More recently still, Michael Saward has argued that the foundation of representation is a *claim* – a claim, publicly advanced by someone, an individual or a group, to speak on behalf of someone else and to look after their interests (Saward 2010). Finally, we have Pierre Bourdieu's notion of representation. According to this idea, it is not the represented that precede the representative, but vice versa (Bourdieu 1991). There is no collective body or identity that is not shaped by representation. It is the pretenders to representation who simultaneously both constitute themselves as representatives and attribute collective will to those whom they would represent, starting from the will to accept them as their representatives. Nor do they stop here: rather the representatives somehow organize the represented, cultivating collective identities, bonds of solidarity, and feelings of shared belonging. The raw material that is exploited to build cleavages is heterogeneous; overlapping allegiances are frequent; stabilizing and politicizing a constituency requires immense effort. Or rather, immense effort was required until television entered the scene, which – as observed by Manin – made it easier to advance claims of representation, without necessarily stabilizing and organizing any collective body or endowing it with an identity.

This is not to say that cleavages may be invented and manipulated at will. First, some raw material is required. Critical junctures are the situations in which the raw material is formed, as, for example, the Industrial Revolution and the class cleavage. Second, those raising a claim suffer competition from other claims. We should also consider that parties are not the only entities that exploit cleavages. Constructivist theory offers us a framework for thinking of the world as crowded with spokespersons, all of whom speak in the name of some supposed collective body and who as such participate in struggles for power. Collective movements, associations, and religious confessions also foster cleavages. There are decentralized forms of mobilization of cleavages, which are decentralized to the point of seeming spontaneous: such as those described by E. P. Thompson (1971). The new communication technologies and the mediatized politics discussed by Manin facilitate the invention of disposable cleavages, which do not even need to be organized, but whose relevance is limited to the duration of an election campaign.

To draw a provisional conclusion: integrating the theory of cleavages with constructivist theories of representation enables us to identify a dynamic, three-stage process. The first stage involves the emergence of the motives for conflict given by collective life, especially at critical junctures. Representation, and the political entrepreneurs and enterprises that run it, have the task of transforming these motives into the glue of an identity and a constituency. It is thanks to claims to representation, which are not necessarily monopolized by parties, that cleavages stabilize, and new social groups become an established part of collective life. In this way, conflicts become politicized. On closer inspection, representation is also conditioned by competing forms of representation. It is also conditioned by the rules of the game, by the prevailing interpretations of the world, by different ways of thinking about politics and collective life, and by historical events. Cleavages can also heal, remain dormant, or become invisible. If we revisit the theory of cleavages from the perspective just outlined, what light can be shed on populism?

3 Cleavage Theory and Populism: Two Hypotheses

In their foundational essay, Lipset and Rokkan viewed European party systems as having remained frozen since the 1920s. However, from the 1970s onwards, the European political landscape has been enlivened by multiple changes, raising the question of what underlying cleavages account for these new developments. In the case of the populist parties, such attributions have proved problematic, in part due to the large number of definitions that have been assigned to populism. The new groups were initially classified as extremist or far-right parties. The term "populism" came into use later on and perhaps this amounted to "stacking the deck", in the sense that it may have conditioned subsequent interpretations. In any case, in terms of cleavage theory, the academic literature has conveyed two main hypotheses:

> Populism is an ancient and recurrent phenomenon, but historically the label has corresponded to different cleavages. Lipset and Rokkan could not have captured the cleavage currently giving rise to populism. It is a new conflict that reflects the situation of our advanced societies and is between the winners and losers of globalization.

> Populism is an ancient and recurrent phenomenon and it is invariably underpinned by the same cleavage, which Lipset and Rokkan failed to observe in their analysis. It is a cleavage produced by recognition of the principle of popular sovereignty and pits the people against the elites.

The first of these hypotheses was argued for by H. P. Kriesi and colleagues (Kriesi 1998; Kriesi et al. 2008; Bornschier 2010). It presumes that in Western democracies, economic, social, and cultural change has profoundly impacted the feelings of voters and reoriented them along a new and different dividing line. The cleavages posited by Lipset and Rokkan reflected the clashes between centre and periphery, church and state, owners and workers, industry and agriculture. In contrast, the new cleavage along which voters divide and take sides is pre-eminently cultural in nature and cuts across the old cleavages. On the one hand, we find voters who are drawn to a universalist and libertarian perspective; on the other, voters who are more inclined to embrace a parochial, authoritarian, and obscurantist perspective. The winners of globalization, including entrepreneurs and workers in sectors that are open to global competition, as well as the educated and cosmopolitan strata, can successfully adapt to the challenges posed by change and are led to virtuously inhabit a broader world, hence, their proclivity for the universalistic values of the libertarian viewpoint. The so-called losers, including entrepreneurs and workers in traditionally protected sectors, unskilled labourers, and the less educated and less well-off strata, are inherently inadequate: they thus tend to identify with conservative outlooks, on both the social and cultural fronts. The working class has been particularly prone to this pattern, ever since the organizations representing the interests of workers ceased to play their traditional guiding role. All of this implies a redesigning of political space. Losers are the ideal clientele for populist parties, which can easily exploit their fears, promising exclusionary, intolerant, and authoritarian measures that are bound to meet their approval.

There is ample scope for objecting to this first interpretation. First, it has trouble explaining left-wing populism. The voters in the latter bloc are certainly nostalgic for the golden age of the welfare state, but it is not true that they are opposed to globalization or the European Union. They may be critical, but they are neither authoritarian nor ethnonationalist. Second, survey data indeed highlights the existence of a conflict between losers and winners. But this conflict has not given rise to specific social groups, horizontal ties, or separate identities. Hence, it may not be said to constitute a cleavage as envisaged by Lipset and Rokkan. It may not even be said that the losers and the lower classes are greatly culturally disadvantaged – after all, mass education has yielded some fruit. The difference between the competent and the incompetent is not clear-cut, nor is there such a sharp divide between libertarians and authoritarians. Electoral data show that a considerable proportion of the populist electorate is made up of voters who might be defined as winners (Mols and Jetten 2017). Populist voters come from all sectors of the population. Polls are never over-reliable, but Zemmour's candidacy in France's presidential election has made visible a large portion of the middle and upper classes who sympathize with the populist far right. There is a significant chunk of the middle class that is educated, conformist, and well-off, but nevertheless appreciates the anti-immigrant and security policies promised by populists.

A second possible application of cleavage theory is implied by the overabundance of literature on populism that has accumulated over the past thirty years. According to this view, the cleavage is a function of democratic revolutions. The opposition between the people and the elites is congenital (Barbieri 2021), but it has undergone several waves, which have cyclically revitalized populism. From time to time, the people reappears as such on the political scene. The most recent such re-emergence is held to be that currently in progress. This is an interesting interpretation: there is no doubt that appeals to "the people" recur in democratic societies. At the same time, however, this explanation lumps together phenomena and ideas associated with experiences that are historically, culturally, and geographically most diverse, from Russia to the United States, and from Latin America to Europe, in the nineteenth century and then again in the twentieth century – that is to say, currently. But above all, to what extent can the ideas of the people, which differ drastically from place to place, as opposed to those of the elites, which are also highly variable, constitute the basis for shared collective identities?

In point of fact, neither of these two extensions of cleavage theory point to the constitution of any "specific social group", nor to any organizational activity aimed at such an end. Globalization, in light of the political upheavals that have accompanied it, may be viewed as a critical juncture. It has certainly provoked new conflicts. Clearly, populist parties are political enterprises. Yet, they do not seem concerned with making losers into a social group with a separate identity. The success of populist parties may simply reflect a temporary shift in opinions. To apply the theory of cleavages, we might do better to suspend our judgement for the time being, emulating Lipset and Rokkan, and wait to see what happens. Alternatively, we might view populism as the effect of a cleavage that has always been there and that we had forgotten about. Has "the people" ever been a specific social group with a collective identity that sets it against the elites? It is hard to say. Perhaps the cleavage is to be sought elsewhere.

4 The Missing Cleavage

Still other propositions may be put forward to reconcile populism with the theory of cleavages, or to associate populism with an underlying cleavage. In the context of this chapter, we discuss the following alternative hypothesis:

> In European history, the cleavage overlooked by Lipset and Rokkan, is a different one: it is the cleavage along which the far-right parties, which were in the minority but still quite vital following World War II, have traditionally formed. What is this cleavage? It is that caused initially by the French Revolution: the cleavage between the representatives of modernity and those who remain nostalgic for the *Ancien Régime*, spanning ultraconservatives, reactionaries, and fascists. The current populist parties are the heirs to this second tradition.

Let us begin by scrutinizing the label "populism". Prior to the late 1970s, it was used to describe two nineteenth-century movements in Russia and the United States, as well as authoritarian regimes in Latin America and the so-called Third World during the first half of the twentieth century. Scholars also used the term to describe a diversity of phenomena that had little in common with contemporary populism (Canovan 1981). The concept began to be extended by Stuart Hall, who in 1979 referred to Thatcherism as "authoritarian populism" because of its nationalist, authoritarian, law and order component and its impatience with immigration (Hall 1979). The current usage likely originated with Pierre-André Taguieff, who in 1984 described the Front National – founded in France in 1972 without acknowledging any kinship with fascism – as "national-populist" (Taguieff 1984; 2002).

Taguieff possibly intended to echo the critique of populism within 1950s American sociology (Jäger 2017). The new party, after a decade of scandalizing public opinion with its discourses but without much success with the electorate, performed very well in the local elections of 1983, going on to win 11 per cent of the vote in the European elections held the following year. This same percentage of electoral share was confirmed in the 1986 general elections. The Front National did not hide its proximity to the Italian neo-fascist party: it had even copied its symbol, the tricoloured flame, simply replacing green with blue. Consistently with this premise, once the party had staked its claim to membership of the "national right", in opposition to "Marxism and cosmopolitan liberalism", its leader, Jean-Marie Le Pen, raised issues such as anti-parliamentarism, order and security, and the threat of immigration. The

Front's rhetoric also lamented the decadence of the country and its customs, the misdeeds of the political class, and the intrusiveness of the state.

One might wonder why, instead of ascribing Le Pen's party to the extreme right, Taguieff chose a different label. No doubts were entertained at the time by Monique Charlot, a French electoral sociologist, who studied the *frontiste* voters (Charlot 1986). The political supply of the Front National was securitarian, nationalist, and xenophobic; like all right-wing parties, it drew most of its clientele from within the middle class: shopkeepers, artisans, farmers, private sector employees, and the upper-middle classes of the bourgeois neighbourhoods of Paris and Lyon. These were voters who mostly came from the moderate right, who in the past had supported extreme-right nationalist candidates in the presidential elections. Men outnumbered women, young people were few, and the intellectual professions were under-represented. In short, Taguieff has been an exception among contemporary observers of the Front National and similar parties that have meanwhile flourished on the European political stage. For a long time to come, scholars will continue talk about the extreme right. They still do so today, even Cas Mudde, perhaps the most cited scholar of populism.[1]

In Europe, the far right and fascism are the same thing, or almost. But what about the relationship between fascism and populism? This is a widely debated topic. At first glance, the two phenomena seem different. The first problem, of course, is to circumscribe the space to which the label of fascism may be applied. This space has been greatly expanded, now extending to all the authoritarian movements that appeared between the two world wars. After all, Nazism and fascism are not the same thing, and we shall only group them together here for simplification purposes. The two movements developed in the aftermath of a huge explosion of violence, which facilitated the extraordinary spread of military skills. Both came to power by forming private militias, and both violently attacked political opponents and stormed the legitimate authorities with the support of the army, police forces, public bureaucracies, judiciary, business circles, and landowners. The situation in the 1920s and 1930s was further marked by a profound economic crisis. Just as dramatic was the ideological tension aroused by the world war and the Russian Revolution. The aversion to representative democracy of Italian fascism, Nazism, and similar movements that arose in France, Belgium, Great Britain, and elsewhere was not disguised in any way. Once the opportunity arose – in Italy, in Germany,

1 See, for example: Ignazi (1992, 2003); Kitschelt and McGann (1995); Schain, Zolberg and Hossay (2002); Merkl and Weinberg (2003); Mudde (2007, 2019).

and in France following the defeat of 1940 – these movements culminated in the establishment of two openly authoritarian and violent regimes.

In contrast, so-called populism has adapted to the democratic regime. At face, the populist parties do not challenge the safeguard mechanisms provided for in the democratic constitutions of the second post-war period and they officially reject the use of violence. On the other hand, they reinterpret representative democracy and distort it. They are critical of the separation of powers; in the name of the majority, they silence minorities; they impose a plebiscitarian idea of representation and democracy (Diehl 2019). Furthermore, their language is aggressive, transgressive, and offensive, Manichean, rude, refractory to any elaborate reflection or argumentation and above all to criticism, and as such incites physical violence in any case. Finally, while anti-Semitism appears to have disappeared, though not always, it has been replaced by anti-Islamism.

Neither should we be confused by populism's evocation of "the people", an expression that has been common currency from the great revolutions onwards. For at least two centuries, there has been no regime and no party, whether right-wing or left-wing, that has refrained from evoking it. Not even authoritarian regimes. The term "people" is vague and polysemic, lending itself to all kinds of ambiguities and exploitive uses. There is a "people" for every taste. And how one defines the people makes a difference. Populist parties have their own way of defining the people, which is not dissimilar to the fascist definition. In the liberal democratic tradition, the people corresponds to the *demos*. It is composed of free and equal individuals, who associate with one another under one and the same law, which they themselves have indirectly contributed to defining. The socialist and communist tradition, which did not disdain the term "people", identified it with the working and lower-status classes: its people were the *plebs*, who aspired to membership of the *demos*. For moderate, conservative, and confessional parties, the people represented the ideal alternative to a society divided into opposing social classes.

The populists' people is also unitary: yet it is woven of entirely different thread. It is an *ethnos* and as such unified, as well as distinct from other peoples by virtue of its peculiar history, culture, religion, and traditions. When observers speak of ethnonationalism, or "nativism", they are referring to an exclusionary and xenophobic variation on the concept of people. This variant has been successful in post-communist Europe, but earlier won a following further west. In Western Europe, the issue of migratory flows has been troubling to large sectors of public opinion since the early 1970s. That populists propose far-right, conservative, and even reactionary ideas is difficult to deny. In their speeches, the meaning of the word people does not lend itself to misunderstandings: it is the same meaning that the fascists attributed to it. Fascism too sometimes opposed the elites. On a planetary scale, for that matter. Italian fascism was permanently at war against the "old and corrupt demoplutocracies".

Once we acknowledge that fascism and populism are not the same thing, but that there is a certain "family resemblance" between them, on what cleavage may we deem one and the other to be based? With regard to fascism, as stated at the outset, Lipset and Rokkan offer no help. They do not even mention the far right. Lipset in other works classifies fascism as a form of extreme protest that is typical of the middle class (Lipset 1960). However, we know too much about fascism to be satisfied with so little. It was also, in some respects, an attempt at modernization. It even set out to create a new man and a new, revolutionary order in competition with liberalism, socialism, and communism. On the other hand, the principle of hierarchy, the cult of the charismatic leader, and a communitarian notion of the people and of the nation are all typical reactionary themes. Populism is undoubtedly rudimentary; it is lacking in intellectuals, who – on the contrary – were well represented in fascism. It does not even offer elaborate programmes. Its political supply is focused on alarmism and fear. But more importantly, as we shall attempt to argue in the next section, it shares fascism's reactionary roots.

5 The Continuity of the Reactionary Tradition

Reactionaryism is an age-old tradition. In England, the trauma of the Civil War was largely reabsorbed by the Glorious Revolution. In France, as in the rest of Europe, the traumatic effects of revolution were longer lasting. Some years ago, Zeev Sternhell, a historian known for his often disputed, but always intriguing, research on the intellectual background of fascism, situated its origins in the trauma of the Enlightenment (Sternhell 1986; 1994). The Enlightenment and the French Revolution essentially overlapped. Together they carved a deep intellectual, political, and moral division in European societies. Nostalgia for a society held together by hierarchy, the authority of the state, national sentiment, religion, and family became a cleavage, following the Congress of Vienna and the Restoration. Ever since, it has fed a rich entanglement of thoughts, feelings, and circles: reactionary, anti-egalitarian, anti-universalist, intolerant, obscurantist, or anti-pluralist. The pantheon of reactionary thought includes distinguished thinkers such as Giambattista Vico, Edmund Burke, Joseph de Maistre, Johann Gottfried Herder, Juan Donoso Cortés, Hippolyte Taine, Charles Maurras, Oswald Spengler, Friedrich Meinecke, Heinrich von Treitschke, Othmar Spann, Carl Schmitt, Alfredo Rocco, and Enrique Gil

Robles. Each country boasts its own great reactionary intellectuals, all of whom are well known internationally, and its own reactionary tradition.

It is more difficult to reconstruct an exhaustive inventory of the associations, movements, parties, and networks that have historically inhabited the reactionary galaxy.[2] Concepts and words have many limitations. Especially in the case of the social sciences, whose language is not much different to that of the everyday. Matters get even more complicated when a word becomes a badge of dishonour. In addition, it is extremely difficult to trace a clear line between reactionaries and conservatives. At first glance, both are nostalgic for the old order. One possible distinction between conservatives and reactionaries could be the loyalty of the former to the principles of representation versus the disloyalty of the latter. However, many reactionaries claim that they are loyal to the representative system, while historically many conservatives sided with autocracy when democratic and socialist parties came to power.

To make life more difficult for their observers, reactionaries form a highly diverse galaxy, composed of elitists and plebeians, secularists and religionists, legitimists and subversives, anti-modernists and even ultramodernists, organicists, pro- and anti-capitalists, nationalists, anti-Semites, and racists. This galaxy has produced political entrepreneurs, leaders, managers, activists, journalists, and an impressive supply of reactionary claims, although such claims have not always been channelled through political parties. Not to mention the even more complex boundaries between conservative and reactionary currents, and fascism, which undoubtedly included reactionary elements, but also a markedly modernist component. Rather than viewing such labels as a reliable tool of classification, they should be understood as the poles that circumscribe a political space, within which actors occupy a range of – unstable – positions.

Against this general backdrop, the family tree of the reactionary far right stretches back a long way. Arguably, the most evident pattern of continuity is observed in France. From the Restoration to the Second Empire, its presence goes without saying. Following the Franco-Prussian War, the reactionary impulse resurfaced with the Boulangist movement in 1882. It continued with Paul Déroulède and the Ligue des Patriotes, which was a mix of anti-German revanchism, Catholic extremism, and authoritarianism, up until the great wave of anti-Semitism surrounding the Dreyfus Affair. At the end of the century, Charles Maurras inspired the founding of Action Française. This was a nationalist, monarchist, anti-Semitic movement that supported the Vichy regime,

2 From the endless literature on this topic, we cite Sternhell (1986) as well as Blinkhorn (1990) and Fawcett (2020).

and subsequently survived until the 1970s. The mid-1930s saw the emergence of the Croix-de-Feux led by Colonel de la Rocque, and Jacques Doriot's Parti Populaire Français. Clearly, a key juncture was the establishment of the État Français headed by Pétain following the German victory of 1940.

This impressively long-standing tradition resumed once again at the time of decolonization, this time under the guise of the reactionary, nationalist awakening in support of *Algerie française*. In 1965, Jean-Louis Tixier-Vignancour, the far-right presidential candidate, won 5 per cent of the national vote. The 1960s also marked the beginning of the heretical adventure of the Nouvelle Droite under the guidance of Alain de Benoist. However, the major turning point was the arrival on the scene of Jean-Marie Le Pen and the Front National in 1972. In recent years, this tradition has expanded thanks to the appearance of Eric Zemmour, a singular case of a nostalgic Jew, who explicitly frames himself as in continuity with Action Française and Vichy and who appeals to a different audience from that of Front National: not the working class, but the conservative Catholic middle class.

The cleavage between reaction and modernity is ubiquitous. It has not spared the United Kingdom, despite the ability of the Conservative Party to host and censor reactionaries. Nevertheless, Oswald Mosley and the British Union of Fascists (BUF) were informed by Italian fascism. In the 1960s, a veteran of the BUF founded the National Front. The splintering of this group in 1980 yielded the British National Party. The more recent UKIP is an anomalous case that has combined anti-European nationalism with an extreme version of neoliberalism, without racist prejudice. Meanwhile, in Germany, where a full-blown representative regime was only introduced after World War I, a robust reactionary current was only to be expected. The history of the Bismarckian and Wilhelmine Reich was a mixture of reaction, modernism, and industrialization, yet the country has suffered no shortage of purely reactionary movements. The pan-German political movement combined nationalism, expansionist ambitions, anti-Semitism and anti-Slavic sentiments.

The anti-Semitic Christian Social Party was founded in the late nineteenth century by Adolf Stoecker, a Lutheran pastor, who wished to mobilize workers in opposition to the SPD. After World War I, the reactionary factions converged to form a river in flood. Revanchism was intertwined with anti-Semitism in the German Nationalist Protection and Defiance Federation and the German National People's Party. A military variant was constituted by the Freikorps, who were forerunners of the Nazi brown shirts. The reactionary current reappeared after World War II under the guise of the NPD (Nationaldemokratische Partei Deutschlands), the DVU (Deutsche Volksunion) founded in 1971, and the Republikaner. Pegida (Patriotic Europeans against the Islamisation of the

Occident) and AfD (Alternative for German) represent the provisional culmination of this lengthy genealogy.

In brief, every European country has its reactionaries. In Catholic countries, the Church traditionally represented a robust repository of anti-modern and reactionary sentiments. Lately, its place has been occupied by Evangelical and Pentecostal movements. The reactionary evolution of nationalism dates back to the turn of the twentieth century. The Italian National Association, founded in 1910, supported first colonialism and later Italy's participation in World War I, before merging with fascism. The latter resurfaced after World War II in the form of the Italian Social Movement (MSI). In Spain in 1933, José Antonio Primo de Rivera founded the Falange Española, a monarchist, Catholic, anti-liberal, and anti-capitalist group. In Austria, the reactionary current manifested itself in the late nineteenth century via the anti-Semitism and anti-liberalism of the Christian Social Party launched by Karl Lueger, burgomaster of Vienna. It continued with the pan-German movement and the Heimwehr militias in the first post-war period, up until the Dollfuss dictatorship. The tradition continued after World War II under the auspices of the National Liberal Party.

Where have all the fascists gone? This question was posed some years ago in the title of a book about the French *nouvelle droite* (Bar-On 2007). But we might make the same enquiry in relation to democratic regimes. Where have the reactionaries and former fascists gone? Sometimes continuity in personal histories help to tease out the answer. We earlier summarized the pedigree of Jean-Marie Le Pen. The first leader of the Austrian FPÖ, Anton Reinthaller, was a former Nazi dignitary and SS officer. Jörg Haider came from a Nazi family. In the 1990s, one of the leading lights in the Italian populist right was Alessandra Mussolini, while behind the localist characteristics of the Northern League, there is no shortage of leaders from the neo-fascist tradition. Currently, we might point to the evident flirtation between the League and the political area comprising Forza Nuova and Casa Pound, which is nostalgic for fascism. No less evident is the nostalgia for the Franco era of the latest addition to the family of so-called European populists: the leaders of Spain's Vox come from the Popular Party, but, unlike the exponents of the latter, are explicit about their Francoist and nationalist convictions.

However, a cleavage is not given by continuity in personal trajectories. Rather it is formed by issues, shared experiences, symbols, and political action. The parties that are active on one side of a cleavage do not necessarily view it as an insurmountable limit. Part of their electoral bases can easily be drawn from further afield. A cleavage is a point of reference, which a political enterprise can exploit and stabilize. It is not necessarily always stabilized by parties. A carefully maintained body of ideas can also stabilize a cleavage. Vice versa, the electoral appeal of parties depends on multiple factors, not solely on their ideal roots, but also on their policy supply. The great European confessional parties (the Italian Christian Democrats, the CDU, the ÖVP, etc.) were originally religious parties, yet they very soon came to represent not just Catholics, but entire social strata (bourgeoisie, middle class, peasants) and often harboured – albeit discreetly – an anti-modern, reactionary wing. Reactionary political entrepreneurs, who for a quarter of a century had identified with fascism and Nazism, enjoyed a terrible reputation after World War II. Therefore, they had to disguise their identity as much as possible. Only recently have certain words, which for half a century had been unpronounceable, been brought back into circulation.

Transferring the concept of cleavage out of Western European politics can be a valid proposition. The necessary precondition is that we reflect very carefully about what cleavages may be salient to other world regions and what critical junctures they may have developed from. We shall not embark on such a challenging venture here. To apply it to Latin American politics, which are infinitely varied, would require a highly ambitious and detailed investigation. The recurrence in Latin America of phenomena labelled as populism can generate confusion about how these movements should be defined. The same caution is recommended for the cleavages and populisms of former socialist Europe. Unless we choose to view populism as a style or technique of political struggle.

Perhaps the task of identifying cleavages is a little easier when it comes to the United States. The racial question undoubtedly constitutes a fundamental cleavage in American society, and the Civil War was a tremendous critical juncture. Yet, while it has conditioned the party system, it has done so in a peculiar way. The rules of electoral competition in the US do not tolerate third, fourth, or fifth parties. At different times, the reactionary tradition has found refuge in both major parties. Up to the 1960s, it prevailed in the Democratic Party in the Southern states. Yet we cannot but observe strong continuity between the reactionary sentiments expressed by the raids of the Ku Klux Klan then and the white supremacism mobilized by Donald Trump today (Huntington 2021).

It might with some justification be argued that the current conditions of European societies offer unprecedented opportunities for reactionary political entrepreneurs to awaken conservative and reactionary sentiments. These are sentiments that must be taken very seriously. First, being reactionary is not a sin, nor a crime. Democracy is incompatible with violence, but it lends itself to many uses. Reactionary sentiments have always been harboured even in the most liberal societies, which are highly diverse, as is appropriate. There is nothing wrong with being conservative or reactionary: for the ordinary voter, this can simply mean being nostalgic for a past that for some reason appears preferable to the present. There have always been entrepreneurs in the field of political representation who were ready to evoke the past, hierarchy, authority, religious faith, tradition and to manoeuvre resentments and fears. Social and cultural change has recently offered such entrepreneurs a series of extraordinary opportunities: the new condition of women, same-sex families, and other rapid shifts in societal customs and norms. For many voters, on the right, but also on the left, regardless of their educational background, and whether losers or winners, it is not easy to adapt. Nor is it easy to adapt to migration, multiculturalism, globalization, and terrorism. The new populist right has made anxiety and fear into the mainspring of its electoral supply: for thirty years, it has devoted itself to replacing class conflict with racial conflict.

The economic recession of 2008, a generalized precarization of labour relations that does not spare the middle class, and the perception of a worsening in living conditions compared to the past, have helped right-wing populists to further this agenda. In the early 1990s, Piero Ignazi distinguished between parties with openly fascist underpinning and formations of the new post-materialist right (Ignazi 1992). In 2022, Aron Buzogáni and Mihai Varga published an interesting article in which they distinguished between two competing orientations within the current configuration of reactionary thinking: one more tied up with the dimension of a European identity, and the other more openly conservative, with a focus on the themes of the nation, the family, the female condition, and traditional morality (Varga and Buzogáni 2022). But while reactionary sentiment is varied, populist parties, via their tactical choices and communication strategies, have skilfully manipulated and confounded different orientations to serve their electoral goals. This is one of the factors underpinning their current success.

6 Is There Populism on the Left Too?

The parties of the populist right represent the most important "new entry" to European political systems in the years spanning the second and third millennia. However, they are not alone. There have been other new entries on the left. When the socialist and social democratic parties chose to weigh in behind the "market turn", new left parties – critical of this turn – appeared in almost all European countries. Prior to the 1990s, socialist and social democratic parties were not anti-capitalist. Rather, they were in favour of the welfare state and state intervention in the economy – until they decided to support the great market turn. At that point, new parties, mostly left-wing, but also environmentalist and of other, more uncertain, categories, moved in to occupy their former space. Let us limit our analysis here to the newcomers on the left.

First, we should acknowledge that in almost all European countries, there has – nevertheless – always been a communist, or at least an anti-capitalist, left. Post-1989, only a small part of it survived. One subset of this remnant has given way to the newcomers, another has allied itself with them. Are the latter also left-wing populists? In any case, it is interesting to note that socialism is never mentioned in the titles of the newcomers' formations: Podemos, Syriza, France Insoumise, Linke, Bloco de Esquerda.[3] For some reason, the word "socialism" must appear outdated. Furthermore, while they are often labelled radicals, the manifestos of the new left-wing parties declare them to be at most reformists, especially by the standards of the 1960s and 1970s. Their leaders are all dissidents from socialist and communist parties. Why ever call them populists? What is the cleavage on which they lean? According to the first theory we considered above, they might be situated along the losers/winners cleavage. According to the second theory, might they be viewed as representing the people/elite cleavage? Is it appropriate to confuse them with far-right populists, just because they love to use the word "people" (Katsambekis and Kioupkiolis 2019)?

There is no cause for scandal here. We all adapt words, categories, and concepts according to our preferences and what we want to say. What complicates the interpretation and classification of these new left parties is that they – unlike far-right populists – call themselves populists. In doing so, they were following Ernesto Laclau, a distinguished intellectual from Argentina who taught for many years in Great Britain, had lived through Peronism, and was close to its left wing. Drawing on his reading of Gramsci and Carl Schmitt, Laclau redefined populism, once again reversing its meaning. While for American sociologists in the 1950s, populism was an illness of democracy, Laclau saw the potential for it to have a therapeutic effect on democratic systems.

His first contribution on the subject dates back to 1977 (Laclau 2014). Drawing inspiration from South America and Peronism, Laclau proposed populism as a political strategy that was also appropriate for the left. He reiterated this in his later writings (Laclau 2005) on the grounds that globalization

3 There is one case that is extremely difficult to classify: the Five Star Movement in Italy. Is it mandatory to classify everything? Perhaps not. In any case, the Five Star Movement is closer to the left than to the right. In the 2013 and 2018 general elections, it attracted voters from both the left and the right. It is currently in decline, but the voters who were previously close to the left seem more willing to remain. The issues it raises are mainly drawn from the repertoire of the left (Biancalana 2022).

rendered the Marxist framework obsolete. In globalized societies, struggles for emancipation must henceforth be based on concepts other than that of social class. Populism serves this purpose; indeed, for Laclau, populism is politics. Pre-empting the constructivist theory of political representation, Laclau proposed that populism is an "empty signifier", which political action is called to fill by piecing together the diverse range of factors afflicting those oppressed by neoliberalism and globalization.

As is well known, Laclau's controversial strategy has inspired many pretenders to political representation. First, the founders of Podemos in Spain. This group initially refused to describe itself as a left-wing party but declared itself populist, drawing on the rhetoric of "the people" and highlighting the opposition between the old politics and the new, between continuity and change, and between political, financial, and business oligarchies and the bulk of ordinary citizens, that is to say, the people. Podemos has also entertained friendly relations with certain populist formations in South America, especially that of Chávez. On the other hand, whatever image of itself Podemos has transmitted, among other methods by exploiting highly original communication technologies, its positions and representative supply are based on socio-economic inequalities and political proposal's intended to fix them. In addition, Podemos has run for election in coalition with historic parties from the Spanish left that are the present-day heirs of the Communist Party (Kioupkiolis 2019; Campolongo and Caruso 2021).

To classify Podemos and the other new left parties in this political family as far-right populist parties is a highly questionable choice. The Fordist working class of the mid-twentieth century was different from what Marx and Engels in 1848 termed the proletariat: the latter was undoubtedly an extremely diverse and fragmented social whole. Laclau's idea was to use populism to politically unify social strata that can in no sense be considered a social class, but yet share flexibility, precariousness, and poverty. But was the raw material from which Marxism and the socialist movement in the second half of the twentieth century assembled the working class so different? Globalization, the process of European unification, the market turn, and austerity may be viewed as comprising a critical juncture. But there is also good reason to assume that the parties of the new left are based on an ancient cleavage that has merely taken a new form. The target of these parties is the lower class. Or, more simply, the victims: the unemployed, the precarious and flexible workers, the working poor, the inhabitants of degraded urban suburbs or of the places that do not matter. The victims extend to the middle class. It is by no means a given that they are culturally backward and therefore more prone to nationalism, xenophobic hatred, authoritarianism, and populism (Langsæther and Stubager 2019).

The cleavage along which the new left parties align is different from the cleavage exploited by the populists of the extreme right. And it is unfair to confound the notion of inclusive, plural, egalitarian, supportive, participatory, rights-oriented, anti-imperialist democracy of the new left with the "illiberal" and plebiscitarian democracy sponsored by the populist right.[4] Of course, they both deploy the term "the people" and a dichotomous rhetoric. Yet both have been present on the political scene for almost two centuries. It is true that a nationalist impulse has sometimes also manifested itself on the left; however, this is not intolerant and xenophobic nationalism, but rather Eurosceptical. Nor does the language of the new left have anything to do with the aggressive language of the extreme right.

7 Conclusion

Populism is clearly a concept that is not only stretched, but over-stretched. In the mid-1990s, when it first began to be extended to far-right parties, it bore the merit of signalling a key shift in the language and style of the political struggle. The previous era had been marked by the language of social classes and imposed by socialist parties. Even competing parties used it, possibly in an attempt to define themselves as inter-classist. The new era, characterized by post-industrialism and the market turn, demanded a new language.

Cleavage theory invites us to seek out the historical roots of political parties. This can represent an extremely useful line of inquiry. Attempts have already been made to identify new cleavages to which populism might be anchored. In this chapter, we have examined the hypothesis that, thanks to populism, an old cleavage has been brought to new life. It is important to note that no right-way European party labelled as "populist" has ever voluntarily described itself as such. The "populist" label has always been imposed by outside observers. Nevertheless, parties have frequently welcomed the label because it frees them from the stigma of fascism, contradicts suggestions that they represent a danger to democracy, and even qualifies them as friends of the people, ultimately pushing them to target the lower classes.

At the same time, while the label has influenced the phenomenon itself, it may also have influenced how it has been interpreted. Some of its indisputable characteristics – its emphasis on the opposition between the people

4 The only clear case of a plebiscitarian style within so-called European left-wing populism is that of Jean-Luc Mélenchon (Cervera-Marzal 2021). But to what extent is such a style on the part of France Insoumise shaped also by the French presidential regime?

and the elites, and its charismatic leadership, a feature shared with North and South American populisms – have shaped interpretation of it, leading other aspects to be underestimated: first and foremost, nationalism and xenophobia. Rereading history allows us to observe the links between what are now called right-wing populists and the reactionary tradition. These ties are cultural, but also social and personal.

The case of what is referred to as left-wing populism is a little different. In at least one case, a party classified in this way has itself embraced the label. But if we look at this party, and the other parties assigned to the same family, their pledges are classical left-wing pledges, albeit a shade radical for our times. Furthermore, their voters come from traditional left-wing parties as do their leaders. In both cases, one wonders whether the populist label is still appropriate. Both sides present crucial novel characteristics with respect to the mainstream parties of the right and left. Yet, these new features are not the same for both and above all they do not justify us in uniting them under a common label.

References

Barbieri, G. (2021) *The fifth cleavage: Genealogy of the populist ideology and parties.* London-New York: Routledge.

Bar-On, T. (2007) *Where have all the fascists gone?* London-New York: Routledge.

Bartolini, S. (2000) *The political mobilization of the European Left, 1860–1980: The class cleavage.* Cambridge: Cambridge University Press.

Bartolini, S. and Mair, P. (1990) *Identity, competition, and electoral availability: The stabilization of European electorates 1885–1985.* Cambridge: Cambridge University Press.

Biancalana, C. (2022) *Political parties and the challenge of disintermediation: Rhetoric and practices of organisational change in Italy.* Baden-Baden: Nomos.

Blinkhorn, M. (ed.) (1990) *Fascists and conservatives: The radical right and the establishment in twentieth-century Europe.* London-New York: Routledge.

Bornschier, S. (2010) *Cleavage politics and the populist right: The new cultural conflict in Western Europe.* Philadelphia: Temple University Press.

Bourdieu, P. (1991) Political representation: Elements of a theory of the political field. In: Bourdieu, P. *Language and symbolic power.* Cambridge, MA: Harvard University Press, 171–202.

Campolongo, F. and Caruso, L. (2021) *Podemos e il populismo di sinistra. Dalla protesta al governo.* Milano: Meltemi.

Canovan, M. (1981) *Populism.* New York: Harcourt Brace.

Cervera-Marzal, M. (2021) *Le populisme de gauche. Sociologie de la France insoumise.* Paris: La Découverte.

Charlot, M. (1986) L'émergence du Front national. *Revue française de science politique, 36*(1), 30–45.

Diehl, P. (2019) Twisting representation. In: de la Torre, C. (ed.) *Routledge handbook of global populism.* London-New York: Routledge, 129–144.

Fawcett, E. (2020) *Conservatism: The fight for a tradition.* Princeton: Princeton University Press.

Hall, S. (1979) The great moving right show. *Marxism Today, 23*(1), 14–20.

Huntington, J. S. (2021) *Far-right vanguard: The radical roots of modern conservatism.* Philadelphia: University of Pennsylvania Press.

Ignazi, P. (1992) The silent counter-revolution: Hypotheses on the emergence of extreme right-wing parties in Europe. *European Journal of Political Research, 22*(1), 3–34.

Ignazi, P. (2003) *Extreme right parties in Western Europe.* Oxford: Oxford University Press.

Inglehart, R. (1977) *The silent revolution: Changing values and political styles among Western publics.* Princeton: Princeton University Press.

Jäger, A. (2017) The semantic drift: Images of populism in post-war American historiography and their relevance for (European) political science. *Constellations, 24*(3), 310–327.

Katsambekis, G. and Kioupkiolis, A. (eds.) (2019) *The populist radical left in Europe.* London-New York: Routledge.

Kioupkiolis, A. (2019) Late modern adventures of leftist populism in Spain: The case of Podemos, 2014–2018. In: Katsambekis, G. and Kioupkiolis, A. (eds.) *The populist radical left in Europe.* London-New York: Routledge, 47–72.

Kirchheimer, O. (1969) The transformation of the Western European party system. In: Burin, F. S. and Shell, K. L. (eds.) *Politics, law and social change: Selected essays of Otto Kirchheimer.* New York: Columbia University Press, 177–200.

Kitschelt, H. and McGann, A. J. (1995) *The radical right in Western Europe: A comparative analysis.* Ann Arbor: University of Michigan Press.

Kriesi, H. (1998) The transformation of cleavage politics: The 1997 Stein Rokkan lecture. *European Journal of Political Research, 33*(2), 165–185.

Kriesi, H., Grande, E., Lachat, R., Dolezal, M., Bornschier, S. and Frey, T. (2008) *West European politics in the age of globalization.* Cambridge: Cambridge University Press.

Laclau, E. (2005) *On populist reason.* London: Verso.

Laclau, E. (2014) Towards a theory of populism. In: Howarth, D. (ed.) *Ernesto Laclau: Post-Marxism, populism and critique.* London-New York: Routledge, 143–98.

Langsæther, P. E. and Stubager, R. (2019) Old wine in new bottles? Reassessing the effects of globalization on political preferences in Western Europe. *European Journal of Political Research, 58*(4), 1213–33.

Lipset, S. M. (1960) *Political man: The social bases of politics.* New York: Doubleday.

Lipset, S. M. and Rokkan, S. (1967) Cleavage structures, party systems and voter alignments: An introduction. In: Lipset, S. M. and Rokkan, S. (eds.) *Party systems and voter alignments.* New York: Free Press, 1–64.

Manin, B. (1997) *The principles of representative government.* Cambridge: Cambridge University Press.

Merkl, P. and Weinberg, L. (eds.) (2003) *Right-wing extremism in the twenty-first century.* London-New York: Routledge.

Mols, F. and Jetten, J. (2017) *The wealth paradox: Economic prosperity and the hardening of attitudes.* Cambridge: Cambridge University Press.

Mudde, C. (2007) *Populist radical right parties in Europe.* Cambridge: Cambridge University Press.

Mudde, C. (2019) *The far right today.* Cambridge: Polity.

Saward, M. (2010) *The representative claim.* Oxford: Oxford University Press.

Schain, M., Zolberg, A. and Hossay, P. (eds.) (2002) *Shadows over Europe: The development and impact of the extreme right in Western Europe.* New York: Palgrave Macmillan.

Schumpeter, J. A. (1942) *Capitalism, socialism and democracy.* London-New York: Harper & Brothers.

Sternhell, Z. (1986) *The anti-Enlightenment tradition.* New Haven: Yale University Press.

Sternhell, Z. et al. (1994) *The birth of fascist ideology: From cultural rebellion to political revolution.* Princeton: Princeton University Press.

Taguieff, P. A. (1984) La rhétorique du national-populisme. Les règles élémentaires de la propagande xénophobe. *Mots*, *9*, 113–139.

Taguieff, P. A. (2002) *L'illusion populiste. De l'archaïque au médiatique.* Paris: Berg International.

Thompson, E. P. (1971) The moral economy of the English crowd in the 18th century. *Past & Present*, *50*(1), 76–136.

Varga, M., Buzogány, A. (2022) The two faces of the 'global right': Revolutionary conservatives and national-conservatives. *Critical Sociology*, *48*(6), 1089–1107.

CHAPTER 5

Sovereignty and Populism

Reinhard Heinisch and Klaudia Koxha

The rise of radical right and left populism has brought sovereignty and sovereignism – the construction and diffusion of sovereignty claims – into renewed focus. Sovereignty is central to populism, both as a core idea attributed to populism ("people centeredness") and as propagated by populists themselves ("constraints on popular sovereignty by liberal/representative democracy"). The idea of unrestrained rule by the people covers multiple dimensions and encompasses the individual dimension (loss of control) and various collective dimensions, the most comprehensive of which is the nation. Sovereignist claims are based on ideologically constructed notions of "people", pertaining collectively to a community, culture, region, or nation to which a special autonomy is attributed but which is threatened a) by internal corrupted and disloyal elites, b) by self-serving or hostile outside elites imposing external authority, and c) by exposure to the uncertain outcomes of the political, social, and economic changes resulting from globalization and modernization. Sovereignty and sovereignism are demand-side and supply-side phenomena in that diffuse fears and aspirations present in the mass public may be shaped by, or filled with specific ideological content through political communication and campaigning.

1 Introduction

What is the relationship between populism and sovereignty, two closely connected concepts that are of central importance in contemporary politics? Sovereignty can be defined as the independent authority and ability of a governing body to manage its affairs according to its own preferences. But why should this concept matter in populism, a system of ideas primarily concerned with the antagonism between the people and nefarious elites? In this chapter, we will examine populism and sovereignty and their relationship from the perspective of contemporary political science scholarship. The chapter will also assess the role of sovereignty in populism research and what can be learned from how scholarship on populism addresses sovereignty.

 | DOI:10.1163/9789004679016_007

2 Our Approach to Populism

As for defining populism, it is useful to recall that scholars have considered it a thin ideology (Mudde 2004), a strategy (Weyland 2021), a discursive framing (Aslanidis 2016), a regime property (Pappas 2019), a political logic or a style (Moffitt and Tormey 2014).[1] Nonetheless, the dichotomy between two vaguely conceptualized but homogeneous entities, the elites and the people, is the unifying feature identified in almost all populism research (Jagers and Walgrave 2007; Hawkins 2009; Akkerman, Mudde and Zaslove 2014). Thus, in populism, the people are the "ultimate source of legitimacy" (van Kessel 2015, 15) for political action, and as such the will of the people is above criticism and above institutional or legal constraints.

Scholars who view populism as an ideology argue that it is based on three core ideas: 1) the portrayal of the elite as corrupt and self-interested, 2) the belief that people are homogeneous, and 3) a Manichean and moralistic cosmology (Mudde and Rovira Kaltwasser 2013; Akkerman, Mudde and Zaslove 2014; Castanho Silva et al. 2018; 2020; Hawkins and Rovira Kaltwasser 2018). Populists are also generally viewed as opponents of liberalism (Mudde and Rovira Kaltwasser 2017; Hawkins et al. 2018; Pappas 2019) by rejecting liberal principles of democracy such as minority rights and the rule of law, and preferring direct popular participation to decision-making without elected representatives. In doing so, populists tend to dismiss the representative function of other parties and portray themselves as the only political actors advocating the will of the people.

Populism is also seen as inherently anti-pluralist in that it employs a logic of de-differentiation by portraying actors in the political arena in terms of homogeneous groups, each with their own alleged mode of behaviour (Schedler 1996). Consequently, feminists, immigrants, pundits, and politicians take on uniform roles in the populist cosmology. However, who exactly belongs to each group remains vaguely or situationally defined. Anti-pluralism and illiberalism give populist positions an absolutist connotation that underscores the authoritarian tendencies of populism (Urbinati 1998). Nevertheless, populism is not per se anti-democratic as long as the political outcomes are consistent with the purported general will (Urbinati 2019; Heinisch and Wegscheider 2020).

1 For an overview, see Bonikowski and Gidron (2016).

Populists' rhetoric often includes a spatial or territorial dimension, as they claim to be the champions of the "heartland" where the "real people" live (Taggart 2000). These representations often vary in terms of what or where exactly these "heartlanders" are (Heinisch, Massetti, and Mazzoleni 2019; Heinisch and Jansesberger 2021). However, insofar as populists are concerned with the authority and sovereignty of the people, the latter are not merely the holders of citizenship, but rather the people in the heartland who have a higher moral claim to having their will respected.

Populism also works with the ideas or frames of crisis and change (Canovan 1999; Mouffe 1999; Mair 2002; Taggart 2002; Mudde and Rovira Kaltwasser 2012; Kriesi 2014). According to Mény and Surel (2000, 181; see also Canovan 2005, 81–82), populists promise change to bring power to the people betrayed by the elite. Such change can express a demand for the removal of a government, for a change in policy, but also for the complete transformation of a polity. In doing so, populists present themselves as credible change agents and derive political legitimacy from this promise (Canovan 1999; Mouffe 1999; Mény and Surel 2002; Rovira Kaltwasser 2014).

Populism seldom appears in its pure form but tends to link itself with radical left and radical right ideas about how to achieve its central goals (Taggart 2000; Stanley 2008). Thus, radical right populism focuses on exclusive nationalism and xenophobia (Rydgren 2018). This nativist world view "holds that states should be inhabited exclusively by members of the native group ('the nation') and that nonnative elements (persons and ideas) are fundamentally threatening to the homogeneous nation-state" (Mudde 2007, 19). Another key ideological characteristic of the radical right is authoritarianism, which encompasses authoritarian submission, authoritarian aggression, and conventionalism (Sanford et al. 1950; Altemeyer 1981).

Right-wing authoritarianism propagates a strictly ordered, hierarchical society that demands submission to authority and social conventions (Mudde 2007; Rydgren 2018). It stems from "uncritical, deferential, obedient support for existing social authorities and institutions" (Duckitt and Bizumic 2013, 843). In the case of the populist radical right, the cause is not anti-elitism and general will per se, but rather the fear of having to compromise with, and be influenced by a) those who are ethnically not part of the autochthonous people (nativism) and b) those who undermine existing authority structures (right-wing authoritarianism). In the next section, we show that these conceptualizations have important consequences for how sovereignty and radical right-wing populism connect.

3 Sovereignty, Sovereignism and Their Relationship with Populism

Sovereignty is one of the oldest and most important concepts in the history of political thought. Jean Bodin in his *Six livres de la République* (1962 [1576]) argues that sovereignty means the concentration of all sovereign rights and legislation in a single supreme power, which is the basic principle of every state. Thus, sovereignty is unlimited in time and indivisible. Whereas for Bodin, this power is concentrated in the sovereign, one ruling figure, who has the monopoly on the use of force but is obliged to the welfare of the state and must provide security, for Thomas Hobbes (2016 [1651]), sovereignty resides in the state itself. It, too, represents the concentration of all sovereign rights and the legislation in a single highest authority that has an absolute, indivisible and unlimited monopoly of power. In Hobbes, the necessity that citizens submit to a statehood (voluntarily or involuntarily) follows from the natural state of human beings and their individual rights to freedom. In the state of nature, the goal of self-preservation and absolute freedom inevitably leads to the struggle for survival of all against all. To escape this cruel state, people submit to a political order, which the sovereign must be capable of enforcing. Both Bodin and Hobbes already recognized that sovereignty is composed of an internal and external dimension. However, whereas both locate sovereignty in an absolute ruler, others, notably John Locke (1988 [1689]) and especially Jean-Jacques Rousseau (2003 [1762]), concentrate sovereign power in free and equal citizens or the people.

For the populist understanding of sovereignty, Rousseau and his work in *Du contrat social ou principes du droit politique* (2003 [1762]) is especially relevant. Accordingly, the people join into a community by social contract and rules following a common will (*volonté générale*). Unlike the mere total will, the *volonté de tous*, the sum of individual special interests, the general will, the *volonté générale*, presents itself as the harmony and convergence of all these interests. This defines the objective good and right will for the whole community and establishes the right of absolute rule of the people over itself. Crucially, for populists, a representative form of rule is thereby not possible, because the common will as a basis of sovereignty can only come from the people that is to be governed, and thus must govern itself. Although Rousseau describes more of an ideal state and sees even his concept as unrealizable, given people's selfish nature, Rousseau's ideas have had a lasting impact. They permeated the thinking of Emmanuel Joseph Sieyès (1890 [1789]) and Thomas Paine (1992 [1791/92]). For the former, sovereignty represents the majority will of the people of a nation-state. The latter sees people in a relationship of mutual trust and responsibility, but who delegate the exercise of power to a government that the people nevertheless control.

The Rousseauian tradition stands in some contrast to later concepts of sovereignty that concentrate this supreme power in an abstract state (Hegel 1972 [1821]; Kant 2016 [1797]), representative government (Mill 2001 [1861]), power of the political decision-maker (Weber 1922), or in accepted legally constituted arrangements (Kelsen 1929). In the modern understanding, sovereignty therefore denotes a condition in which a political entity has the legally recognized authority to pursue its own course of action. Conceptually, contemporary liberal democracy owes much to its Anglo-Saxon roots and is thus much more committed to the sum and weighting of individual interests. As such, it has remained sceptical of the often authoritarian or metaphysical ideas of wanting to establish or at least recognize a general will, as an expression of popular sovereignty.

The central connection with populism is the purported erosion of political legitimacy if the distance between the governing body and the people increases such that it fails to represent the will of the people (Urbinati 2010, 73). This may be the result of declining popular interest in political participation, of technocratic and expert-led decision-making that reduces popular input, or of backroom deal-making and insider politics. Populists are also sceptical of deliberative bodies involving a select group of citizens performing a consultative function. Populists consider these institutions as elite committees "impersonating citizens" (Urbinati 2010, 74). Instead, populists view these developments as indications of an authoritative body's declining ability to implement the will of the people and therefore question the legitimacy of the governing body's authority. Accordingly, the source of illegitimacy in all these cases is the alleged infringement on popular sovereignty because decision-making no longer aligns with the manifest popular preferences.

Sovereignty possesses a collective dimension that is directed both outwards (national sovereignty) and inwards (popular sovereignty) (Philpott 2003; Piirimäe 2010). In the former, sovereignty represents the authority recognized by other such sovereign bodies such as when nations become independent. According to Bull's widely used definition, "external sovereignty" denotes the "independence of outside authorities" (Bull 1977, 8). Popular sovereignty, by contrast, pertains to the internal dimension describing the state in which the people transfer the exercise of sovereignty via a social contract, elections, referenda, or other expressions of the popular will to a legislative body or an executive.

In the populist discourse, popular sovereignty represents a central pillar but it is nonetheless conceptually ambivalent because of populism's inherent scepticism of representation and delegation of power. Populism is people-centred but "the people" remain an abstraction. They are not merely a collection of individuals, but, as mentioned above, a homogeneous collective capable of expressing a combined will that alone is seen as the legitimate basis of all political action and is binding on political decision-makers. Thus, the popular will does not emerge through arbitration and compromise, as envisaged by the liberal representative tradition, but precedes political decision-making. It is already given and has a transcendental quality, since "the people" already know what they want. It is the task of political leaders to recognize this will and act on it, which is the political promise of populism. Plebiscites merely confirm the will of the people, which populists have claimed as well-known all along.

Yet, when populists speak of popular sovereignty, the locus remains necessarily ambiguous. The governing bodies that represent the people and make decisions are often the very institutions that populists criticize for being made up of self-serving elites. Instead of representation, populists favour devolving power to the direct decision-making of the people. At the same time, however, populists refuse to anchor sovereignty in the individual because this would not distinguish them from liberals and inevitably commit them to pluralism and diversity, which their inherently anti-pluralist stance negates. Therefore, populists must anchor power at a collective level that is close to, but also above, the individual. However, this creates a constant tension between the individual and the collective level, which successful populists must manage by discursive means. Incidentally, the Covid-19 pandemic made this tension quite clear, as measurable majorities favoured strict health and vaccination campaigns while vocal and sizable minorities demanded the opposite, often putting populist actors in a dilemma (Wondreys and Mudde 2022). In response, populists have taken up classical liberal positions, emphasizing individual rights, respect for diversity of opinion about vaccines, and arguing for a kind of individual autonomy to make health decisions without regard to the greater good of the community.

Economic sovereignty nominally goes hand in hand with national sovereignty and popular sovereignty and with the formal authority that comes with them. However, economic sovereignty can become decoupled. This means that a collective body has popularly legitimized political or legal sovereignty vis-à-vis powerful economic actors or powerful international market forces but is de facto incapable of going against these forces. Even advanced economies often find themselves embroiled in political debates about the loss of economic sovereignty to supranational institutions and integrated markets. While issues of national sovereignty tend to be associated with the political right, economic sovereignty and economic autonomy from global markets are important concerns for the political left.

3.1 *Sovereignism: Instrumentalizing Sovereignty*

Populist discourses about the erosion or usurpation of popular sovereignty have been called "sovereignism" (Basile, Borri and Verzichelli 2020), which described a characteristic of radical populist actors to distinguish themselves from established parties and from each other. Sovereignist claims are based on ideologically constructed notions of "people", pertaining collectively to a community, culture, region, or nation to which a special autonomy is attributed but which is threatened a) internally, by corrupted and disloyal elites, b) externally, by self-serving or hostile outside elites imposing authority from without, and c) by exposure to the uncertain political or socio-economic outcomes resulting from globalization and modernization. Because of populism's Manichean world view, the purported threats to sovereignty are linked to conspiratorial accounts of how politics "really" works. The threat posed by an alleged "deep state" in Trump's diction is a well-known example. In its coverage of his 2018 State of the Union address, the Fox News television network portrayed the president's agenda as Trump "saving sovereignty and the citizenry from the deep state" (Williams 2018).

Sovereignism, too, expresses itself in three dimensions: the popular, the national, and the economic. In popular sovereignism, unaccountable elites whose interests become divorced of those of the "true people" represent the threat to the legitimate political power and authority of sovereign people (Spruyt, Keppens and Van Droogenbroeck 2016, 336). Charges of systematic programmatic misrepresentations (Mudde 2004) lie at the heart of populist calls for radical change (Canovan 2002; Abts and Rummens 2007; Barr 2009; van Kessel 2015). In fact, it is the assertion about the erosion of sovereignty that supplies the raison d'être for, and the justification of urgent and radical action in populist discourse.

Similarly, national sovereignism centres on the alleged dichotomy between the "own people" and the cultural "others" (Basile, Borri and Verzichelli 2020). Although not a concern unique to populists but also to nationalists and nativists, populists appropriate this agenda to appeal to voters outside their traditional base, particularly those who are disillusioned with, and alienated from the mainstream right. Heartland constructions also serve to rally majority populations against ethnic and cultural minorities (Heinisch, Massetti and Mazzoleni 2018; 2019).

Radical right-wing populists who hold public office employ the defence of national sovereignty also as a weapon against liberal democracy and liberalism in general. Liberal democratic institutions, non-governmental organizations and critical media at the national and international level are the villains in the sovereignist discourses led by the likes of Viktor Orbán (Krekó and Enyedi 2018). Accordingly, political criticism of the ruling party or government is framed as a conspiracy by internal and external liberal elites aimed at undermining national sovereignty and subverting the voting preferences of the political majority. National sovereignty arguments imply the imposition of a culturally alien agenda that promotes anti-patriotic and anti-religious sentiments, as well as sexually "deviant" and "decadent" lifestyle preferences (Enyedi 2016).

A particularly pernicious form of national sovereignism is anti-Semitism exemplified by the discourses of Poland's Law and Justice Party (PiS) and Hungary's Fidesz (Pintilescu and Magyari 2020; Langer 2021). National sovereignism is where right-wing populist and other right-wing discourses intersect and often become indistinguishable. The success of national sovereignist discourses has influenced also mainstream parties of the right which have either began "parroting the pariah" (van Spanje 2018) or adopted such positions outright.[2]

A confluence of popular and national sovereignism occurs in newer democracies where political institutions and national independence are still fragile. An example of this is Kosovo and the success of the Self-Determination Party (Vetëvendosje), a formation that combines a populist political style, a leftist/social democratic agenda, and contentious politics as a means of spreading its message (Yabanci 2016). When it was in opposition, criticism of the political establishment/elite was closely related to this elite's cooperation with the international community in resolving the Kosovo-Serbia conflict. Specifically, Vetëvendosje objected to international efforts of having Kosovo labelled a multi-ethnic and thus multinational state (Koxha 2020).

Left-wing populism too, engages in sovereignist discourses but the framing is often different. Given its transnational aspiration, left-wing populism has ideological difficulties linking the betrayal of people's sovereignty to a particular geographic or national territory. Instead, the focus lies on groups, classes, or movements of people that can act transnationally for a common purpose (Blokker 2019). In this case, sovereignty resides in people and structures beyond nation-state, based on the leftist idea of "people without borders" (Blokker 2019, 345). In Latin American populism, for example, the case of Chávez represents such an attempt at constituting one common Latin American people based on cultural affinity. In contrast, DiEM25, a pan-European, progressive movement

2 For an overview, see Bale and Rovira Kaltwasser (2021).

that seeks to construct a "European people", claiming they are unified by the fact that "all decisions are made beyond the sight and control of citizens, and our enslavement to our economic conditions becomes an immutable fact of life" (Hufton 2017). In general, these and similar leftist populist claims are de facto expressions of economic sovereignism.

Economic sovereignism refers to the idea that economic policies should primarily be of benefit for a nation's "own" people (Basile and Mazzoleni 2020). This approach is also pursued by leftist populists to frame economic policy failures, to appeal to in-group solidarity, and to provide a means of connecting internationally with other leftist parties and even nationalist groups. Rejecting international trade agreements, "bringing back jobs" from other countries, and closing the national labour market to non-national workers are examples of such a sovereignist discourse. In making such policy proposals, populists seek to capitalize on the sentiments of working-class voters and those feeling economically disadvantaged (Betz and Meret 2012; Moffitt 2016; Brubaker 2017). The economic sovereignism of the left differs from that of the right in that it does not antagonize foreign workers, but instead focuses on the role of the state. The latter is often brought into the discourse to block privatization policies and budget cuts by criticizing the failure to provide social and financial security for citizens. A well-known example of this is Podemos in Spain. It capitalizes on feelings of those who feel economically disadvantaged and emphasizes the loss of economic sovereignty due to austerity policies and forced labour migration (López-Sala 2017). We conclude with the recognition that populism effectively engages with all three dimensions of sovereignty.

3.2 *The Role of Sovereignty in Populism Research*

The most important contribution of populism studies to understanding the role of sovereignty in contemporary political contexts is understanding how claims about sovereignty and threats to it are constructed and disseminated. Scholarship has focused on each of the three dimensions: popular sovereignty, national sovereignty, and economic sovereignty. One sub-field, often treated as a separate research area because of its importance, is devoted to studying Euroscepticism and the erosion of sovereignty through integration and internationalization.

3.2.1 Populism, Popular Sovereignty, and Change Agency

Scholarship on populism has studied the concept of popular sovereignty in populism from the start because it serves two important functions. First, the populist claim that the sovereign "people" are the only source for legitimating political power (Spruyt, Keppens and Van Droogenbroeck 2016, 336) provides populists with an authoritative base from where they question the legitimacy of exiting political arrangements. Accordingly, people embody "the heart of democracy" (Akkerman, Mudde and Zaslove 2014), which places populists simultaneously inside and outside established liberal politics. They share with mainstream actors a commitment to sovereignty and democracy thus appearing like a force from within, however populism's interpretation and agenda place its protagonists also outside conventional political bounds. The populist discourse which relies on a master frame of an antagonism between elites and people requires evidence of popular grievances and systemic shortcomings to support charges of declining legitimacy (Heinisch and Mazzoleni 2021). Whether populism is understood as ideology, discourse, logic, or political strategy, the idea that popular sovereignty is at risk is central to all of these approaches and allows populism to connect with other reformist political movements that criticize a particular status quo.

Popular sovereignty plays a crucial role in populism also because it supplies both the reason and urgency for the radical change narrative that is central to all types of populist discourse. However, populism's call to restore sovereignty is unsettling to many because people are naturally inclined to reduce or avoid conditions of uncertainty (Frenkel-Brunswik 1949; Stanley Budner 1962; Jost et al. 2003; Gründl and Aichholzer 2020). In fact, empirical evidence suggests that the need for security and conformity are strong predictors of voting for populist radical right parties in Europe (Webster and Kruglanski 1994). Therefore, populists need to mitigate the potentially frightening prospect of change with the promise of a return to something familiar (Jost et al. 2007; Jost, Maurer and Hassler 2020). Their conceptual solution is to promise restoring popular sovereignty by acting in the present to return to a status quo ante in the future, i.e. to a time and place before elites supposedly usurped power as the central emotional hook (Heinisch and Mazzoleni 2021).

While it proposes radical change, it simultaneously frames change as the restoration of a familiar but long lost state. Populism appeals to this sense of safety and clarity not by invoking revolutionary chaos but rather promising a return to the "proper" ordering of the community. In the case of leftist populism the narrative can be more varied. In Bolivia under Evo Morales we saw the promise centred to an idealized community of *originarios* governed by indigenous codes of resources allocation and justice. In other cases such as Venezuela the promise entailed the return to a (e.g. Bolivarian) revolutionary and emancipatory project that had been taken away or thwarted by neo-imperialist forces. The return to popular sovereignty means restoring people's mastery over their own lives (Kallis 2018; Basile, Borri and Verzichelli 2020).

Resentment and grievance can be powerful motivations that populists know how to manipulate (Betz 1993; 2002; van Kessel 2015; Wodak 2015).

Whereas grievance, resentment, and fear are typically the emotional and psychological push factors for populist-induced change, the restoration of popular sovereignty is the pull factor (Betz 2002; Eberl et al. 2021). Thus, the populist appeal lies in the lure of a future "where it is crystal clear who belongs and who does not, where there is no confusion and no reason for confusion" (Bauman 2001, 12). Trump's slogan "making America great again" is the distilled essence of this promise. The restoration of popular sovereignty is the essence of the three-part populist narrative: the construction and propagation of sovereignty claims, the threat narrative, and the promise of change and salvation.

3.2.2 Populism and National Sovereignty

In its external dimension, sovereignty is most often associated with the formal recognition of a state by other sovereign states (Krasner 2001, 6–12). Thus, Westphalian sovereignty implies the absence of authority of one state over another. Analogous to the binary and antagonistic relationship between the people and elites, populist discourses about national sovereignty call for the defence of national borders against external "threats", which can be constructed in political, cultural, and economic terms or combinations of the three.

The distinction between external and internal, foreign and national fits with the binary ideological orientation so characteristic of populism. Yet, in comparison to nationalists and nativists, whose main concern is citizenship status, culture, and ethnicity, populists go a step further. Their emphasis is the cultural "heartlander" (Taggart 2000; Heinisch, Massetti, and Mazzoleni 2019; Heinisch and Jansesberger 2021) who is the antithesis to all things foreign. The "heartlander" represents an aspiration of what the community could be like had it not been lost to cosmopolitan manipulation (Bauman 2001). Populism often extols the "commonsense" of the people of the "heartland" (Taggart 2000). Few populist politicians have been more overt about this than Donald Trump, whose narrative about "real heartland Americans" has been a central theme in his politics. We find similar accounts in all populist radical right parties (Arzheimer and Carter 2006; Halla, Wagner and Zweimüller 2017; Ramos, Schumann and Hewstone 2021). The purported antagonism between the heartlander and cultural others leads to a Manichean discourse in which citizens are asked to choose between these two mutually exclusive groups: "us" and "them" (Heinisch and Jansesberger 2021). In radical right populism, the dangerous "other" is not only the non-native (Mudde 2007; Rydgren 2018) but also the cosmopolitans. They represent an elite that is conceived of as detached from the interests of ordinary people (Hochschield 2018).

A closely related concept is that of cultural integration, which in radical right populist rhetoric implies the ability of foreign-born people to "disappear" into a constructed heartland population (Erkurt 2019; OE24 News 2016). To the extent that people stand out due to custom, appearance, unwillingness to adapt, or the size of the subgroup, radical right populists find targets to mobilize their constituents (Ruzza 2018; Redgrave et al. 2019). Radical right populist parties like the Austrian Freedom Party have been analyzed from this perspective, as they demand the complete cultural submission of Muslims to existing cultural and culinary conventions (Hafez and Heinisch 2018).

A central aspect in this discourse is border security and restricting immigration (Krzyżanowski and Wodak 2011), which allows populists to make claims about "law and order" and demand for "preservation of one's own culture" against what is seen as "foreign" and "harmful". Related to immigration is social policy, whose central demand is to address "welfare abuse" and to regulate labour market mobility for the benefit of "one's own people" (Bale 2008). Schumacher and Van Kersbergen (2016) point out that such demands have a "back to the nation-state" function that is also central to identity, cultural, and religious politics (Hafez 2014).

National sovereignty also plays a role in radical left populism as research on Latin American populism has shown. In two of the most prominent cases, that of Peron in Argentina and Chávez in Venezuela, national sovereignty is understood as a *trinom* that equates people with the nation and ultimately the both of them with the leader. The Peronist doctrine illustrates this best: "Whoever is not a Peronist is not an Argentinian" (de la Torre 2017).

Political science research shows how radical populism instrumentalizes the concept of external sovereignty and turns it inward. Through the process of othering, groups already present in the population are framed as cultural aliens and thus as externals to whom the sovereignty argument is applied as if they were outsiders. In this view, external sovereignty is no longer constructed as the independence of a decision-making body from external influences, but rather as the inability to make independent decisions due to cultural infiltration largely from within.

3.2.3 Populism and Economic Sovereignty

While national sovereignty is concerned with the political and cultural other, economic sovereignty refers to the idea that governing authorities should be able to make economic decisions independently of other actors. Both radical left-wing (Prentoulis 2016) and right-wing populists have taken up this theme, especially in the context of globalization (Quiggin 2001; Hoekman and Nelson 2018; Rodrik 2021), the introduction of trade agreements and international governance arrangements (Goldstein and Gulotty 2019), and European integration. These issue areas and especially the global financial and euro crises (Kriesi 2014) along with the accession of Eastern European countries to the EU on the basis of the principle of conditionality have received considerable attention in the literature (Harmsen and Spiering 2004, 28; Riishøj 2007; Harmsen 2010).

In this regard, Eurosceptic claims about the loss of economic sovereignty, the "democratic deficit" in decision-making, and more generally the fear of being controlled by "foreign" interests are closely linked to the sovereignist logic that distant political elites do not care about these developments or are intentionally complicit in them (Beichelt 2004; Rovny 2004; Krouwel and Abts 2007; Szczerbiak and Taggart 2008; Leconte 2010). Against this, populists promise change in the form of "handing back the power to the people" through direct democratic tools. Moreover, as radical right populist parties are both populist and nativist, they can base their objection to the EU on both populist and nativist arguments and thus shift their Eurosceptic narrative as is expedient in political contestation. Since adopting an explicit EU-rejectionist position is politically risky especially for an office-seeking populist party, recent research suggests that populists pursue a more ambivalent strategy couched in the language of democracy and accountability so to appear more mainstream (Heinisch, McDonnell, and Werner 2021).

Nonetheless, economic sovereignty presents parties on the right with a strategic dilemma since "economically they tend to endorse liberalization, but socially and culturally they tend to be nationalists and opposed to the opening up of borders" (Kriesi et al. 2006, 927). The radical right and populists have fewer such constraints (De Koster, Achterberg and Van der Waal 2013). They even adopt leftist positions when talking about threats to economic sovereignty, as was exemplified by Donald Trump who routinely broke with his own party on questions of trade and economic protectionism.

4 What Can Be Learned from How Scholarship on Populism Addresses Sovereignty?

Clearly, the discussion of populism and sovereignty resonates across the social sciences. Sociology asks how in Western societies an individual's sense of autonomy and structures of power coexist. Populism research then shows us how this sense of individual autonomy and agency can be manipulated to political or economic advantage by actors who have neither authority nor legitimacy (Korczynski and Ott 2006, 914).

Anthropology has emphasized that sovereignty often means having the right to govern and the right over life. However, this power has not always rested exclusively with the state. In a world of economic globalization and interdependence, new forms of sovereignty are emerging in the framing of biopolitical regimes in that market forces and corporations decide about how to punish those who fail to perform or fall behind (Hansen and Stepputat 2006). According to this view, sovereignty is not viewed as being threatened or eroded through internationalization but as constituting a new collective authority capable of enforcing its will.

To some, the legal notion of sovereignty is misleading because de facto the exercise of sovereignty depends on the specific contexts such as political culture, processes of state formation, and democratic practices. In this respect, many parts of the world, notably postcolonial societies, differ from established Western democracies. Thus, the concept of sovereignty may take on different meanings or at least contextual hues. Populism studies are illuminating in this respect as they trace populism's capacity to adapt sovereignist claims to cater to particular contexts. Moreover, the restoration of national sovereignty is a commonly stated populist objective but there is considerable variation in the way populists propose to do so. Fundamental concepts such as "the people" and "the elites" are constructed in different ways. In fact, it is not even clear that all populists would object to the loss of nation-state sovereignty if this simultaneously means the empowerment of a people as the ultimate locus of sovereign power (Hansen and Stepputat 2006).

Transnational populists in particular manage to construct notions of sovereignty beyond the nation-state in which "the people" as the locus of sovereignty are a transnational collective. Yet, such ideas run into the same questions about legitimacy (Kuyper and Moffitt 2020) that fuel the narratives about authority becoming too removed from ordinary people. The central point in all these forms of populism is that it is based on the claim that sovereignty has been betrayed and usurped. This forms the basis for populism's call to action, the goal of which is to restore sovereignty. Without sovereignty, populism would lose its raison d'être. Research on populism has brought this multifaceted relationship to light.

5 Conclusion

The rise of radical right and left populism has brought sovereignty and sovereignism – the construction and proliferation of sovereignty claims – back into focus. We show how populism is based on claims of betrayed and usurped sovereignty, which in turn provides the basis for populism's call to action, the goal of which is always the restoration of sovereignty. Without sovereignty, populism would lose its raison d'être. However, we have emphasized that the concept of sovereignty is highly contested in the social sciences. Scholars argue about legal and de facto sovereignty and about whether the notion of sovereignty anchored in the nation-state should be discarded in the context of globalization, since market forces are, in effect, another form of sovereignty that is more authoritative than the nation-state.

In the case of populism, the dimensions that resonate most strongly in populist discourse are those of popular sovereignty, national sovereignty, and economic sovereignty, which often overlap. As we have argued, populists on the right may even take left-wing positions when it comes to threats to economic sovereignty. Given the tension between the individual's increasing sense of autonomy and the coexistence of power structures, populists must anchor power at a collective level that is close to, but also above the individual. However, this creates a constant tension between the individual and collective levels, which successful populists must manage discursively. Populists also rely on the promise of restoring sovereignty by promising an aggrieved people a return to a familiar state and place to ease people's fear of change. In this sense, sovereignty for populism is both a goal and a means.

References

Abts, K. and Rummens, S. (2007) Populism versus democracy. *Political Studies, 55*(2), 405–424.

Akkerman, A., Mudde, C. and Zaslove, A. (2014) How populist are the people? Measuring populist attitudes in voters. *Comparative Political Studies, 47*(9), 1324–1353.

Altemeyer, R. A. (1981) *Right-wing authoritarianism.* Winnipeg, CA: Manitoba Press.

Arzheimer, K. and Carter, E. (2006) Political opportunity structures and right-wing extremist party success. *European Journal of Political Research, 45*(3), 419–443.

Aslanidis, P. (2016) Is populism an ideology? A refutation and a new perspective. *Political Studies, 64*(1_suppl), 88–104.

Bale, T. (2008) Turning round the telescope: Centre-right parties and immigration and integration policy in Europe. *Journal of European Public Policy, 15*(3), 315–330.

Bale, T. and Rovira Kaltwasser, C. (eds.) (2021) *Riding the populist wave: Europe's mainstream right in crisis.* Cambridge: Cambridge University Press.

Barr, R. R. (2009) Populists, outsiders and anti-establishment politics. *Party Politics, 15*(1), 29–48.

Basile, L. and Mazzoleni, O. (2020) Sovereignist wine in populist bottles? An introduction. *European Politics and Society, 21*(2), 151–162.

Basile, L., Borri, R. and Verzichelli, L. (2020) "For whom the sovereignist Bell Tolls?" Individual determinants of support for sovereignism in ten European countries. *European Politics and Society, 21*(2), 235–257.

Bauman, Z. (2001) *Community: Seeking safety in an insecure world.* Cambridge: Polity.

Beichelt, T. (2004) Euro-skepticism in the EU accession countries. *Comparative European Politics, 2*(1), 29–50.

Betz, H. G. (1993) The new politics of resentment: Radical right-wing populist parties in Western Europe. *Comparative Politics, 25*(4) 413–427.

Betz, H. G. (2002) Conditions favouring the success and failure of radical right-wing populist parties in contemporary democracies. In: Mény, Y. and Surel, Y. (eds.) *Democracies and the populist challenge.* London: Palgrave Macmillan, 197–213.

Betz, H. G. and Meret, S. (2012) Right-wing populist parties and the working class vote: What have you done for us lately? In: Rydgren, J. (ed.) *Class politics and the radical right.* London-New York: Routledge, 107–121.

Blokker, P. (2019) Varieties of populist constitutionalism: The transnational dimension. *German Law Journal, 20*(3), 332–350.

Bodin, J. (1962 [1576]) *The six bookes of a commonweal.* Cambridge, MA: Harvard University Press.

Bonikowski, B. and Gidron, N. (2016) Multiple traditions in populism research: Toward a theoretical synthesis. *APSA Comparative Politics Newsletter, 26*(12), 7–14.

Brubaker, R. (2017) Why populism?. *Theory and society, 46*(5), 357–385.

Budner, S. (1962) Intolerance of ambiguity as a personality variable. *Journal of Personality, 30*(1), 29–50.

Bull, H. (1977) *The anarchical society: A study of order in world politics.* New York: Columbia University Press.

Canovan, M. (1999) Trust the people! Populism and the two faces of democracy. *Political Studies, 47*(1), 2–16.

Canovan, M. (2002) Taking politics to the people: Populism as the ideology of democracy. In: Mény, Y. and Surel, Y. (eds.) *Democracies and the populist challenge.* London: Palgrave Macmillan, 25–44.

Canovan, M. (2005) *The people.* Cambridge: Polity.

Castanho Silva, B., Andreadis, I., Anduiza, E., Blanuša, N., Corti, Y. M., Delfino, G., Rico, G., Ruth, S. P., Spruyt, B., Steenbergen, M. and Littvay, L. (2018) Public opinion surveys: A new scale. In: Hawkins, K. A., Carlin, R. E., Littvay, L. and Rovira Kaltwasser, C. (eds.) *The ideational approach to populism.* London: Routledge, 150–177.

Castanho Silva, B., Jungkunz, S., Helbling, M. and Littvay, L. (2020) An empirical comparison of seven populist attitudes scales. *Political Research Quarterly, 73*(2), 409–424.

De Koster, W., Achterberg, P. and Van der Waal, J. (2013) The new right and the welfare state: The electoral relevance of welfare chauvinism and welfare populism in the Netherlands. *International Political Science Review*, *34*(1), 3–20.

de la Torre, C. (2017) Populism and nationalism in Latin America. *Javnost – The Public*, *24*(4), 375–390.

Duckitt, J. and Bizumic, B. (2013) Multidimensionality of right-wing authoritarian attitudes: Authoritarianism–conservatism–traditionalism. *Political Psychology*, *34*(6), 841–862.

Eberl, J. M., Huber, R. A. and Greussing, E. (2021) From populism to the "plandemic": Why populists believe in COVID-19 conspiracies. *Journal of Elections, Public Opinion and Parties*, *31*(sup1), 272–284.

Enyedi, Z. (2016) Populist polarization and party system institutionalization: The role of party politics in de-democratization. *Problems of Post-communism*, *63*(4), 210–220.

Erkurt, M. (2019, July 31) Isst du Schwein, kommst du rein. *Falter*. https://www.falter.at/zeitung/20190731/isst-du-schwein--kommst-du-rein/a713311f2d. (accessed: May 09, 2023)

Frenkel-Brunswik, E. (1949) Intolerance of ambiguity as an emotional and perceptual personality variable. *Journal of Personality*, *18*(1), 108–143.

Goldstein, J. and Gulotty, R. (2019) The globalisation crisis: Populism and the rise of an anti-trade coalition. *European Review of International Studies*, *6*(3), 57–83.

Gründl, J. and Aichholzer, J. (2020) Support for the populist radical right: Between uncertainty avoidance and risky choice. *Political Psychology*, *41*(4), 641–659.

Hafez, F. (2014) Shifting borders: Islamophobia as common ground for building pan-European right-wing unity. *Patterns of Prejudice*, *48*(5), 479–499.

Hafez, F. and Heinisch, R. (2018) Breaking with Austrian consociationalism: How the rise of rightwing populism and party competition have changed Austria's Islam politics. *Politics and Religion*, *11*(3), 649–678.

Halla, M., Wagner, A. F. and Zweimüller, J. (2017) Immigration and voting for the far right. *Journal of the European Economic Association*, *15*(6), 1341–1385.

Hansen, T. B. and Stepputat, F. (2006) Sovereignty revisited. *Annual Review of Anthropology*, *35*, 295–315.

Harmsen, R. (2010) Concluding comment: On understanding the relationship between populism and Euroscepticism. *Perspectives on European Politics and Society*, *11*(3), 333–341.

Harmsen, R. and Spiering, M. (eds.) (2004) *Euroscepticism: Party politics, national identity and European integration*. Leiden: Brill.

Hawkins, K. A. (2009) Is Chávez populist? Measuring populist discourse in comparative perspective. *Comparative Political Studies*, *42*(8), 1040–1067.

Hawkins, K. A. and Rovira Kaltwasser, C. (2018) Measuring populist discourse in the United States and beyond. *Nature Human Behaviour, 2*(4), 241–242.

Hawkins, K. A., Carlin, R. E., Littvay, L. and Rovira Kaltwasser, C. (eds.) (2018) *The ideational approach to populism: Concept, theory, and analysis*. London-New York: Routledge.

Hegel, G. W. F. (1972 [1821]) *Grundlinien der Philosophie des Rechts. Naturrecht und Staatswissenschaft*. Ullstein, Frankfurt: Helmut Reichelt.

Heinisch, R. and Jansesberger, V. (2021) Does ethno-territorial identity matter in populist party support? Evidence on the demand-side from 19 populist radical right and populist radical left national and regionalist parties. *European Politics and Society*, online first.

Heinisch, R. and Mazzoleni, O. (2021) Analysing and explaining populism: Bringing frame, actor and context back in. In: Holtz-Bacha, C., Heinisch, R. and Mazzoleni, O. (eds.) *Political populism*. Baden-Baden: Nomos, 111–131.

Heinisch, R. and Wegscheider, C. (2020) Disentangling how populism and radical host ideologies shape citizens' conceptions of democratic decision-making. *Politics and Governance, 8*(3), 32–44.

Heinisch, R., Massetti, E. and Mazzoleni, O. (2018) Populism and ethno-territorial politics in European multi-level systems. *Comparative European Politics, 16*(6), 923–936.

Heinisch, R., Massetti, E. and Mazzoleni, O. (eds.) (2019) *The people and the nation: Populism and ethno-territorial politics in Europe*. London-New York: Routledge.

Heinisch, R., McDonnell, D. and Werner, A. (2021) Equivocal Euroscepticism: How populist radical right parties can have their EU cake and eat it. *JCMS: Journal of Common Market Studies, 59*(2), 189–205.

Hobbes, T. (2016 [1651]) *Leviathan, or the matter, forme and power of a commonwealth ecclesiastical and civil*. Cambridge: Cambridge University Press.

Hochschild, A. R. (2018) *Strangers in their own land: Anger and mourning on the American right*. New York-London: New Press.

Hoekman, B. and Nelson, D. R. (2018) Reflecting on populism and the economics of globalization. *Journal of International Business Policy, 1*(1), 34–43.

Hufton, S. (2017, September 5) A treatise on European government: On the international and the problems of the treaties. *OpenDemocracy*. https://www.opendemocracy.net/en/treatise-on-european-government-international/.(accessed: May 09, 2023)

Jagers, J. and Walgrave, S. (2007) Populism as political communication style: An empirical study of political parties' discourse in Belgium. *European Journal of Political Research, 46*(3), 319–345.

Jost, J. T., Glaser, J., Kruglanski, A. W. and Sulloway, F. J. (2003) Political conservatism as motivated social cognition. *Psychological Bulletin, 129*(3), 339.

Jost, J. T., Napier, J. L., Thorisdottir, H., Gosling, S. D., Palfai, T. P. and Ostafin, B. (2007) Are needs to manage uncertainty and threat associated with political conservatism or ideological extremity? *Personality and Social Psychology Bulletin*, *33*(7), 989–1007.

Jost, P., Maurer, M. and Hassler, J. (2020) Populism fuels love and anger: The impact of message features on users' reactions on Facebook. *International Journal of Communication*, *14*, 1–22.

Kallis, A. (2018) Populism, sovereigntism, and the unlikely re-emergence of the territorial nation-state. *Fudan Journal of the Humanities and Social Sciences*, *11*(3), 285–302.

Kant, I. (2016 [1797]) *Metaphysik der Sitten*. Berlin: Hofenberg.

Kelsen, H. (1929) *Vom Wesen und Wert der Demokratie*. Berlin: Mohr Siebek.

Korczynski, M. and Ott, U. (2006) The menu in society: Mediating structures of power and enchanting myths of individual sovereignty. *Sociology*, *40*(5), 911–928.

Koxha, K. (2020) *How do radical-left populist parties respond to cultural cleavages? A case study of Podemos, Die Linke and Vetëvendosje*. MA thesis, University of Salzburg.

Krasner, S. D. (2001) *Problematic sovereignty: Contested rules and political possibilities*. New York: Columbia University Press.

Krekó, P. and Enyedi, Z. (2018) Explaining Eastern Europe: Orbán's laboratory of illiberalism. *Journal of Democracy*, *29*(3), 39–51.

Kriesi, H. (2014) The populist challenge. *West European Politics*, *37*(2), 361–378.

Kriesi, H., Grande, E., Lachat, R., Dolezal, M., Bornschier, S. and Frey, T. (2006) Globalization and the transformation of the national political space: Six European countries compared. *European Journal of Political Research*, *45*(6), 921–956.

Krouwel, A. and Abts, K. (2007) Varieties of Euroscepticism and populist mobilization: Transforming attitudes from mild Euroscepticism to harsh Eurocynicism. *Acta Politica*, *42*(2), 252–270.

Krzyżanowski, M. and Wodak, R. (2011) *The politics of exclusion: Debating migration in Austria*. New Brunswick: Transaction Publishers.

Kuyper, J. and Moffitt, B. (2020) Transnational populism, democracy, and representation: Pitfalls and potentialities. *Global Justice: Theory Practice Rhetoric*, *12*(2), 27–49.

Langer, A. (2021) The eternal George Soros: The rise of an antisemitic and Islamophobic conspiracy theory. In: Önnerfors, A. and Krouwel A. (eds.) *Europe: Continent of conspiracies*. London-New York: Routledge, 163–184.

Leconte, C. (2010) *Understanding Euroscepticism*. Houndmills, Basingstoke: Palgrave Macmillan.

Locke, J. (1988 [1689]) *Two treatises of government*. Cambridge: Cambridge University Press.

López-Sala, A. (2017) The new emigration issue in public and political debate in Spain. Official discourses and new forms of mobilization. In: Glorius, B. and Domínguez-Mujica, J. (eds.) *European mobility in times of crisis*. Bielefeld: Transcript Verlag, 267–286.

Mair, P. (2002) Populist democracy vs party democracy. In: Mény, Y. and Surel, Y. (eds.) *Democracies and the populist challenge*. London: Palgrave Macmillan, 81–98.

Mény, Y. and Surel, Y. (2000) *Par le peuple, pour le peuple: le populisme et les démocraties*. Paris: Fayard.

Mény, Y. and Surel, Y. (2002) The constitutive ambiguity of populism. In: Mény, Y. and Surel, Y. (eds.) *Democracies and the populist challenge*. London: Palgrave Macmillan, 1–21.

Mill, J. S. (2001 [1861]) *Considerations on representative government*. Kitchener: Kitchener Books.

Moffitt, B. (2016) The performative turn in the comparative study of populism. *Political Studies, 41*(1), 3–23.

Moffitt, B. and Tormey, S. (2014) Rethinking populism: Politics, mediatisation and political style. *Political Studies, 62*(2), 381–397.

Mouffe, C. (1999) Deliberative democracy or agonistic pluralism? *Social Research, 66*(3), 745–758.

Mudde, C. (2004) The populist zeitgeist. *Government and Opposition, 39*(4), 541–563.

Mudde, C. (2007) A Fortuynist foreign policy. In: Liang, C. S. (eds.) *Europe for the Europeans: The foreign and security policy of the populist radical right*. London-New York: Routledge, 209–222.

Mudde, C. and Rovira Kaltwasser, C. (2012) Populism and (liberal) democracy: A framework for analysis. In: Mudde, C. and Rovira Kaltwasser, C. (eds.) *Populism in Europe and the Americas*. Cambridge: Cambridge University Press, 1–26.

Mudde, C. and Rovira Kaltwasser, C. (2013) Exclusionary vs. inclusionary populism: Comparing contemporary Europe and Latin America. *Government and Opposition, 48*(2), 147–174.

Mudde, C. and Rovira Kaltwasser, C. (2017) *Populism: A very short introduction*. Oxford: Oxford University Press.

OE24 News (2016, January 22) Schnitzel-Pflicht? FPÖ: Schweinefleisch im Kindergarten als Pflicht. https://www.oe24.at/oesterreich/politik/fpoe-schweinefleisch-im-kindergarten-als-pflicht/221053134. (accessed: May 09, 2023)

Paine, T. (1992 [1791/92]) *Rights of man: Being an answer to Mr. Burke's attack on the French revolution*. New York: Woodstock Books.

Pappas, T. S. (2019) *Populism and liberal democracy: A comparative and theoretical analysis*. Oxford: Oxford University Press.

Philpott, D. (2003) Sovereignty. *The Stanford encyclopedia of philosophy*.

Piirimäe, P. (2010) The Westphalian myth and the idea of external sovereignty. In: Kalmo, H. and Skinner, Q. (eds.) *Sovereignty in fragments: The past, present and future of a contested concept*. Cambridge: Cambridge University Press, 64–80.

Pintilescu, C., & Magyari, A. K. (2020) Soros conspiracy theories and the rise of populism in post-socialist Hungary and Romania. In: Astapova, A. Colăcel, O., Pintilescu,

C. and Scheibner, T. (eds.) *Conspiracy theories in Eastern Europe*. London-New York: Routledge, 207–231.

Prentoulis, M. (2016) From the EU to Latin America: Left populism and regional integration. *Soundings*, *63*(63), 25–37.

Quiggin, J. (2001) Globalization and economic sovereignty. *Journal of Political Philosophy*, *9*(1), 56–80.

Ramos, M. R., Schumann, S. and Hewstone, M. (2021) The role of short-term and longer term immigration trends on voting for populist radical right parties in Europe. *Social Psychological and Personality Science*, online first.

Redgrave, H., Paulsen, L., Comerford, M. and Tipple, C. (2019) *The glue that binds: Integration in a time of populism*. Tony Blair Institute for Global Change, report.

Riishøj, S. (2007) Europeanization and Euroscepticism: Experiences from Poland and the Czech Republic. *Nationalities Papers*, *35*(3), 503–535.

Rodrik, D. (2021) Why does globalization fuel populism? Economics, culture, and the rise of right-wing populism. *Annual Review of Economics*, *13*, 133–170.

Rousseau, J. J. (2003 [1762]) *On the social contract*. New York: Dover.

Rovira Kaltwasser, C. (2014) The responses of populism to Dahl's democratic dilemmas. *Political Studies*, *62*(3), 470–487.

Rovny, J. (2004) Conceptualising party-based Euroscepticism: Magnitude and motivations. *Collegium: News from the College of Europe*, *29*, 31–48.

Ruzza, C. (2018) Populism, migration, and xenophobia in Europe. In: de la Torre, C. (ed.) *The Routledge international handbook of global populism*. London-New York: Routledge, 201–216.

Rydgren, J. (ed.) (2018) *The Oxford handbook of the radical right*. Oxford: Oxford University Press.

Sanford, R. N., Adorno, T. W., Frenkel-Brunswik, E. and Levinson, D. J. (1950) The measurement of implicit antidemocratic trends. In: Adorno, T. W., Frenkel-Brunswik, E., Levinson, D. J. and Sanford, R. N. (eds.) *The authoritarian personality*. New York: Harper & Brothers, 222–279.

Schedler, A. (1996) Anti-political-establishment parties. *Party Politics*, *2*(3), 291–312.

Schumacher, G. and Van Kersbergen, K. (2016) Do mainstream parties adapt to the welfare chauvinism of populist parties? *Party Politics*, *22*(3), 300–312.

Sieyès, E. J. (1890 [1789]) Extract from "What is the third estate?". In: Whitcomb, M. (eds.) *Translations and reprints from the original sources of European history*, vol. 6. Philadelphia: University of Pennsylvania Press, 32–35.

Spruyt, B., Keppens, G. and Van Droogenbroeck, F. (2016) Who supports populism and what attracts people to it? *Political Research Quarterly*, *69*(2), 335–346.

Stanley, B. (2008) The thin ideology of populism. *Journal of Political Ideologies*, *13*(1), 95–110.

Szczerbiak, A. and Taggart, P. (2008) Theorising party-based Euroscepticism: Problems of definition, measurement and causality. In: Szczerbiak, A. and Taggart, P. (eds.) *Opposing Europe? The Comparative Party Politics of Euroscepticism, Vol. 2: Comparative and Theoretical Perspectives*. Oxford University Press, Oxford, pp. 238–262.

Taggart, P. (2000) *Populism*. Buckingham: Open University Press.

Taggart, P. (2002) Populism and the pathology of representative politics. In: Mény, Y. and Surel, Y. (eds.) *Democracies and the populist challenge*. London: Palgrave Macmillan, 62–80.

Urbinati, N. (1998) Democracy and populism. *Constellations*, *5*(1), 110–124.

Urbinati, N. (2010) Unpolitical democracy. *Political Theory*, *38*(1), 65–92.

Urbinati, N. (2019) Political theory of populism. *Annual Review of Political Science*, *22*, 111–127.

van Kessel, S. (2015) *Populist parties in Europe: Agents of discontent?* New York: Palgrave Macmillan.

van Spanje, J. (2018) The parroting the pariah effect: Theoretical framework. In: van Spanje, J. *Controlling the electoral marketplace: political campaigning and communication*. Cham: Palgrave Macmillan, 67–78.

Weber, M. (1922). Die drei reinen Typen der legitimen Herrschaft. *Preussische Jahrbücher*, *187*(1), 1–12.

Webster, D. M. and Kruglanski, A. W. (1994) Individual differences in need for cognitive closure. *Journal of Personality and Social Psychology*, *67*(6), 1049–1062.

Weyland, K. (2021) Populism as a political strategy: An approach's enduring – and increasing – advantages. *Political Studies*, *69*(2), 185–189.

Williams, R. P. (2018, February 13) Trump's agenda: Saving sovereignty and citizenship from the deep state. *FoxNews*. https://www.foxnews.com/opinion/trumps-agenda-saving-sovereignty-and-citizenship-from-the-deep-state. (accessed: May 09, 2023)

Wodak, R. (2015) *The politics of fear: What right-wing populist discourses mean*. London: Sage.

Wondreys, J. and Mudde, C. (2022) Victims of the pandemic? European far-right parties and COVID-19. *Nationalities Papers*, *50*(1), 86–103.

Yabanci, B. (2016) Populism and anti-establishment politics in Kosovo: A case study of Lëvizja Vetëvendosje. *Contemporary Southeastern Europe*, *3*(2), 17–23.

CHAPTER 6

Populism and Accountability

Enrique Peruzzotti

1 Introduction

One central concept of contemporary social and political science is that of accountability (Schultz 1998; Przeworski, Stokes and Manin 1999; O'Donnell 2003; Mulgan 2000; Borowiak 2011; Olsen 2015; Fox 2022). The presupposition that popular sovereignty requires that rulers be accountable to the people is a universal tenet of democratic theory (March and Olsen 1995, 162). There is less agreement, however, on how to produce governmental accountability. As processes of democratic consolidation unfolded in the third-wave democracies of Asia, Africa, Eastern and Central Europe, and Latin America, a liberal model of accountability as limited government gained ground, as many analysts called attention to existing rule of law deficits in the recently established regimes. The diagnosis of the liberal model is that deficits of legal accountability were central to understanding the problems that many of those new democracies were confronting.

To improve their political performance, those regimes should make a concerted effort at producing stronger mechanisms to prevent or sanction governmental wrongdoing (O'Donnell 2003; Schedler, Diamond and Plattner 1999; Schmitter 2009; Magyar 2016). The theory and practice of populism entail a normative and epistemological break with those concepts and theories of democracy and accountability (Peruzzotti 2017c). Contemporary populism predicates an alternative model of democracy that requires the dismantling of many of the constitutive features of the liberal model. The challenge that populism poses to mainstream approaches to democracy and accountability is seen by defenders of liberal democracy as the confirmation that the third wave of democratization has exhausted itself and a shift from democracy to authoritarianism is underway.

Critics of populism see it as antithetical to any notion of accountable government, calling attention to the negative effects that populism interventions have on liberal democratic institutional arrangements. Once in power, they argue, populist administrations set into motion a dynamic of regime hybridization (or disfiguration) that, if left unchallenged, can threaten the very survival of liberal democracy (Levitsky and Loxton 2013; Mudde and Rovira

 | DOI:10.1163/9789004679016_008

Kaltwasser 2017, 96; Urbinati 2014; Müller 2017; Peruzzotti 2017b; Weyland 2020). Proponents of populism, instead, consider the efforts at redesigning the constitutional landscape of existing regimes promoted by populist administrations are but an expression of the constituent power of the people and seek to place constitutionalism at the service of the common good of people (Anria 2018; Colón-Ríos 2020).

Is populism actually hostile to any notion of accountability as its liberal critics contend? Or is there a specific populist understanding of the concept? The links between populism and accountability have not been sufficiently explored, in part because of the major challenge that populism as a governmental exercise poses to liberal mechanisms of governmental accountability. At the same time, those processes of institutional reform are made in the name of democratic accountability. What is the meaning that populism assigns to the concept of accountability? The chapter seeks to address that question by contrasting liberal and populist approaches to accountability. The first section reconstructs the liberal model of accountability by focusing on the widely popular conceptual framework of horizontal/vertical mechanisms proposed by Guillermo O'Donnell. The second section resorts to O'Donnell's categories to present the main tenets of the populist notion of accountability. The third section concludes with some reflections on the limitations of both approaches.

2 The Liberal Model: Accountability as Limited Government

The liberal model of constitutionalism was widely adopted by the new democracies of the third wave (Ackerman 1994; Schedler, Diamond and Plattner 1999; Fukuyama 2006, 39–51). The agenda of the transition and consolidation periods was dominated by an overriding concern in societies that had experienced brutal forms of authoritarianism: preventing the newly democratized societies from succumbing to dictatorship again. The legacy of political violence and massive human rights violations that served as the background of the third democratizing wave made it impossible to reduce the question of democratization to the holding of free and competitive elections as had been the case of previous democratizing experiences. There was a more demanding notion of democracy that entailed not only elections but rule of law institutions to control government officials and protect the fundamental rights of citizens. It is within that context that the question of governmental accountability as a tool to discipline and control public authorities gained prominence, to the extent that it dominated the agenda of democratization studies (Schedler, Diamond and Plattner 1999; Arato 2000; Mulgan 2000; Mainwaring and Welna 2003;

Schmitter 2004; Levine and Molina 2011; Odugbemi and Lee 2011; Goodman and Pegram 2012).

The tacit diagnosis was that the democratization process was successful in establishing regular free and competitive elections but unable to consolidate effective rule of law mechanisms (Mendez, O'Donnell and Pinheiro 1999; Schedler, Diamond and Plattner 1999; Ungar 2001; Peruzzotti and Smulovitz 2006; Uildriks with Tello Peon 2010). Electoral mechanisms were in place and functioning relatively well, yet that was not the case for those institutions responsible for preventing governmental wrongdoing. Accountability agencies were incapable of effectively fulfilling their constitutional role and their weaknesses seriously compromised democratic dynamics. As O'Donnell succinctly stated, the deficits of new regimes are of a liberal rather than democratic nature (1997). In his view, many of the novel democracies lacked an effective system of institutional mechanisms to control and discipline elected authorities and public officials.

The combination of effective electoral institutions and ineffective rule of law mechanisms prompted a distinctive path to regime institutionalization whose outcome was a type of polyarchy that lacked effective mechanisms of governmental control. While those democracies constituted an obvious advance when contrasted with the dictatorial regimes they replaced, they fell short when compared to Western representative polyarchies (which provided the normative model to emulate). Consequently, the literature called attention to the need for another transition, a "transition to accountability" to borrow Jonathan Fox's term, that would complement the initial transitions to electoral rule (Fox 2007, 11). The notion of a "transition to accountability" refers to pro-accountability efforts and reforms to address existing rule of law deficits (Ackerman 2004; Isunza Vera and Olvera 2006; Peruzzotti and Smulovitz 2006; Fox 2007).

The transitions to accountability framework were deeply influenced by O'Donnell's work, which set the contours of what would become the dominant approach to governmental accountability in Latin America. He contributed to the accountability agenda by providing: a) an analytical model for the analysis of accountability, and particularly, of legal accountability; b) a typology of the different sorts of illegal encroachments that a system of governmental accountability should help prevent; c) a typology of a type of democratic regime where such encroachments assume a systemic nature to the extent that they determine the logic of the political processes; and d) a road map to guide efforts at democratic betterment. Let's briefly review his contribution in those four areas.

a) O'Donnell developed a highly influential analytical framework for the analysis of accountability as control (O'Donnell 1999a; 2003; 2006). Following a spatial metaphor, he distinguished between horizontal and vertical mechanisms of accountability. Horizontal mechanisms refer to intrastate exchanges among accountability agencies while vertical ones involve the control of an external actor over the state, be it the electorate, the media, or civil society (O'Donnell 1999b, 68). He sought to highlight the central role played by a certain subset of horizontal mechanisms of accountability for democratic life: those "state agencies that are legally enabled and empowered, and factually willing and able, to take actions that span from routine oversight to criminal sanctions or impeachment concerning actions or omissions by other agents or agencies of the state that might be qualified as unlawful" (O'Donnell 1999b, 38). He distinguished between balance and mandate agencies: the first ones were oriented to prevent the unlawful transgression of the power jurisdiction of one power by another, while the second ones are legally responsible for overseeing, preventing, and sanctioning unlawful actions of other state agencies (such as comptrollers, prosecutors, supreme audit institutions, legislative committees, anti-corruption agencies, etc.). In his view, both sets of agencies were crucial for enforcing that wide range of rules and regulations that are an essential part of a functioning system of institutional control to limit and control public power.

b) O'Donnell provided a diagnosis about the ways that the lack of horizontal accountability affected democratic political processes. In his view, in societies where the network of state mechanisms of legal accountability is unable to control unlawful actions, the dynamics of democratic rule are undermined due to the generalization of three different types of illegal encroachments: 1) the malfunctioning of balance mechanisms result in permanent executive encroachments over the jurisdiction of the legislative and judiciary powers, distorting the equilibrium among powers; 2) the weakness of mechanisms of rights protections and an autonomous judiciary generate brown areas characterized by the predominance of privatized circuits of power and encroachments on the rights of the citizens subjected to those de facto powers (O'Donnell 1999b, 142–143); and 3) the lack of effective mechanisms of intrastate control results in illegal encroachments by unscrupulous elected officials, bureaucrats, or social groups on state institutions. If the previously mentioned second type of encroachment refers to a situation of colonization of civil society by particularistic powers, this one expresses a parallel process of privatization of state institutions and the emergence of brown areas within the state (O'Donnell 1999b, 140).

c) O'Donnell proposed the concept of delegative democracy to call attention to a situation where the three above described encroachments were systematic enough to merit the distinguishing of a new sub-type of polyarchy. Delegative polyarchy is a democratic regime where elections, as well as their surrounding freedoms, are institutionalized but where that horizontal accountability is notoriously weak. The nature of illegal encroachments is of such magnitude that the structure of representative government cannot operate and is consequently replaced by a short-lived and crisis-ridden form of plebiscitary exercise that O'Donnell refers to as delegative democracy (O'Donnell 1994).

d) Lastly, he established the parameters that should guide the agenda of democratic betterment: the strengthening of that subset of horizontal accountability mechanisms oriented to the control of the described forms of governmental wrongdoing. He referred to such a process as a "second transition" from delegative to representative polyarchy (O'Donnell 1992). He envisioned such a transition as a process of "actualization" of existing constitutional arrangements, given that he considered that seen from a formal perspective, delegative democracies do not differ from representative polyarchies: their constitutions are organized around the principle of separation of powers, mutual checks and balances, universal citizenship rights, and the authority of public law. Their problems are not derived from their constitutional design; rather, they are produced by the nocive influence that informal institutions exert on horizontal agencies.

3 The Populist Model: Accountability as Unlimited Elected Government

As democratic discontent proliferated regarding the performance of many third-wave democracies, populism appeared as a plausible solution to the democratic malaise (Peruzzotti 2017b). Populism proposed an alternative path to reconstruct the linkages between state and society than that of the hegemonic liberal model. The latter proposal found an echo in societies marked by generalized citizen disenchantment with mainstream parties and politicians. The populist challenge put an end to the democratic consensus of the third wave: liberal democracy was no longer seen as the only possible game in town;

its legitimacy was questioned on alleged democratic grounds by those who claim to be advancing a more radical understanding of democracy.

The populist theory of democracy contains an implicit constitutional conception from which a populist understanding of accountability can be extracted. What is the main premise of populist constitutionalism? To consider the idea of limited government as undemocratic for it imposes an illegitimate constraint on the constituent power of the people. Populist constitutionalism is predicated on the premise of the absolute primacy to the constituent power vis-à-vis the legal and constitutional order (Arato 2016, 3; Corrias 2016, 9; Peruzzotti 2019; Colón-Ríos 2020). It considers that in a proper democracy, the principle of popular sovereignty should prevail over any other consideration and that the goal of any constitutional project is to allow for the expression of an unconstrained popular will (Corrias 2016, 10; Müller 2017, 598). The programmatic call that derives from such constitutional doctrine is a dramatic U-turn concerning the agenda towards democratic betterment discussed in the first section: if the main concern of the quality of democracy approach was to make the principle of limited government effective; populism hopes to achieve the exact opposite: the establishing of a constitutional order that would bring to life the idea of "unlimited elected government". The latter does not necessarily mean expanding institutional channels for democratic participation. Constitutional reforms frequently seek to strengthen the power of the elected executive figure as it is seen as the power that incarnates popular aspirations. Embodiment in leadership, not democratic participation, is the way the constitution of popular subjects is envisioned (Laclau 2007; Arato 2016, 283)

What does the principle of "unlimited elected government" mean for an agenda of democratic accountability? Can a populist conception of accountability be derived from it? To address these questions and reconstruct the implicit accountability theory of the populist constitutional doctrine, each of the previously reviewed elements of the liberal approach will be contrasted with those of the populist one. Consequently, O'Donnell's conceptual framework for accountability will be employed to derive a populist conception of democratic accountability. The analysis addresses each of the dimensions of the model he elaborates to analyze the question of democratic accountability in Latin America: a) the analytical distinction between horizontal and vertical forms of accountability to show how the populist conception relies on a different valuation of each of those dimensions and on the way they should relate to one another; b) the populist diagnosis about the alleged accountability deficits of real existing democracies and the strategy to overcome them; c) the target of the critical democratic theory of populism as contrasted with that proposed by O'Donnell's; and, finally, d) the road map of constitutional reforms populist government propose to bring the principle of unlimited elected government to life.

a) How does the populist model relate to O'Donnell's conceptual framework for accountability? As previously seen, the model focuses on the interrelations between two broad forms of accountability (vertical and horizontal). While O'Donnell grants logical priority to *vertical electoral accountability*, since he considers that without it there would be no democratic regime (O'Donnell 2003, 49), it considers that a proper democratic regime (representative polyarchy) relies on a particular combination of horizontal and vertical. The populist perspective, while agreeing with the former, relies on a different understanding regarding the preconditions that should be present for vertical electoral accountability to properly function. O'Donnell considered processes of democratic consolidation successfully established free and competitive elections but failed at institutionalizing other indispensable elements (of a vertical as well as of a horizontal nature) that the representative polyarchy model sees as indispensable for the proper exercise of vertical accountability. O'Donnell makes reference to some of the vertical components that are absent in delegative polyarchies, however, his analysis calls attention to how the systemic malfunctioning of a sub-type of mechanisms (legal horizontal ones) compromise the overall effectiveness of the system of democratic accountability, producing a suboptimal form of the democratic regime (O'Donnell 2003, 49; 2006). The central presupposition of his model is that democratic accountability cannot be the unilateral accomplishment of a single mechanism, no matter how central it might be in defining the democratic nature of the regime. In his view, the workings of democratic accountability depend, to be effective, on a complex system of linkages and interactions among a diversity of accountability mechanisms. Elections per se do not produce democratic accountability; they can only develop their accountability potential in a political regime where the multiple vertical and horizontal components of the accountability system operate in a coordinated manner, complementing and reinforcing one another (O'Donnell 2006). The democratic theory of populism agrees with O'Donnell in granting logical priority to vertical electoral mechanisms while postulating a simpler and unilateral model of democratic accountability: it assumes that horizontal and vertical forms of accountability are in a zero-sum interaction since they are the expression of opposing political principles. It considers that the polyarchic model of representative government is an anathema to democratic rule for it is a form of political regime purposely designed to prevent the tyranny of the majority, that is, to undermine vertical electoral accountability. In contrast to O'Donnell, it considers that only by disentangling vertical electoral mechanisms from horizontal ones can the full democratic potential of elections be realized.

b) The populist diagnosis consequently turns the liberal agenda of democratic betterment upside down: to place vertical electoral accountability at the service of the democratic principle, mechanisms of horizontal accountability are to be removed for they are considered illegitimate encroachments on the will of the people. The transformative agenda of populism, however, does not stop at the dismantling of horizontal controls but also targets the structure of vertical accountability of representative polyarchy (political parties, parliament, the public sphere, etc.). Vertical electoral accountability is disentangled with the principle of representation to put it at the service of that of identification (Peruzzotti 2008). Populism comes to life whenever a successful form of unmediated identification between leader and people is established (Peruzzotti 2019; Ostiguy, Panizza and Moffitt 2021). Such a process of identification can only take place in an unmediated manner, that is, free from any interference from the structures of intermediation of representative government. So, while it is true that populism relies heavily on vertical electoral accountability (Saffon and Bertomeu 2021, 7), the proper implementation of an interference-free process of identification requires the dismantling of the structure of vertical accountability of representative democracy.

c) The critical democratic theory of populism targets the polyarchic model that was the normative reference point of the liberal approach to accountability. Populism postulates a model to transcend representative democracy altogether. The "second transition" argument is thus replaced by a radical project of constitution making that seeks to drastically redefine the structure of the constitutional machine room that regulates the exercise of governmental power.[1]

1 The restructuring of the constitutional machinery that regulates the exercise of power is compatible with processes of rights expansion and inclusive public policies. That is particularly the case of so-called inclusionary forms of populism, which often result in the broadening of the catalogue of rights to address the concerns of previously ignored sectors of the population, such as indigenous communities, formal and informal workers, LGBT individuals or women. The plebiscitarian structure of authority that populism seeks to implant is not necessarily incompatible with processes of citizenship expansion: inclusive forms of populism are an example of processes of democratization that were frequently promoted by non-democratic or semi-democratic means.

d) The latter means that the agenda of democratic betterment is replaced by one of constitutional refoundation. Populists in power will seek to craft a constitutional order that reflects their conception of democratic power. They will seek to drastically redefine the constitutional machinery that regulates the exercise of power by promoting reforms in two directions. A first track of reforms targets existing horizontal accountability structures to strengthen executive authority over other state powers and accountability agencies (Müller 2017, 600). The overall intent of this track of reforms is to weaken horizontal accountability and, ultimately, to erase the distinction between law and power: in this conception, the constitutional order can only reflect the existing majoritarian will that the person of the executive embodies. Efforts to reduce the autonomy of courts and other agencies of legal accountability are a central aspect of the reforms. Given that their main responsibility is upholding the distinction between constitutional and ordinary politics, apex courts are frequently the first target of such efforts. There are alternative ways to undermine their institutional autonomy: 1) removing or packing the supreme court or constitutional tribunals, 2) reducing the jurisdiction of apex courts, and/or 3) manipulating their voting/appointment procedures. Those strategies are subsequently extended to lower courts and agencies of legal accountability such as comptrollers, public prosecutors, electoral courts, or ombudsmen (Arato and Cohen 2021). The second track of reforms seek to decouple vertical accountability mechanisms from the rules and regulations of representative government to accomplish a plebiscitary reorganization of the electoral system that would ultimately leave (presidential) elections as the sole vertical mechanism of accountability. Elections are to serve the principle of identification:[2] they are no longer conceived as part of the structure of mediated politics of representative polyarchies where different accountability mechanisms interact with one another (such as the role of the institutionalized opposition in the legislature, the existence of an autonomous and deliberative public sphere, and the presence of an independent and plural civil society). Instead, they stand alone (in combination with other forms of unmediated vertical communication such

2 Carl Schmitt rightly called attention to the dual character of elections, arguing that they can either serve the principle of representation or of identification (Schmitt 2008, 251). Such recognition weakens the claim that elections are the central institution of representative government (Manin 1997), for elections are equally central for other democratic models, such as populism and delegative democracy.

as mobilizations and referenda), as the quintessential channel of political accountability.

The presented structure of accountability is shared by exclusionary and inclusionary forms of populism alike. While populist governments might disagree on the orientation of public policies or on the willingness to expand or restrict rights to certain constituencies, they share the same conception on how power should be exercised. It is not uncommon to see similar sets of reforms, such as the undermining of the autonomy of courts or the independence of the media (Arato 2016, 206; Waisbord 2014; Müller 2017, 599; Sadurski 2018), in governments that are on the ideological antipodes, such as those of Hugo Chávez or Viktor Orbán. Efforts at constitutional refounding are not always successful: given that most contemporary populist governments operate in already democratized societies, their push to restructure the institutional landscape of the existing regimes might encounter different sorts of resistance (Peruzzotti 2013). Those efforts are many times unsuccessful: populist political parties in Western Europe, for instance, have been unable to fundamentally reshape the political order. While they have shown little respect for checks and balances, independent journalism, or the courts, existing institutional structures have constrained their impact on minority rights, press freedom, or independent courts (Akkerman 2021, 235). A similar argument has been made with respect to the experience of Trump in the US and of some Latin American cases (Peruzzotti 2017a; Weyland and Madrid 2019).

4 Populism, Elections, and Accountability

In the previous section, two ideal types of accountability models were developed to contrast the differences between the liberal and populist approaches to accountability. Relying on the influential O'Donnell's distinction between vertical and horizontal forms of accountability, the analysis presented the way in which each of the dimensions was understood by each model. From the analysis, it became clear that a populist understanding of accountability stands in open opposition to the liberal notion of accountability as limited government and its concomitant concerns with mechanisms of horizontal control. The populist model relies on a unilateral emphasis on vertical electoral accountability at the expense of the other dimensions of the concept. It is ironic that populism's reassertion of electoral accountability takes place in a political environment characterized by the generalized decline of the accountability performance of elections (Ginsberg and Shefter 1999; Dalton and Wattenberg 2002; Warren and Urbinati 2008; Foa and Mounk 2016; Rosanvallon 2017; Scheppele 2018).

The decline experienced by elections is in great part attributed to the crisis of the intermediary role played by political parties: parties seem to have lost their clout in significant sectors of the electorate, as citizen mistrust and disaffection towards professional politicians expands in contemporary democratic systems (Schmitter 2001; Dalton and Wattenberg 2002; Cheresky 2015). The crisis of parties has significantly altered the political dynamics of old and new democracies alike, resulting in a scenario marked by the weakening of traditional political identities and a growing individualization of political behaviours, electoral fragmentation and volatility, increased electoral absenteeism, generalized mistrust on the institutions of representative government, the personalization of politics, and the increasing clout of outsiders (Dalton 2007; Rosanvallon 2017; Mair 2013; Cheresky 2015; Schmitter 2020).

The populist response appears as an effort to preserve the centrality of elections by adapting their operation to the contemporary situation of political orphanages. In this light, the strategy at democratic hybridization of populism constitutionalism could be understood as a problematic attempt to make elections fit to the contemporary condition of crisis of representation. Its recipe consists of preserving the centrality of electoral representation by engaging in a formidable process of plebiscitary simplification of the institutional landscape of existing democracies. The latter can be understood as an attempt to alleviate the burdens that increased complexity and pluralization exert on political arrangements, by reducing all conflicts and claims to a binary antagonism: that of the people versus its illegitimate enemies. Such effort at political simplification (Urbinati 2014) is meant to unburden representative politics, for the political system now is limited to "represent" only a part of society: the one that populist consider it legitimately expresses popular aspirations. In the end, populism's response to the erosion of electoral democracy is more elections: populist administrations create an atmosphere that Conaghan and de la Torre refer to as "hyper-electoralism" to describe leaders that are in a permanent campaigning mode and that make frequent resort to elections and referendums to ratify their political standing (Conaghan and de la Torre 2008; also López Maya and Panzarelli 2013, 251–252).

Populism's bet for a plebiscitary redefinition of democracy does not solve the crisis of representation but aggravates it, for its antagonistic politics turns the deficit of legitimation into a constitutive feature of political life. The political polarization that results from the antagonistic behaviour and discourse of populist leaders usually gives rise to a militant and disloyal opposition that is willing to resort to any means to overthrow what they consider is an illegitimate and threatening government.

5 Populism, Liberalism, and Democratic Accountability

The formula of populist constitutionalism challenged the liberal model of accountability that dominated debates on the matter since the transitions from authoritarianism. The liberal model had emphasized the horizontal dimension of accountability over the vertical one, since it has attributed the malfunctioning that many new democratic regimes to the weaknesses of their rule of law arrangements. As crises of representation proliferated, it was clear that existing democracies were affected by other sorts of deficits beside horizontal ones. As feelings of political exclusion and loss of influence grew in many sectors of society, it became evident that there were also troublesome deficits of vertical accountability. It is in such an atmosphere that populism builds its reputation as a democratic critique of really existing democracies, redirecting the attention from liberal to properly democratic deficits. The political theory of populism considers that deficits of vertical accountability are intrinsic to the structure of representative democracy and that a proper response to the crisis of representation is to drastically reformulate the constitutional structure of existing democracies.

Guided by a questionable zero-sum reformulation of the linkages between vertical and horizontal mechanisms, populist reforms seek to strengthen the vertical electoral dimension at the expense of the horizontal one, while simultaneously instituting an impoverished structure of vertical accountability. Populism justifies its option for a more unmediated democratic model in the need to liberate the constituent power of the people from the constraints that the structure of indirect government poses upon it. Populism's prioritization of constituent over constituted power, however, does not necessarily result in the expansion of institutional channels for democratic participation but in the strengthening of the power of the elected executive. The strategy of concentrating and extending executive power and undermining the mediating structures of representative government (parties, parliament, the public sphere, civil society) is justified as the only way to overcome the veto powers that oligarchic elites held over any efforts to promote redistributive reforms and inequality alleviation to excluded majorities.

The populist critique might be right in their diagnosis regarding the power of elites to capture democratic institutions, yet its call for a relaxation of checks and balances not only weakens vetoes to redistribution but also the capacity of citizens to make claims (Saffon and Bertomeu 2021, 29). Populism's prioritization of constituent over constituted power, however, does not necessarily result in the expansion of institutional channels for democratic participation but in the strengthening of the power of the elected executive. While some of the institutional innovations promoted by populist administrations might enhance certain dimensions of vertical accountability and the adoption of redistributive politics, the plebiscitary nature of their conception of democracy ends up undermining whatever accountability gains are achieved.

The shortcomings of the populist proposal and the authoritarian risks it involves should not justify the uncritical embracement of the liberal model of accountability. Rather, the present crisis of democracy should be seen as an opportunity to explore democratic innovations that could promote a positive democratic transformation. Any transformative project should preserve the valuable elements of the liberal model while simultaneously addressing some of its shortcomings. At the same time, reforms should avoid the populist route towards illiberalism while being receptive to its legitimate concerns on how to enhance the vertical dimension of accountability.

A stronger notion of accountability cannot be built by turning its back to the principle of representation, for representation is a constitutive feature of democratic politics. Rather than opposing representation, efforts towards the construction of more inclusive polities should focus on the improvement of representative practices and institutions. Given that representation "helps constitute democratic capacities and practices" (Plotke 1997, 30), the expansion of democratic claims will inevitably result in more complex representative arrangements. Instead of engaging in counterproductive projects at institutional simplification, efforts should be geared in the opposite direction: expanding and improving representative practices and institutions to make them more open, effective, and fair. The latter requires abandoning the zero-sum conception to accountability that informs the populist perspective to avoid the trap of an agenda that seeks to strengthen one dimension at the expense of the other. Efforts at improving the political and legal dimensions of accountability should not be at odds with one another but the priority of any effort at democratic deepening.

The liberal notion of legal accountability cannot be abandoned since it is crucial for the exercise of political agency. Reforms of existing constitutional frameworks should be oriented to strengthening such features while simultaneously devising ways for avoiding the oligarchic capture of democratic institutions. The former resonates with the populist concern to grant a greater role to constituent politics, a goal that can only be attained by extending and improving channels for civic participation and social accountability.[3] That might require exploring sub-types of horizontal and vertical mechanisms that were not sufficiently emphasized by the liberal or populist models while simultaneously improving the signalling role of existing vertical mechanisms like elections and the public sphere. Such efforts will inevitably result in an expansion of the field of political intermediation and of accountability mechanisms.

The populist critique of the mainstream approach served to expand the debate on accountability beyond the question of controlling unlawful governmental encroachments, calling attention to the question of the nature and quality of vertical arrangements. Populist critics were right in signalling properly democratic deficits that the liberal model overlooked. The former's response, however, was predicated on a troublesome constitutional doctrine and notion of what constitutes democratic accountability. Far from solving the accountability deficits, the populist constitutional recipe aggravates them, undermining whatever gains in horizontal accountability had been accomplished and undermining the accountability role of vertical structures as well to the extent that it run the risk of promoting an authoritarian reversal. While accountability remains a central feature of democracy, debates on accountability need to move beyond liberal and populist approaches so a stronger and more productive notion can be established.

References

Ackerman, B. (1994) *The future of liberal revolution*. New Haven: Yale University Press.

Ackerman, J. (2004) Co-governance for accountability: Beyond "exit" and "voice". *World Development*, *32*(3), 447–463.

Akkerman, T. (2021) Populist parties in power and their impact on liberal democracies in Western Europe. In: Heinish, R., Holtz-Bacha, C. and Mazzoleni, O. (eds.) *Political populism: Handbook of concepts, questions, and strategies of research*. Baden-Baden: Nomos, 227–238.

Anria, Santiago (2018) *When Movements Become Parties: The Bolivian* MAS *in Comparative Perspective*, Cambridge, Cambridge University Press.

3 Such as the development of novel representative circuits such as those of public interest representation or of participatory institutions and of novel linkages between vertical and horizontal mechanisms such as those envisioned by the different formats of social accountability politics.

Arato, A. (2000) Revolution, restoration, and legitimation: Ideological problems in the transition from state socialism. In: Arato, A. *Civil society, constitution, and legitimacy*. Lanham: Rowman & Littlefield, 81–127.

Arato, A. (2016) *Post-sovereign constitution-making: Learning and legitimacy*. Oxford: Oxford University Press.

Arato, A. and Cohen, J. (2021) *Populism and civil society: The challenge to constitutional democracy*. Oxford: Oxford University Press.

Blokker, P. (2019) Populist constitutionalism. In: de la Torre, C. (ed.) *Routledge handbook of global populism*. London-New York: Routledge, 113–128.

Borowiak, C. (2011) *Accountability and democracy: The pitfalls and promise of popular control.* Oxford: Oxford University Press.

Cheresky, I. (2015) *El nuevo rostro de la democracia.* Buenos Aires: Fondo de Cultura Económica.

Colón-Ríos, J. I. (2020) Constitution making through law. In: Negretto, G. L. (ed.) *Redrafting constitutions in democratic regimes: Theoretical and comparative perspectives.* Cambridge: Cambridge University Press, 33–52.

Conaghan, Catherine, and De la Torre, C. (2008), "The Permanent Campaign of Rafael Correa: Making Ecuador's Plebiscitary Presidency" *The International Journal of Press/Politics*, *13*(3), 267–284.

Corrias, L. (2016) Populism in a constitutional key: Constituent power, popular sovereignty, and constitutional identity. *European Constitutional Law Review*, *12*(1), 6–26.

Dalton, R. J. (2007) *Democratic challenges, democratic choices: The erosion of political support in advanced democracies.* Oxford: Oxford University Press.

Dalton, R. J. and Wattenberg, M. P. (eds.) (2002) *Parties without partisans: Political change in advanced industrial democracies.* Oxford: Oxford University Press.

Foa, R. S. and Mounk, Y. (2016) The democratic disconnect. *Journal of Democracy*, *27*(3), 5–17.

Fox, J. (2007) *Accountability politics: Power and voice in rural Mexico.* Cambridge: Cambridge University Press.

Fox, J. (2022) *Accountability keywords.* Accountability Research Center.

Fukuyama, F. (2006) *The end of history and the last man.* New York: Free Press.

Ginsberg, B. and Shefter, M. (1999) *Politics by other means: Politicians, prosecutors, and the press from Watergate to Whitewater.* London-New York, W. W. Norton & Co.

Goodman, R. and Pegram, T. (eds.) (2012) *Human rights, state compliance, and social change: Assessing national human rights institutions.* Cambridge: Cambridge University Press.

Isunza Vera, E. and Olvera, A. J. (2006) *Democratización, rendición de cuentas y sociedad civil. Participación ciudadana y control social.* México DF: Miguel Ángel Porrúa.

Laclau, E. (2007) *On populist reason.* London: Verso.

Levine, D. and Molina, J. E. (eds.) (2011) *The quality of democracy in Latin America*. Boulder: Lynne Rienner.

Levitsky, S. and Loxton, J. (2013) Populism and competitive authoritarianism in the Andes. *Democratization, 20*(1), 107–136.

López Maya, M. and Panzarelli, A. (2013) Populism, renterism, and socialism in twenty-first century: The case of Venezuela. In: de la Torre, C. and Arnson, C. (eds.) (2013) *Latin American populisms of the twenty-first century*. Baltimore-Washington, DC: Johns Hopkins University Press-Woodrow Wilson Press, 239–268.

Magyar, B. (2016) *Post-communist mafia state: The case of Hungary*. Budapest: CEU Press.

Mainwaring, S. and Welna, C. (eds.) (2003) *Democratic accountability in Latin* America. Cambridge: Cambridge University Press.

Mair, P. (2013) *Ruling the void: The hollowing of Western Democracy*. London: Verso.

Manin, B. (1997) *The principles of representative government*. Cambridge: Cambridge University Press.

March, Johan P. and Olsen J.P. (1995) *Democratic Governance*, New York, The Free Press.

Mendez, J. E., O'Donnell, G. and Pinheiro, P. S. (eds.) (1999) *The (un)rule of law and the underprivileged in Latin America*. South Bend: Notre Dame University Press.

Mudde, C. and Rovira Kaltwasser, C. (2017) *Populism: A very short introduction*. Oxford: Oxford University Press.

Mulgan, R. (2000) Public accountability: An ever-expanding concept? *Public Administration, 78*(3), 555–573.

Müller, J.-W. (2017) Populism and constitutionalism. In: Rovira Kaltwasser, C., Taggart, P., Ochoia Espejo, P. and Ostiguy, P. (eds.) *The Oxford handbook of populism*. Oxford: Oxford University Press, 590–206.

O'Donnell, G. (1992) Transitions, continuities, and paradoxes. In: Mainwaring, S., Valenzuela, S. and O'Donnell, G. (eds.) *Issues in democratic consolidation: The new South American democracies in comparative perspective*. South Bend: Notre Dame University Press, 17–56.

O'Donnell, G. (1994) Delegative democracy. *Journal of Democracy, 5*(1), 55–69.

O'Donnell, G. (1997) Hoy ser progresista es ser liberal y viceversa. In: Quiroga, H. and Iazzetta, O. (eds.) *Hacia un nuevo consenso democrático. Conversaciones con la política*. Rosario: Homo Sapiens Ediciones, 55–71.

O'Donnell, G. (1999a) Horizontal accountability in new democracies. In: Schedler, A., Diamond, L. and Plattner, M. F. (eds.) *The self-restraining state: Power and accountability in new democracies*. Boulder: Lynne Rienner, 29–52.

O'Donnell, G. (1999b) Illusions about consolidation. In: O'Donnell, G. *Counterpoints. Selected essays on authoritarianism and democracy*. South Bend: Notre Dame University Press, 75–194.

O'Donnell, G. (2003) Horizontal accountability: The legal institutionalization of mistrust. In: Mainwaring, S. and Welna, C. (eds.) *Democratic accountability in Latin America*. Oxford: Oxford University Press, 34–54.

O'Donnell, G. (2006) Notes on various accountabilities and their interrelations. In: Peruzzotti, E. and Smulovitz, C. (eds.) *Enforcing the rule of law*. Pittsburgh: University of Pittsburgh Press, 334–343.

Odugbemi, S. and Lee, T. (eds.) (2011) *Accountability through public opinion: From inertia to public action*. Washington, DC: The World Bank.

Olsen, J. P. (2015) Democratic order, autonomy, and accountability. *Governance: An International Journal of Policy, Administration, and Institutions*, *25*(4) 425–440.

Ostiguy, P., Panizza, F. and Moffitt, B. (eds.) (2021) *Populism in global perspective: A performative and discursive approach*. London-New York: Routledge.

Peruzzotti, E. (2008) Populismo y representación. In: de la Torre, C. and Peruzzotti, E. (eds.) *El retorno del pueblo. Populismo y nuevas democracias en América Latina*. Quito: Flacso Ecuador, 97–124.

Peruzzotti, E. (2013) Populism in democratic times: Populism, representative democracy, and the debate on democratic deepening. In: de la Torre, C. and Arnson, C. (eds.) *Latin American populism in the XXI century*. Baltimore-Washington, DC: Johns Hopkins University Press-Woodrow Wilson Center Press, 61–84.

Peruzzotti, E. (2017a) Conceptualizing Kirchnerismo. *Partecipazione e Conflitto*, *10*(17), 47–64.

Peruzzotti, E. (2017b) Populism as democratization's nemesis: The politics of regime hybridization. *Chinese Political Science Review*, *2*(3), 314–327.

Peruzzotti, E. (2017c) Regime betterment or regime change? A critical review of recent debates on liberal democracy and populism in Latin America. *Constellations*, *24*(3), 389–400.

Peruzzotti, E. (2019) Laclau's theory of populism: A critical review. In: de la Torre, C. (ed.) *The Routledge handbook on populism*. London-New York: Routledge, 33–43.

Peruzzotti, E. and Smulovitz, C. (eds.) (2006) *Enforcing the rule of law: Social accountability in the new Latin American democracies*. Pittsburgh: Pittsburgh University Press.

Plotke, D. (1997) Representation is democracy. *Constellations*, *4*(1), 19–34.

Przeworski, Adam, Susan Stokes, and Bernard Manin (eds.) (1999) *Democracy, Accountability, and Representation*, Cambridge, Cambridge University Press.

Rosanvallon, P. (2017) La democracia del siglo XXI. *Nueva Sociedad*, *269*, 148–162.

Sadurski, W. (2018) Constitutional crisis in Poland. In: Graber, M. A., Levinson, S. and Tushnet, M. (eds.) *Constitutional democracy in crisis?* Oxford, Oxford University Press, 257–275.

Saffon, M. P. and Bertomeu, J. F. (2021) The mix of Latin American populist constitutionalism, mimeo.

Schedler, A., Diamond, L. and Plattner, M. (eds.) (1999) *The self-restraining state: Power and accountability in new democracies*. Boulder: Lynne Rienner.

Scheppele, K. L. (2018) The party's over. In: Graber, M. A., Levinson, S. and Tushnet, M. (eds.) *Constitutional democracy in crisis?* Oxford: Oxford University Press, 495–524.

Schmitt, C. (2008) *Constitutional theory*. Durham-London: Duke University Press.

Schmitter, P. C. (2001) Parties are not what they once were. In: Diamond, L. and Gunther, R. (eds.) *Political parties and democracy*. Baltimore: Johns Hopkins University Press, 67–89.

Schmitter, P. C. (2004) The quality of democracy: The ambiguous virtues of accountability. *Journal of Democracy*, *15*(4), 47–60.

Schmitter, P. C. (2009) Defects and Deficits in the Quality of Neo-Democracy in Gary Bland and Cynthia J. Arnson, Eds. *Democratic deficits. Addressing challenges to sustainability and consolidation around the world*. Washington DC, The Woodrow Wilson International Center for Scholars and RTI International.

Schmitter, P. C. (2020) Crisis and mutation in the institutions of representation in "real-existing democracies". In: Chu, Y. H. and Zheng, Y. *The decline of the Western-centric world and the emerging new global order*. London-New York: Routledge, 58–73.

Schultz, J. (1998) *Reviving the fourth state: Democracy, accountability, and the media*. Cambridge: Cambridge University Press.

Uildriks, N. with N. Tello Peon (2010) *Mexico's unrule of law: Implementing human rights in police and judicial reform under democratization*. Lanham: Lexington Books.

Ungar, M. (2001) *Elusive reform: Democracy and the rule of law in Latin America*. Boulder: Lynne Rienner.

Urbinati, N. (2014) *Democracy disfigured: Opinion, truth, and the people*. Cambridge, MA: Harvard University Press.

Waisbord, S. (2014) *Vox populista*. Buenos Aires: Gedisa.

Warren, M. E. and Urbinati, N. (2008) The concept of representation in contemporary democratic theory. *Annual Review of Political Science*, *11*, 387–412.

Weyland, K. (2020) Populism's threat to democracy: Comparative lessons from the United States. *Perspectives on Politics*, *18*(2), 389–406.

Weyland, K. and Madrid, R. L. (eds.) (2019) *When democracy trumps populism*. Cambridge: Cambridge University Press.

PART 3

Actors

CHAPTER 7

Populism and Participation

Cecilia Biancalana

1 Introduction[1]

On the one hand, the concept of participation, in general, and of political participation, in particular, is one of the most important in sociology and political science. On the other hand, in the last decades, the rise and success of populist parties and movements contributed to change in many ways a number of solid beliefs, shared by the academic community, on politics and society. It is then worth asking whether, and in which ways, populism questioned our understanding of political participation.

Participation is closely intertwined with democracy; however, the literature on populism focused much more on the latter (e.g. Canovan 1999; Mény and Surel 2001; Rovira Kaltwasser 2012; Huber and Schimpf 2021), leaving aside an in-depth analysis of the relationship between populism and participation. The literature on the relationship between democracy and populism consisted of two main strands. While one argues that populism may mitigate what has been called a "crisis of representation" (Mair 2002; Kriesi 2014), the other sees populism as a threat to liberal democracy and the rule of law (Urbinati 2019). It has been claimed that this ambivalent relationship depends on the definition given to democracy, and that the variable that determines whether populism is conceived as a threat to or a corrective for democratic governments is the preference for a "liberal" or "radical" conception of democracy (Rovira Kaltwasser 2012). Moreover, it must be recalled that the relationship between populism and democracy is contingent and varies in different historical, institutional, and social contexts: there are numerous factors that can influence whether populist actors can erode or enhance the quality of democracy (Huber and Schimpf 2021), whose analysis falls beyond the scope of this contribution.

1 This chapter is based on a lecture given at the "Participation et démocratie" summer school held in Lausanne in May 2019. A first version of this chapter was published in Italian in 2020 in the journal *Iride*. I want to thank Alfio Mastropaolo and the participants to the "Populism as a Challenge to Key Concepts in Social and Political Sciences" workshop (Lausanne, November 2021) for their precious comments made about an earlier version of this text.

 | DOI:10.1163/9789004679016_009

Yet, despite the relative lack of studies on populism and participation compared to the ones dedicated to populism and democracy, it is clear that the two strands are closely intertwined. Indeed, according to Dahl (1971), two different dimensions of democratization exist. The first is "public contestation" and refers to the development of a system of political competition, which implies the possibility to oppose the government and to offer alternative points of view. The second is "inclusiveness" and denotes the breadth of the right to *participate* in the system of public contestation. Inclusiveness refers mainly to the right to participate in elections and hold office, but also, more generally, to the capacity of the people "to participate on a more or less equal plane in controlling and contesting the conduct of the government" (Dahl 1971, 4).

If, on the one hand, through populist mobilizations, disadvantaged groups may make their voices heard and promote the implementation of policies that they prefer, on the other, the idea of a homogeneous people with unified interests, typical of populism, excludes parts of the population and fosters plebiscitary dynamics. For this reason, populism seems to be negative with regard to public contestation, but potentially positive in terms of fostering inclusiveness (Rovira Kaltwasser 2012).

Populism stems indeed from the tensions between what democracy promises (a government of the people, by the people, for the people) and its daily practices, in which the people are consulted only on election day and do not have the power to meaningfully influence political decisions (Canovan 1999). Populism, with its promise to restore the sovereignty of the people, attempts to fill this gap and thus can address the groups of citizens who feel excluded from politics. And this can have consequences on citizens' participation.

The aim of this contribution is to deepen the hypothesis according to which, instead of stifling participation, populism can in principle reinforce it instead. After having defined the two broad concepts of populism and participation, and through a review of the existing studies on the subject, our goal will be to understand how, and with which potential consequences. Our interpretation is that, if it is true that populism can foster participation, it is worth asking if it holds true regarding different "variants" of populism, and in different geographical areas. Moreover, it is worth asking which kind of participation populism promotes, whether it is only a matter of rhetoric, and which is the meaning that citizens who support populism would give to participation.

2 Populism: a Contested Concept

It has become commonplace to start a contribution on populism by acknowledging the contested nature of the concept (Moffitt and Tormey 2014, 382; Albertazzi and McDonnell 2015, 4). "Populism" is indeed a term that in recent years has more and more entered citizens', politicians' and journalists' vocabulary; not to mention academia, where it has become almost impossible to count the volumes and essays consecrated to this topic. However, such a wide use did not correspond to a consensus on its definition. If we assume that the popularity of the concept is not a mere matter of fashion, then we must admit that it is capable of grasping some important features of the transformations of democracy, and of the challenges they are facing. But, when one tries to give a clear, precise, and parsimonious definition of the concept, the complexity of the phenomenon to be defined emerges. In the case of populism, the difficulty lies not only in the definition of the content, but in its very nature.

There are different approaches in the definition of the nature of populism. Populism has been defined as a "thin ideology" based on the Manichean opposition between the people and the elite, and on the assertion that politics should be an expression of the general will of the people. This is the famous definition by Cas Mudde (2004), that reached a sort of hegemony in the studies of populism.[2] Populism has been defined as a political discourse or a style of communication based on the opposition between the people and the elite, simplification and a direct appeal to the people (Moffitt and Tormey 2014; Aslanidis 2016), whose success can be ascribed to some facets of the processes of mediatization (Mazzoleni 2008). Populism can be also seen as a political strategy, aimed at seizing power and governing (Weyland 2001). Similarly, Jansen (2011; 2017), starting from the Latin American case, defined "populist mobilisation" as a way of animating political support, a mode a political practice, a set of actions that politicians and supporters do.

It is not the aim of this contribution to try to clarify the debate on the nature of the concept of populism. As for the purpose of this contribution, we can say that the "core" of the concept lies in the opposition between the people and the elite, and in the claim to restore the people's sovereignty, which has been betrayed by the elites. *The way in which people's sovereignty must be restored, and in which populists claim to give voice to the people, is a matter of participation.*

2 For a critique, see de la Torre and Mazzoleni (2019).

Populism has been defined as a "chameleonic" (Taggart 2000) phenomenon: each actor, according to his characteristics and to the context in which it operates, can define the people and the elites, or the way in which to restore the people's sovereignty, in a different way. And indeed, despite its commonalities, we know that populism credits a varied history in different continents. For instance, while populism is a relatively recent phenomenon in most European countries, it has much longer roots in the United States and the nations of Latin America, where it has been linked to modernization processes and where charismatic populist leaders first emerged. Moreover, this heterogeneity of legacies across regions is made more complex by the growing number of political systems affected by populism and its ability to adapt to local circumstances.

Nevertheless, we can identify a basic difference between right-wing and left-wing populism. While right-wing populism excludes parts of the population as not being a legitimate part of the people, left-wing populist parties tend to emphasize an inclusive *demos* (Rooduijn and Akkerman 2017). While right-wing populists combine a populist world view with nativist and authoritarian tendencies (Mudde 2007), according to Waisman (2021) "forms of left-wing populism, which are more likely to be found in Southern Europe and Latin America, are movements of incorporation". In sum, right-wing populist parties propose solutions that involve exclusion, whereas left-wing populist parties promote inclusion (Mudde and Rovira Kaltwasser 2017). Consequently, we can argue that even populists' conceptions of participation can be various, based on contextual differences between countries and on the "variant" of populism concerned. We can hypothesize that, as left-wing populism is associated with a more inclusionary conception of the people (Caiani and Graziano 2019), it might favour political participation more than its right-wing counterpart (de la Torre 2010). However, it remains to be seen what "participation" means.

3 Participation: A Multifaceted Concept

The concept of political participation is as broad as that of populism but, perhaps, less controversial. Political participation is one of the crucial properties of democratic societies. "Citizen participation is at the heart of democracy. Indeed, democracy is unthinkable without the ability of citizens to participate freely in the government process" (Verba et al. 1995): not only through political participation are representatives elected and citizens can communicate their needs to them, but participation is also a way in which people express their identity.[3] However, debates arose also on the definition of participation (Teorel, Torcal and Montero 2007). For instance, should participation be limited to actions aimed at influencing political personnel? Should it include any attempt made by citizens to influence political outcomes? Should it necessarily imply an action, that is, an observable behaviour, pursued by citizens? Of course, each definition of participation is more or less congruent with a particular normative view of democracy. The lack of consensus on a single definition of participation can contribute to explain the relative scarcity of studies on populism and participation. As in the case of populism, here we will consider participation as a complex and multifaceted phenomenon. Moreover, we will also take into consideration its symbolic or immaterial dimensions.

Consequently, we can identify two main meanings of the concept of political participation: "taking part" in the life of the community and "being part" of that community (Cotta 1979). In other words, we can distinguish between a kind of "instrumental" participation, whose purpose is to influence political decisions and select the political class – to influence the authoritative allocations of values for a society (Easton 1953) – and an "expressive" one, which results in a sense of collective belonging. Indeed, through participation people identify in a group – that can be as broad as the nation in the case of elections or as narrow as a local committee – and express their identity on the outside, vis-à-vis political opponents (Raniolo 2007). As for the "taking part", the literature traditionally divides between "conventional" or "institutionalized" forms of participation (such as voting, discussing politics, or joining a party) and "unconventional" or "non-institutionalized" ones (such as participating in a march or strike) (Kaase and Marsh 1979). A distinction can be also made between "electoral" and "non-electoral" forms of participation (Teorel, Torcal and Montero 2007).

Looking at the empirical reality, this results in a vast array of practices: nowadays, people take part to the life of the community first and foremost by voting in elections, or in initiatives and referendums. It is the electoral dimension of participation, the most common but less and less popular (Delwit 2013). Also to counter the decreasing turnout and to bring citizens closer to politics, in the last decades, local and national institutions promoted experiments of participatory and deliberative democracy, whose aim is exactly to expand the possibilities of citizens' participation beyond elections (Bobbio 2005; Pateman 2012). Citizens can participate, in various ways and at different levels, in

3 Even though this is a rather recent acquisition. We know that, in the 1970s, participation was considered by some to be a threat to democracies as it ran the risk of "overloading" them (Crozier, Huntington and Watanuki 1975).

organizations such as parties and social movements. They can self-organize outside the political arena to protect rights and commons, or participate in demonstrations or other forms of protest. People can participate with different degrees of intensity. Of course, it is one thing to vote, and other to be elected. It is one thing to belong to a party, an another to be an activist. And, in any case, people are expressing themselves and their identity when they take part in these kinds of activities – activities that have as their ultimate goal to influence the allocation of authoritative values in a society.[4]

Sometimes, the expression of an identity is the very driving force of participation, and this often explain why people participate despite the negative incentives, and even when individual participation does not make the difference (Olson 1965; Hirschman 1982). Indeed, although "assuming that individuals act in politics to pursue their interests [...] is considered sufficiently plausible to build sophisticated models of interpretation of phenomena on these premises", voting or doing politics cannot be explained only in utilitarian terms (Pizzorno 1983, 5). According to Pizzorno, to explain political action a "logic of identification" should replace a "logic of utility": "those who vote and those who fight for political power aim, albeit with a very different commitment, to ensure the recognition of a collective identity" (ibid., 39).

4 Three Research Paths on the Link between Populism and Participation

How does populism challenge the concept of political participation? We have said that the link between the two is found in the fact that the actors defined as populists claim to give voice to the people and aim to restore their sovereignty; the *how* this is done is a matter of participation. As for the relationship between the two concepts, a review of the existing literature points out that it is possible to identify three main paths that correspond to three main research strands in political science. In the first, it is possible to focus on the supply side, that is, on the participation of populist actors and their participation practices. The second focuses on the demand side, that is, on populist voters and sympathizers and on their participation needs and behaviours. Finally, the third strand adopts a "systemic" perspective, that is, it focuses on the impact of the presence of populist parties on political systems in terms of increased or decreased participation. In this section, we will review the existing studies that

4 This issue is particularly taken into consideration in the works on social movements.

focused on these three dimensions in order to disentangle and understand the link between populism and participation.

4.1 *Do Populist Actors Push for a Greater Citizens' Participation?*

In the first place, we can ask ourselves whether or not populist actors are in favour of a greater participation of citizens in the decision-making processes. In this respect, answers are different when we look at different "variants" of populism, and at different geographical areas.

At least in Western Europe, until a decade ago, we would have had no problem in saying that populist parties do *not* push for greater citizen participation. Dealing with this issue, in a well-known article from 2004 Mudde stated quite assertively that "in contrast to popular misperceptions, the populist voters do not strongly favour any form of participatory democracy, be it deliberative or plebiscitary" (Mudde 2004, 558). According to Mudde, for populists, politics should be the expression of the *volonté générale* of the people. The question is: *How*? How to transform the people's general will into political action? Mudde sees two roads that populists can take: leadership and participation. There is, following his line of reasoning, a clear dividing line between the 1968 and New Left movements, on the one hand, and the contemporary radical right, on the other – both considered by the author as populist. The fundamental difference between what Mudde calls "the current populist zeitgeist" and the New Left parties is the interpretation of the people. While the New Left referred to "an active, self-confident, well-educated, progressive people", the current populism is the rebellion of the "silent majority" (ibid., 557). Thus, while for the former the will of the people would be achieved through a greater participation in the political process, for the latter it suffices that the demands of the people are implemented, without the need for the citizens "to be bothered with politics all the time" (ibid., 558).

Therefore, if in the first case the *volonté générale* is transformed into political action through citizens' involvement in the decision-making processes, in the second case it is sufficient that there is a leader who knows, interprets, and embodies the wishes and needs of the people, bringing them in the political arena. Therefore, if what the former asked in order to see the *volonté générale* realized was "more participation and less leadership", for the second is "more leadership and less participation". For this reason, according to Mudde, populists do not favour any form of participatory democracy, focusing on the output – rather than the input – of the democratic process.

> The heartland of contemporary populism is thus focused primarily on the *out*put and not on the *in*put of democracy. What they demand is

> *responsive* government, i.e. a government that implements policies that are in line with their wishes. However, they want the politicians to come up with these policies without bothering them, i.e. without much participation from them.
>
> MUDDE 2004, 558

This seems to have changed over the past decade. Some social changes, such as individualization and cognitive mobilization, that make people more confident of their competences and more and more sceptical towards the authority of expert knowledge, including political knowledge, and technological changes such as the spread of the internet and the digital revolution, have led to the emergence of new forms of direct and unmediated of participation, inside and outside parties. According to Tormey (2015), we are moving from a "vertical" to a "horizontal" mode of politics. Nadia Urbinati states:

> [W]e are witnessing, on the one hand, the re-emergence of charismatic leaders [...] and, on the other, a process going in quite the opposite direction as it claims to promote the diffusion of politics in view of *reaffirming ordinary citizens' voice* against the established political elites.
>
> URBINATI 2015, 477, emphasis added

This also applies to some new parties, defined as populist, that have arisen in recent years. This is the case, for instance, with Italy's Five Star Movement and Spain's Podemos.[5] The case of the Five Star Movement (FSM) is telling, as it was born exactly on the promise of bringing into the Italian political system elements of direct and participatory democracy. FSM did not only promote a broader use of initiatives and referenda. Against the backdrop of a political system seen as closed to citizens' inputs, in 2013 FSM managed to elect a new political class made of common citizens – complete outsiders – to the highest levels of political representation. Moreover, according to its rhetoric, citizens must – through the internet – direct the work and actions of those representatives. For this reason, FSM equipped itself with a platform for online participation, significantly called *Rousseau* (Deseriis 2017; Mosca 2020), perhaps the most developed one in the world, through which the party organized members' consultations on topics ranging from the selection of the president of the republic to decisions on alliances.

5 For a comparison, see Vittori (2017).

Research has demonstrated, however, that over time FSM has undergone, like most new parties based on the promises of direct participation, a process of institutionalization that led it to scale down its claims and to adapt to the constraints of government. Scholars have also pointed out that the rhetoric and practices of the party do not match (Biancalana 2022), and that especially regarding (online) participation, if members *formally* have a lot of power, the outcomes of online consultations rarely contest the leadership, due to the fact that the "rules of the game" are not shared, that members have no control on the management of the platform, and that the questions are often framed to make members accept decisions taken elsewhere (Biancalana and Vittori 2021).

Thus, if it is not possible to say that all populist parties today stand on the side of "participation", and if it is necessary to point out which kind participation they are promoting, there is no doubt that some populist parties pushed for greater citizen participation to public affairs. As anticipated, the distinction between right-wing and left-wing populism can be useful to disentangle the relationship between populism and participation. We can hypothesize that the former would focus on the outputs of, while the latter on the inputs into, democracy. Indeed, studies have demonstrated that while the populist right prefers the electoral to the protest arena, the left promotes its claims in both, and this finding can be linked with the values that underlie the two kinds of populism: authoritarian and libertarian, respectively (Pirro and Portos 2021). As we will see, supporters of left-wing populist parties are also more active in direct-democratic voting (Trüdinger and Bächtiger 2022).

From the point of view of European scholarship, the American and especially Latin American context seem to present partially different patterns. As anticipated, in Latin America populism historically aimed to "include the excluded", often at the cost of disfiguring democracy (de la Torre 2016). In a context in which large sectors of the population were excluded from politics and the public sphere, especially in the 1930s and 1940s, populists sought to incorporate the people, also through mass rallies that were considered as a direct expression of sovereignty (see in this respect the case of Peronism). The occupation of public spaces in the name of a leader happened also at the turn of the twentieth century in the case of some episodes of non-institutional collective action in Ecuador, Venezuela, and Bolivia (de la Torre 2015). In this respect, we can consider these mobilizations as a top-down form of participation, guided or manipulated by a strong leader, that present a substantial ambivalence towards constitutional democracy.

Finally, a question that is worth asking is whether populist actors take advantage of the participatory opportunities offered by the internet more than others. As anticipated, both Podemos and FSM are known for having extensively used the opportunities offered by the internet, not only for communication purposes, but also for organization and participation. Two recent American cases, Occupy Wall Street and the Tea Party, considered as forms of populism (Grattan 2016), also used new technologies to reach their supporters.

Regarding the relationship between traditional media and populism, this has been analyzed in Gianpietro Mazzoleni's research on "media populism" (Mazzoleni 2008). According to Mazzoleni, some structural characteristics of contemporary media systems (such as spectacularization, personalization, and dramatization) are particularly congruent with populist traits and contribute to give populist leaders notoriety, legitimacy, and visibility. In short, there is a sort of (albeit unintentional) "convergence of goals" between news media and populist actors, which can favour the success of the latter. According to Gerbaudo (2018), there is also an "elective affinity" between populism and social media. Social media would provide, on the one hand, a means for disaffected individuals to express themselves and, on the other hand, a space to gather and form partisan online crowds.

However, if the online communication of populist parties has been widely analyzed (e.g. de Vreese et al. 2018), research on their online participation is less common. We know that populism is opposed to all forms of mediation, and that the internet can favour disintermediation processes (Chadwick 2007). Indeed, in his recent book on digital parties Gerbaudo (2019) traces some links between digital and populist parties, asserting that in the latter hyper-valourization of participation "combines populist ideas such as popular sovereignty, the people's will and the fight against the elite with a strong cyber-libertarian feel". But this topic remains underdeveloped.

4.2 *Populist Supporters' Patterns of Participation*

In the second place, in order to understand the link between populism and participation, we can ask ourselves whether the voters or sympathizers of populist parties have specific traits, such as asking for more participation, or a different kind of participation, than others. As one of the traits of populism is an antipathy towards mediation, we can start by asking whether the voters or supporters of populist parties or, more broadly, citizens holding populist attitudes are characterized by a greater demand for direct democracy than others. Direct democracy – such as referendums and initiatives – could be considered by populists as tools to give people a greater voice, and indeed a number of major Western European right-wing populist parties express clear support for greater direct democracy (Bowler et al. 2017).

Some studies conducted in Western Europe seem to support the claim that populist voters share their parties' position on direct democracy. Comparing

Belgium, the Netherlands, and Germany, Pauwels (2014) found that a preference for more direct decision-making through referendums is a factor that can be linked with populist voting. Mohrenberg, Huber, and Freyburg's (2021) analysis of representative survey data in four European democracies (France, Germany, Switzerland, and the United Kingdom) reveals that individuals with stronger populist attitudes indeed support direct democracy more than citizens with no strong populist attitudes. Analyzing a 2016 Dutch referendum, Jacobs et al. (2018) confirm that citizens with a higher degree of populist attitudes are more likely to favour referendums.

Focusing on the UK, Webb found that what he defines as "stealth democrats" – "lower social status [people], who are less well-educated, less politically interested and efficacious individuals who recoil from political debate and have little desire to participate in political activity beyond the minimum necessary to hold untrustworthy elites in check" (Webb 2013, 750) – are favourably disposed towards direct democracy. However, when given the opportunity to take part in a national referendum, they didn't show much inclination to vote. According to Webb their demand for the principle of greater participation "may owe more to a sense of frustration with, and perhaps incomprehension about, the obscure complexities of the political process, with its all its attendant noise, conflict and undoubted venality, than to an authentic desire to become involved in the detail of political decision making" (ibid., 768).

Populists' availability to participate in direct-democratic voting is indeed an under-researched topic. Trüdinger and Bächtiger (2022) recently analyzed the discrepancy between the attitudes and the actions of populist individuals regarding direct democracy. A gap between the attitudes and the actions might indicate that their preferences for direct democracy reflect an opposition to the institutions and actors of the representative system, more than an authentic demand for more participatory democracy. Focusing on Germany, they found that the stronger the populist attitudes people exhibit, the more they are in favour of direct citizen participation. In particular, the more likely individuals are to vote for Alternative for Germany, the more they support direct democracy. However, Alternative for Germany's voters have a lower tendency to participate in direct-democratic voting with respect to others. On the contrary, supporters of Die Linke, a left-wing populist party, have a higher inclination to participate. This would testify to yet another diversity between left-wing and right-wing populists, with supporters of left-wing populist parties more concretely active in direct-democratic voting.

Outside of Western Europe, results point to a far more tenuous linkage. Focusing on Australia, Canada, and New Zealand, Bowler et al. (2017) found that right-wing populist voters do not support their parties' direct democracy policies. Nevertheless, populists' appeal for greater direct democracy "may nonetheless serve as rhetoric that adds to these parties' aura of challenging the status quo and empowering the ordinary voters, despite the latter not necessarily caring about having direct votes on policy matters" (Bowler et al. 2017, 87).

What meaning direct democracy would have to populist supporters is, of course, a matter of debate. Is it a need for participation or simply a desire to make governments and elites accountable? Is it the expression of a frustration towards representative democracy or the desire to have a say on important issues, or both? It depends also on their position towards government. When in opposition, they could use direct democracy to counter the decisions of the corrupt elite; when in power, to impose the will of the majority and to support populist leaders favouring plebiscitary dynamics. Through survey data collected on the occasion of a Dutch referendum held in 2018, Werner and Jacobs (2021) found that populists' support for referendums seems to be less driven by instrumental motives compared to that of non-populists, and that populists are more likely than non-populists to accept the outcome of a referendum, even when this outcome is unfavourable.

Going beyond direct democracy, a study based on survey data from nine European countries (Anduiza, Guinjoan and Rico 2019) found evidence in favour of a positive association between populist attitudes and non-institutional modes of political participation (such as petition signing and the online expression of political views), and a null or a negative effect for the most institutionalized one, that is voting. The authors' interpretation is that populist attitudes involve an emphasis on the importance of a popular will *directly expressed* and of a defence of a collective identity (the people) morally outraged by an evil elite. These elements could generate motivation to participate in politics through identity, purpose, and emotion, that is, through non-institutionalized forms of participation that would be preferred to institutional channels, such as elections.

Pirro and Portos (2021) also focused on non-electoral participation and ask whether, and to what extent, populist party voters engage in non-institutional modes of political participation (demonstrating, petitioning, political consumerism, and online activism). They looked at nine European countries (France, Germany, Greece, Italy, Poland, Spain, Sweden, Switzerland, and the United Kingdom) and found that populist party voters, and especially the ones on the left, were more engaged in non-electoral participation than non-populist party voters.[6]

6 On non-institutional participation and populism in the Latin American case, see the cases of Ecuador, Venezuela, and Bolivia discussed in de la Torre (2015).

Finally, Anduiza, Guinjoan, and Rico (2019) also found that the presence of populist attitudes increases participation, particularly for individuals with low levels of education and income, narrowing or even reversing the traditional socio-economic inequality in participation. This would be in line with the hypothesis of Rovira Kaltwasser (2012, 200) that populism could favour inclusiveness through the fostering of the participation of disadvantaged groups, in particular, in societies with high levels of socio-economic exclusion. It remains to be discussed whether this inclusion would mean only an *incorporation* of the people, which would result in a lessening on the dimensions of accountability and division of power.

To sum up, be it the expression of a need for participation or of a frustration towards representative democracy, populism, contrarily to what one can think, *is not apolitical* and can lead to a full engagement in politics (Taggart 2018, 81). Indeed, one of the few studies linking populism and political identities shows that populist supporters are politicized citizens open to anti-establishment appeals (Meléndez and Rovira Kaltwasser 2019). This question of the relationship between populism and political identities is actually an important "missing link" in the study of populism.

4.3 *Does Populism Increase Electoral Turnout?*

Finally, we can ask, What is the impact of populism on political and party systems? In terms of participation, we can ask, for instance, whether the presence or the success of a populist party increases electoral turnout. According to Mudde and Rovira Kaltwasser (2017, 83), "populism tends to favor political participation" because it gives voice to and mobilizes those who felt underrepresented by the political establishment.

Going back in time, an association between populism and increased electoral participation was observed in Argentina in the case of Perón in the 1940s and 1950s. However, the interpretation of this datum cannot be separated from the degree of consolidation of a country's democratic institutions. If in a context of stable institutions populism can make democratic politicians remember the principle that sovereignty belongs to the people, then when institutions are weak it can damage them, leading to a drop in the system's legitimacy. Indeed, "electoral participation might increase without creating democratic political cultures, or respecting the rule of law. In this sense, populist inclusion under Perón did not foster or strengthen democracy" (Mazzoleni and de la Torre 2019). After all, we have seen that inclusion is only *one dimension* of democracy.

Nevertheless, focusing on consolidated democracies, we can identify three hypotheses on the relationship between populism and electoral participation.

The first is that those who feel excluded from political systems, and who therefore would abstain without the populist alternative (what Hirschman would call *exit*), would instead use populists as a way to make their voices heard (*voice*). The second is that *other* parties and their supporters would mobilize against a populist party, when it is perceived, for instance, as a threat to the rights of minorities, thus increasing electoral participation. The third posits that, as populism fosters a distrust of politics and representative institutions, it discourages voting.

As it could be expected, the results of the studies on this topic do not give univocal results. A study focused on right-wing populism, based on the analysis of European Social Survey data in 33 European countries in the period 2002–2012, shows that although there is, in general, no positive influence of these parties on the electoral participation (no effect in Western Europe, a negative effect in Eastern Europe), they, at least in Western Europe, encourage some social groups to vote. However, they are not the social groups traditionally identified as supporters of populist parties (people with lower levels of education, manual workers, the unemployed, dissatisfied democrats, and people prone to holding negative views on immigration), but groups with higher levels of education and an interest in politics. This could represent a confirmation of the second hypothesis: When populism is seen as a threat, opponents mobilize against it. On the contrary, in Eastern Europe this effect is not detected: social groups habitually opposed to populism are discouraged from voting as populist parties grow stronger (Immerzeel and Pickup 2015). Huber and Ruth (2017) also expected to find a positive relationship between the presence of populist parties and changes in the electoral turnout but were unable to confirm this association. However, using data from 31 European countries from 1990 until 2014 they showed that the presence of populist parties increased the participation of voter groups with lower socio-economic status in terms of income and education (thus confirming the hypothesis of Rovira Kaltwasser).

Finally, estimating the effect of populist parties on the aggregate level of voter turnout for 315 national parliamentary elections between 1970 and 2016 in 31 European countries, Leininger and Meijers (2021) found that the presence of a populist party on the ballot paper did not affect the average level of voter turnout in the election. They did, however, find robust empirical support for a positive effect of the parliamentary presence of populist parties on turnout in Central and Eastern European countries. It remains unclear, however, whether this was because of the mobilization of former non-voters attracted by populists or because of the increased presence of voters that oppose such parties and choose to go to the ballot box to counter populism. Aggregate level data give us no information on individuals' motivation and underestimate the contextual factors on which populism relies.

5 Conclusions

What can we learn, then, from the examination of the nexus between populism and participation? The aim of this contribution was to provide an advancement of the theoretical knowledge on populism, by highlighting the challenges that it poses to participation. Populism and participation are multifaceted concepts. Populists claim to restore the sovereignty of the people in multiple ways, depending on the characteristics of the social, institutional, and political context in which they operate, and on the different type of populism (e.g. right-wing and left-wing) at stake. These manifold ways are reflected in their different views and practices of participation. Populism is not apolitical and does not equate to apathy. Due to its aversion to any kind of mediation, populism – and especially its left-wing variant – can promote the direct participation of citizens. Due to the defence of a collective identity that it can activate, it can foster non-electoral forms of participation.

However, all that glistens is not gold. In poorly consolidated democracies, inclusion can increase through populist electoral mobilization at the expense of public contestation. Participation can be used by populists, for instance, with referenda or insurrections, to impose the will of the majority against checks and balances, and to support populist leaders favouring plebiscitary dynamics. To conclude, I will highlight some lessons that can be drawn and present an agenda for future research on the challenge that populism poses to participation.

5.1 *If Populism Fosters Participation, Which Kind of Participation?*

When dealing with participation, we have seen that is important to specify the kind of participation we are speaking about. A simple quantitative increase in participation can underlie plebiscitary dynamics, or mere inclusion. The risk of a plebiscitary turn can be seen with respect to electoral participation,[7] popular mobilizations, and in intra-party decision-making processes.

In the Latin American case, it has been demonstrated that the incorporation of the people was at odds with the dimensions of accountability and division of power typical of liberal democracies. Even though they wanted to redeem

7 For some Latin American cases, see Mazzoleni and de la Torre (2019).

democracies, populists' view of a homogeneous people contributed to the creation of authoritarian governments in that area (de la Torre 2016), showing a tension between empowerment of the people and plebiscitary dynamics. In the same vein, the Tea Party mobilizations, which seemed to achieve great public support, proved to be a form of *astroturfing* – that is, manipulated mobilizations that appear to originate from grassroots participants – contributing to the reinforcement of neoliberal democracy (Grattan 2016).

As regards intra-party democracy, in the case of the Five Star Movement we have seen that if members *formally* have a lot of power inside the participatory platform *Rousseau*, in reality they control neither the management of the platform nor the "rules of the game" (e.g. the framing of the questions), and this has led to the fact that the outcomes of online consultations rarely contested the leadership, and that online participation resulted in members accepting decisions taken elsewhere. More generally, it has been demonstrated that populist parties develop scarcely democratic intra-party structures (Böhmelt, Ezrow and Lehrer 2022).

In 1970, Pateman defined as "pseudo-participation" a situation in which no participation in decision-making actually takes place: for decision-makers, the concern is to create a *feeling* of participation and openness, while retaining power in their own hands (Pateman 1970). Pateman, dealing with participation in industries, defines it as a situation in which participation is limited to an endorsement of a decision made elsewhere; for instance, a situation in which the supervisor instead of merely telling the employees of a decision, allows them to question him about it and to discuss it, but without changing the desired outcome. The risk with populism is then to have a "plebiscitary" or "pseudo" kind of participation.[8] On the side of actors, therefore, it is important to distinguish between rhetoric and practices of participation.

5.2 *Populist Actors Favouring Participation: Is it Just Rhetoric?*

A request of more participation, for instance, in party documents or in leaders' or representatives' discourse, does not automatically mean that more participation is requested by supporters (as shown in the research by Webb, Bowler and colleagues) or even that it is actually in the plans of populist parties themselves. It is then important to distinguish between rhetoric and practices (Kittilson and Scarrow 2003) of participation. Coherently with their claim that politics should be an expression of the general will of the people, populist

8 Research that counters this assumption undertaken by Zaslove et al. (2021) surprisingly finds that people who hold stronger populist attitudes are also more supportive of *deliberative* forms of participation.

actors can request more participation in a rhetorical or strategic attempt to give voters the impression that their voice will be heard. However, this doesn't mean that the narrative is not important. Writing about party reforms, Gauja (2017) acknowledged that the symbolism of change can be just as important as the substance. Narratives can indeed have an impact both on citizens' perceptions and on parties themselves. For instance, rhetoric, discourses, and symbols of participation can shape collective identities.

5.3 *What Is the Meaning of the Act of Participating?*

Looking at the demand side, a last question that is worth asking is related to the meaning given to participation by populist supporters. In this sense, an overlooked dimension is the one related to collective identities and identification. We have seen that one of the triggers of participation, often considered more in the studies on social movements than in the ones on parties in general and populism in particular, is the identification with a group. Therefore, it is worth asking if we can speak about a collective identity when we deal with populism. What are the dimensions of that collective identity? Is it just an anti-establishment identity (Meléndez and Rovira Kaltwasser 2019), or is it based in a desire to defend the identity of the people – whatever "people" can mean (Biancalana and Mazzoleni 2020)? And how can this identity be considered to be a trigger of participation? One insight is that populist ideas can "provide both identity and purpose [...], two important elements behind any process of political mobilization" (Anduiza, Guinjoan and Rico 2019, 110). Identity can thus mediate the relationship between populism and participation. One thing is certain – more study of this is needed.

References

Albertazzi, D. and McDonnell, D. (2015) *Populists in power*. London-New York: Routledge.

Anduiza, E., Guinjoan, M. and Rico, G. (2019) Populism, participation, and political equality. *European Political Science Review*, *11*(1), 109–124.

Aslanidis, P. (2016) Is populism an ideology? A refutation and a new perspective. *Political Studies*, *64*(1_suppl), 88–104.

Biancalana, C. (2022) *Political parties and the challenge of disintermediation: Rhetoric and practices of organizational change in Italy*. Baden-Baden: Nomos.

Biancalana, C. and Mazzoleni, O. (2020) Unifying and multiplying the people: The strategy of ambiguity in national-populist discourse within a cross-border area. *Nationalism and Ethnic Politics*, *26*(3), 279–298.

Biancalana, C. and Vittori, D. (2021) Cyber-parties' membership between empowerment and pseudo-participation: The cases of Podemos and Five Star Movement. In: Barberà, O., Sandri, G., Correa, P. and Rodríguez-Teruel, J. (eds.) *Digital parties: The challenges of online organisation and participation.* New York: Springer, 109–126.

Bobbio, L. (2005) La democrazia deliberativa nella pratica. *Stato e mercato, 25*(1), 67–88.

Böhmelt, T., Ezrow, L. and Lehrer, R. (2022) Populism and intra-party democracy. *European Journal of Political Research,* online first.

Bowler, S., Denemark, D., Donovan, T. and McDonnell, D. (2017) Right-wing populist party supporters: Dissatisfied but not direct democrats. *European Journal of Political Research, 56*(1), 70–91.

Caiani, M. and Graziano, P. (2019) Understanding varieties of populism in times of crises. *West European Politics, 42*(6), 1141–1158.

Canovan, M. (1999) Trust the people! Populism and the two faces of democracy. *Political Studies, 47*(1), 2–16.

Chadwick, A. (2007) Disintermediation. In: Bevir, M. (ed.) *Encyclopedia of governance.* Thousand Oaks: Sage Publications, 232–233.

Cotta, M. (1979) Il concetto di partecipazione politica: linee di un inquadramento teorico. *Italian Political Science Review/Rivista Italiana di Scienza Politica, 9*(2), 193–227.

Crozier, M. J., Huntington. S. P. and Watanuki, J. (1975) *The crisis of democracy: Report on the governability of democracies to the Trilateral Commission.* New York: New York University Press.

Dahl, R. A. (1971) *Polyarchy: Participation and opposition.* New Haven: Yale University Press.

de la Torre, C. (2010) *Populist seduction in Latin America.* Athens: Ohio University Press.

de La Torre, C. (2015) The contested meanings of insurrections, the sovereign people, and democracy in Ecuador, Venezuela, and Bolivia. In: de la Torre (ed.) *The promise and perils of populism: global perspectives.* Lexington: University Press of Kentucky, 349–371.

de la Torre, C. (2016) Populism and the politics of the extraordinary in Latin America. *Journal of Political Ideologies, 21*(2), 121–139.

de la Torre, C. and Mazzoleni, O. (2019) Do we need a minimum definition of populism? An appraisal of Mudde's conceptualization. *Populism, 2*(1), 79–95.

de Vreese, C. H., Esser, F., Aalberg, T., Reinemann, C. and Stanyer, J. (2018) Populism as an expression of political communication content and style: A new perspective. *internationalJournal of Press/Politics, 23*(4), 423–438.

Delwit, P. (2013) The end of voters in Europe? Electoral turnout in Europe since WWII. *Open Journal of Political Science, 3*(1), 44–52.

Deseriis, M. (2017) Direct parliamentarianism: An analysis of the political values embedded in Rousseau, the "operating system" of the Five Star Movement. *JeDEM – e-Journal of e- Democracy and Open Government*, 9(2), 47–67.

Easton, D. (1953) *The political system: An inquiry into the state of political science*. New York: Alfred A. Knopf.

Gauja, A. (2017) *Party reform: The causes, challenges, and consequences of organizational change*. Oxford: Oxford University Press.

Gerbaudo, P. (2018) Social media and populism: An elective affinity? *Media, Culture & Society*, 40(5), 745–753.

Gerbaudo, P. (2019) *The digital party: Political organisation and online democracy*. London: Pluto Press.

Grattan, L. (2016) *Populism's power: Radical grassroots democracy in America*. Oxford: Oxford University Press.

Hirschman, A. O. (1982) *Shifting involvements: Private interests and public action*. Princeton: Princeton University Press.

Huber, R. A. and Ruth, S. P. (2017) Mind the gap! Populism, participation and representation in Europe. *Swiss Political Science Review*, 23(4), 462–484.

Huber, R. A. and Schimpf, C. H. (2021) Populism and democracy: Theoretical and empirical considerations. In: Heinisch, R., Holtz-Bacha, C. and Mazzoleni, O. (eds.) *Political populism: Handbook of concepts, questions and strategies of research*. Baden-Baden: Nomos, 131–148.

Immerzeel, T. and Pickup, M. (2015) Populist radical right parties mobilizing "the people"? The role of populist radical right success in voter turnout. *Electoral Studies*, 40, 347–360.

Jacobs, K., Akkerman, A. and Zaslove, A. (2018) The voice of populist people? Referendum preferences, practices and populist attitudes. *Acta Politica*, 53(4), 517–541.

Jansen, R. S. (2011) Populist mobilization: A new theoretical approach to populism. *Sociological Theory*, 29(2), 75–96.

Jansen, R. S. (2017) *Revolutionizing repertoires*. Chicago: University of Chicago Press.

Kaase, M. and Marsh, A. (1979) Political action: A theoretical perspective. In: Barnes, S. H., Kaase, M., Allerback, K. R., Farah, B., Heunks, F., Inglehart, R., Jennings, M. K., Klingemann, H. D., Marsh, A. and Rosenmayr, L. (eds.) *Political action: Mass participation in five Western democracies*. Beverly Hills: Sage, 27–56.

Kittilson, M. C. and Scarrow, S. E. (2003) Political parties and the rhetoric and realities of democratization. In: Cain, B. E., Dalton, R. J. and Scarrow, S. E. (eds.) *Democracy transformed? Expanding political opportunities in advanced industrial democracies*. Oxford: Oxford University Press, 59–80.

Kriesi, H. (2014) The populist challenge. *West European Politics*, 37(2), 361–378.

Leininger, A. and Meijers, M. J. (2021) Do populist parties increase voter turnout? Evidence from over 40 years of electoral history in 31 European democracies. *Political Studies, 69*(3), 665–685.

Mair, P. (2002) Populist democracy vs party democracy. In: Mény, Y. and Surel, Y. (eds.) *Democracies and the populist challenge*. London: Palgrave Macmillan, 81–98.

Mazzoleni, G. (2008) Populism and the media. In: Albertazzi, D. and McDonnell, D. (eds.) *Twenty-first century populism: The spectre of Western European democracy*. London: Palgrave Macmillan, 49–64.

Meléndez, C. and Rovira Kaltwasser, C. (2019) Political identities: The missing link in the study of populism. *Party Politics, 25*(4), 520–533.

Mény, Y. and Surel, Y. (eds.) (2001) *Democracies and the populist challenge*. London: Palgrave Macmillan.

Moffitt, B. and Tormey, S. (2014) Rethinking populism: Politics, mediatisation and political style. *Political Studies, 62*(2), 381–397.

Mohrenberg, S., Huber, R. A. and Freyburg, T. (2021) Love at first sight? Populist attitudes and support for direct democracy. *Party Politics, 27*(3), 528–539.

Mosca, L. (2020) Democratic vision and online participatory spaces in the Italian Movimento 5 Stelle. *Acta politica, 55*(1), 1–18.

Mudde, C. (2004) The populist zeitgeist. *Government and Opposition, 39*(4), 541–563.

Mudde, C. (2007) *Populist radical right parties in Europe*. Cambridge: Cambridge University Press.

Mudde, C. and Rovira Kaltwasser, C. (2017) *Populism: A very short introduction*. Oxford: Oxford University Press.

Olson, M. (1965) *The logic of collective action: Public goods and the theory of groups*. Cambridge, MA: Harvard University Press.

Pateman, C. (1970) *Participation and democratic theory*. Cambridge: Cambridge University Press.

Pateman, C. (2012) Participatory democracy revisited. *Perspectives on Politics, 10*(1), 7–19.

Pauwels, T. (2014) *Populism in Western Europe: Comparing Belgium, Germany and the Netherlands*. London-New York: Routledge.

Pirro, A. L. and Portos, M. (2021) Populism between voting and non-electoral participation. *West European Politics, 44*(3), 558–584.

Pizzorno, A. (1983) Sulla razionalità della scelta democratica. *Stato e mercato, 7*, 3–46.

Raniolo, F. (2007) *La partecipazione politica*. Bologna: Il Mulino.

Rooduijn, M. and Akkerman, T. (2017) Flank attacks: Populism and left-right radicalism in Western Europe. *Party Politics, 23*(3), 193–204.

Rovira Kaltwasser, C. (2012) The ambivalence of populism: Threat and corrective for democracy. *Democratization, 19*(2), 184–208.

Taggart, P. (2000) *Populism*. Buckingham: Open University Press.

Taggart, P. (2018) Populism and "unpolitics". In: Fitzi, G., Mackert, J. and Turner, B. S. (eds.) *Populism and the crisis of democracy: Volume 1: Concepts and theory*. London-New York: Routledge, 79–87.

Teorel, J., Torcal, M. and Montero, J. R. (2007) Political participation: Mapping the terrain. In: Van Deth, J. W., Montero, J. R. and Westholm, A. (eds.) *Citizenship and involvement in European democracies: A comparative analysis*. London-New York: Routledge, 358–381.

Tormey, S. (2015) *The end of representative politics*. Hoboken, New Jersey: John Wiley & Sons.

Trüdinger, E. M. and Bächtiger, A. (2022) Attitudes vs. actions? Direct-democratic preferences and participation of populist citizens. *West European Politics*, online first.

Urbinati, N. (2015) A revolt against intermediary bodies. *Constellations*, *22*(4), 477–486.

Urbinati, N. (2019) *Me the people*. Cambridge, MA: Harvard University Press.

Verba, S., Schlozman, K. L. and Brady, H. (1995) *Voice and equality: Civic voluntarism in American politics*. Cambridge: Cambridge University Press.

Vittori, D. (2017) Podemos and the Five Stars Movement: Divergent trajectories in a similar crisis. *Constellations*, *24*(3), 324–338.

Waisman, C. H. (2021) The generative contexts of populist regimes. In: Heinisch, R., Holtz-Bacha, C. and Mazzoleni, O. (eds.) *Political populism: Handbook of concepts, questions and strategies of research*. Baden-Baden: Nomos, 149–161.

Webb, P. (2013) Who is willing to participate? Dissatisfied democrats, stealth democrats and populists in the United Kingdom. *European Journal of Political Research*, *52*(6), 747–772.

Werner, H. and Jacobs, K. (2021) Are populists sore losers? Explaining populist citizens' preferences for and reactions to referendums. *British Journal of Political Science*, online first.

Weyland, K. (2001) Clarifying a contested concept: Populism in the study of Latin American politics. *Comparative politics*, *34*(1), 1–22.

Zaslove, A., Geurkink, B., Jacobs, K. and Akkerman, A. (2021) Power to the people? Populism, democracy, and political participation: a citizen's perspective. *West European Politics*, *44*(4), 727–751.

CHAPTER 8

Populist Leadership

Carlos de la Torre

1 Introduction

Since Gino Germani wrote his pioneer comparison between Peronism and fascism in the 1950s the question of leadership has been at the centre of the scholarship on populism. In dialogue with the work of classical sociologists such as Max Weber and Emile Durkheim, and with his contemporaries like Talcott Parsons, Germani (1971) focused on the socio-economic causes of populism, on the dislocations of modernization that produced masses in the state of anomie, and on charismatic leadership. Critics questioned his view of followers as irrational masses and used Marxism to focus on the class alliances of populism (Murmis and Portantiero 1971). Historians and historically oriented social scientists built on Laclau's (1977) path-breaking early work to analyze the discourse of populist leaders (Braun 1985; de la Torre 1993; Álvarez Junco 2002).

The emergence of right-wing European populist parties in the 1980s and the renaissance of right-wing and left-wing populism in Latin America at the turn of the twenty-first century drew the attention of an increasing number of political scientists, communication scholars, and sociologists. Depending on their geographical focus and epistemological orientations, scholars built on theories of the relative autonomy of politics (Weyland 2001), Freedman's theory of ideology (Mudde 2004), deconstructionism (Laclau 2005), and performance theories (Moffitt 2016; Ostiguy 2017). After Trumpism and the realization that some of the largest democracies such as India, Brazil, the United States, and the Philippines were in populist hands, there was a proliferation of books and academic articles on this previously marginal topic of research and theorization.

Despite the surge in the number of publications there is no agreement on a definition nor on the role of leadership in populism. This chapter reconstructs how different approaches view the role of the leader. After mapping these debates, Max Weber's concept of charismatic leadership is reconstructed to make sense of how passions, emotions, and interests are intertwined in populism. It then distinguishes populist from other types of leaders in current audience democracies where personalities are more important than party platforms. The chapter distinguishes right and left populism, uses examples

 | DOI:10.1163/9789004679016_010

from the Americas and Europe, and differentiates populism as movements and parties challenging power, populism in office, and populist regimes.

Populism is studied as a gradation based on performance and discourse. The chapter distinguishes light from full-blown populists. The former, similar to other leaders of what Bernard Manin (1997) theorized as audience democracies, put personalities ahead of platforms and occasionally use populist tropes and styles. Full-blown populists politicize all social interactions as the confrontation between antagonist camps and are considered what George MacGregor Burns (1978, 37) defined as transformational leaders. They "raise the level of human conduct and ethical aspiration of both leader and led, and thus has a transforming effect on both". Whereas light populists accept the rules and norms of the constitutional democratic game, full-blown populists have missions that could not be constrained by institutions, procedures, and norms that they consider protect the power of elites. Hence, when they get to office they clash with the institutional fabric of constitutional democracy, with the private media, and with the institutions of civil society that they aim to regulate. Well-functioning institutions and strong public spheres and social movements might restrain their projects of regime change. Yet when the institutional framework of democracy is in crises, and citizens do not trust parties, congress, the courts, and the media, a populist in office might attempt to bring about regime change by transforming constitutions, adjusting electoral rules, and enacting laws to supervise the media, universities, social movements, and non-governmental organizations.

2 Is the Leader Central to Populism?

The first studies of populism were influenced by interpretations of fascism. Hans Gerth (1940, 418), for example, described Hitler's personal charisma in the following terms: "[H]e does not follow already existing rules; he creates new ones. He is a revolutionary who does not accept the existing order but sets up instead an order of his own. His authority is not a delegated authority but one residing in himself." In contrast to Gerth, Talcott Parsons was more interested in the social conditions that produced charismatic movements. He combined Weber's theory of rationalization with Durkheim's notion of anomie. He argued that rapid social change makes it particularly difficult for large numbers of people to have sufficiently settled routines and modes of orientation. "The accompaniment of this is in turn is widespread psychological 'insecurity' and anxiety. Charismatic movements of various sorts seem to function in the situation as mechanism of 'reintegration' which give large numbers of disorganized, insecure people, a definite orientation, give 'meaning' to their lives" (Parsons 1942a, 76). Fascist movements, he argued, involved a large number of common people "imbued with a high emotional, indeed often fanatical, zeal for a cause. [...] Though their primary orientation is political, have many features in common with great religious movements in history" (1942b, 138).

Parsons reduced the socio-psychological to pathological and irrational reactions to stress provoked by rapid social change. He wrote: "[I]t is a generalization well established in social sciences that neither individuals nor societies can undergo major structural changes without the likelihood of producing a considerable element of 'irrational' behavior" (Parsons 1955, 127). The expected responses to the stress produced by major structural transformations were anxiety, aggression focused on what was felt to be the source of strain, and a desire to re-establish a fantasy where everything will be all right, preferably as it was before the disturbing situation.

Parsons viewed followers as irrational, formless, and unstable masses. He developed binary oppositions such as organization-disorganization, rational-irrational, and normal-pathological. Gino Germani (1971; 1978) built on Parsonian modernization theory to compare fascism and national populism in societies undergoing abrupt transitions to modernity. He argued that rapid processes of modernization such as urbanization and industrialization produced masses in a state of anomie that became available for top-down mobilization. He maintained that the social base of Peronism was the new working class, made up of recent migrants who were not socialized into working-class culture and therefore could be mobilized from the top by a charismatic leader. Germani interpreted national populism as a phase in the transition to modernity that incorporated the excluded and gave them a sense of participation in heteronomous authoritarian movements controlled from above.

Differently from breakdown theories that focus on processes of social change, political-strategic concepts centre their attention on strategy and action (Barr 2019, 45). Kurt Weyland was a theorist who argued for the relative autonomy of politics from the economy and society. He defined populism as a "political strategy through which a personalistic leader seeks or exercises government power based on direct, unmediated, uninstitutionalized support from large numbers of mostly unorganized followers" (2001, 14). In a later piece he wrote that "the clear predominance of a powerful leader is a cornerstone of populism" (Weyland 2017, 56). The main goal of populist leaders is to get and to stay in power. Hence, they are more pragmatic than ideological.

Whereas Weyland focuses on strategic action, definitions of populism as a political style emphasize its dramaturgical dimensions. Populism, they argue, is a style of doing politics based on performances that "flaunt the low" (Ostiguy 2017). If elites appropriate for themselves the high considered as good manners (refined sophisticated tastes and styles, technocratic and rational discourses), populists use words and performances that shock elites as vulgar, distasteful, low, and unlearned. Moffitt (2016, 51–52) argues that leaders "should be our main focus when studying the phenomenon, given that they are the figures that ultimately 'do' populism".

The ideational approach does not consider that the role of the leader is a key definitional attribute of populism. Mudde (2004, 543) defined it as "an ideology that considers society to be ultimately separated into two homogeneous and antagonistic groups, 'the pure people' versus 'the corrupt elite,' and which argues that politics should be an expression of the *volonté générale* (general will) of the people". Mudde and Rovira Kaltwasser (2012, 8–9) wrote that "populism is in essence a form of moral politics, as the distinction between 'the elite' and 'the people' is first and foremost moral (i.e. pure vs. corrupt), not situational (e.g. position of power), socio-cultural (e.g. ethnicity, religion), or socio-economic (e.g. class)". If populism is a set of ideas about politics it encompasses political parties, and social movements like the Indignados in Spain who did not have leaders.

Ernesto Laclau (2005) sees populism as a gradation. Instead of analyzing the content of its ideology, its policies, or its class base, he focuses on its formal logic. He argues that populism is a logic of articulation that aims to rupture existing institutional systems, builds enemies, and reduces political and social conflicts to the confrontation between two antagonistic camps. Populism creates strong identities of the people by constructing them as antagonistic to a series of enemies. The populist leader, according to Laclau, encompasses "a *multiplicity* of concrete, very different meanings – not necessarily coherent amongst themselves from the standpoint of theoretical logic, but derived from games of oppositions, historically and contextually situated" (Ostiguy and Moffitt 2021, 55).

Because conceptual debates about the role of the leader in populism might not be resolved it is more fruitful to focus on it as a distinct practice, as something that is done, particularly when leaders get to power and attempt to create regimes. In what follows I offer a middle-range, ideal-typical definition of populism as a set of practices.[1]

1 For a discussion of ideal types, see the chapter by Mazzoleni.

2.1 *Creating Enemies*

Populists do not face political rivals with whom one could disagree; they confront existential enemies. They are different from fascists, who physically eliminate their enemies. Populists do not kill their opponents. When seeking power, their antagonist is broadly cast as the establishment (Urbinati 2019). Once in power, their enemies become political, economic, and cultural elites who supposedly hold real power.

Populists differ on whom they construct as their enemies (de la Torre 2019, 9–12). Right-wing populists often face two types of enemies: cosmopolitan elites (above) and dependents of colour (below). Racist arguments are used to cast whole populations not only as inferior but as inherently culturally different and inassimilable. If the right politicized fears to the danger of contamination of culture, religion, and race, the left focuses on the resentments produced by socio-economic and political exclusions, and by systemic inequalities. They politicize anger, indignation, and envy to cast the elites as servants of imperialism and the IMF in the Global South, or the Troika made up of the European Central Bank, the EU commission, and the IMF in Europe.

2.2 Populism's *Pars Pro Toto* Dynamic

Populists do not aim to give power to everyone in the population. They aim to empower only a section of the population, – the excluded ones who, according to the leader, represent the right and truthful people. The logic of populism excludes anyone whom the leader does not consider to be part of "the people".

2.3 *Populist Leadership*

Takis Pappas (2019, 106) writes that "extraordinary leadership thus emerges as the most important predictor for populism's overall successful performance". Similarly, Urbinati (2019) argues that for populism to move from the margins of the political system to the centre of power it needs a leader. A leader is built as the authentic and truthful personification of the right people. Populist inclusion is on the condition of accepting the guidance of the wise leader.

Embodying the people means that the leader performs their ordinariness by acting and talking like common folk. Simultaneously, leaders perform their extraordinariness by their physical or mental attributes, their successes in non-political realms, and by their alleged dedication to work for their people's redemption. Populist leaders are in the democratic camp in so far as the vote is their source of legitimacy and elections can be lost. Yet simultaneously, full-blown populist leaders who are constructed and see themselves as redeemers consider that they are carrying projects of irreversible transformation that cannot be constraint by constitutional rules and procedures. If they lose the popular vote, they claim fraud because the people can only vote for their avatars and not for their enemies.

2.4 *Differentiating Populisms*

Not all populisms are the same. As several chapters of this volume argue, right-wing and left-wing populisms are different. Light and full-blown populists should also be distinguished. The former occasionally use populist tropes and discourses. For example, Lula da Silva – who is not a populist – strategically uses a populist language of the people against the oligarchy when he engages in conflicts with the opposition (Panizza 2013). Light populists are almost indistinguishable from other politicians in contemporary audience democracies that appeal to trust in their personas and use the mass media to directly appeal to electors. They politicize failures of democracy staying within the parameter of existing constitutional norms and procedures. Full-blown populists like Hugo Chávez or Donald Trump aim to rupture existing institutions by polarizing society and the polity into two camps of enemies and by constructing a leader as the symbol of all the demands for change and renewal. When seeking power, full-blown populists appeal to constituencies that the elites despise or ignore. They use institutional mechanisms and mass mobilization to try to bring change using words and performances to shock and disturb the limits of the permissible and to confront conventions. Once in office, they see existing norms, procedures, and institutions as constraints on the will of the people, which they claim to embody.

Populists attempting to achieve power, populists in office, and populist regimes are not the same (de la Torre 2019). When challenging power, populists politicize issues that other politicians ignore or do not address. Once in office, populists follow a similar playbook involving attempting to concentrate power in their office (such as the presidency), change electoral rules, revise existing or create new constitutions, enter into wars with the private media, and aim to regulate civil society. The success of populists in revamping institutions and the normative foundations of democracy depend on the context in which they emerge. Strong civil society institutions and organizations and solid media corporations where professionals have autonomy to pursue watchdog journalism often constrain populists. When institutions and norms are in crisis because democracy does not deliver and inequality and corruption thrive, populists in office change constitutions, concentrate power in the presidency, and control the public sphere and organizations of civil society. Populist regimes combine a democratic commitment to elections as the only legitimate tool to elect and remove politicians with undemocratic views of political rivals as enemies, and of the leader as the incarnation of the people above institutions and laws.

3 Populist Charismatic Leadership

Charisma has been used to analyze populist leadership, yet, with few exceptions (Zúquete 2007; 2008; Garrido 2017; Burbano de Lara 2019; Pappas 2019; de la Torre 2021), the affinities between charisma and populism have rarely been theorized. Charisma is a social relation and not a possession of an individual: "who counts as charismatic depends on the audience" (Grint 2014 198). When studying charisma, it is a challenge not to reduce followers to irrational masses or charisma to the attribute of an individual. In what follows, Weber's notion of charisma is reconstructed to analyze populist leadership as a social relationship. The charismatic social link often encompasses most of the following dimensions.

3.1 *The Redemptive Mission of the Leader*

Differently from rational bureaucratic leaders whose legitimacy lies in their office, "the bearer of charisma enjoys loyalty and authority by virtue of a mission believed to be embodied in him" (Weber 1978, 1117). Charismatic leaders become moral archetypes, exemplary figures who ought to be followed (Zúquete 2007). The leader must prove their charisma "in the eyes of their adherents" (Weber 1978, 1112). Having performed a heroic act often proves their charisma. Hugo Chávez's unsuccessful coup attempt in 1992 against President Carlos Andrés Pérez transformed him into the symbol of the fight against the corrupt neoliberal political establishment. His military red beret became an icon of defiance against a failed two-party system, and many Venezuelans started to wear it proudly.

In the absence of a heroic performance, leaders and their close circle of followers try to mythologize their achievements and life stories. Pedro Zúquete (2007) writes that Jean Marie Le Pen's inner circle worked as apostles to sanctify his image. In the eyes of the militants of the Front National Jean Marie Le Pen appeared "as a true authentic leader. His life story, his role as the founder of the party, and all the perceived campaign of hatred against him dramatically bolster his leadership credentials. […] He offers a powerful example to follow and to emulate" (Zúquete 2007, 106).

Populist charismatic leaders, even when they don't, claim to come from humble and working-class origins and to be like regular people. Due to their hard work, superior intelligence, and interest in serving their nation and their people, they transformed their ordinariness into extraordinariness. Eva Perón was an illegitimate child born in the province of Buenos Aires in Argentina. Like many of her contemporaries, she migrated to the city. She became a radio and movie actress before marrying General Juan Perón. When she was the first lady (1946–1952), she wore expensive designer dresses and jewellery while dedicating her life to serve the poor by creating a charity foundation, advocating for women's right to vote, and giving incendiary speeches against the oligarchy. Evita was transformed into the Mater Dolorosa of the workers and the poor, an extraordinary woman, and even a saint.

Often performing common acts (like sharing food with the poor) proves the uniqueness of populist politicians. Joseph Estrada, an actor who became the president of the Philippines, was unlike other middle-class politicians, who saw the poor as repugnant and as carriers of disease. He shared food with them. His ordinariness showed his extraordinariness (Garrido 2017).

3.2 *Charisma and Myths*

Charismatic leaders invoke and are linked to myths. Some are religiously inspired, others more secular. The persona of Hugo Chávez symbolized the myths of Simón Bolívar, the liberator of Venezuela and Latin America, and of Jesus Christ, the Savior. His political movement, the new constitution, and Venezuela were re-baptized as Bolivarian. His followers saw him as the carrier of Bolívar's unfinished projects of national and continental liberation. Chávez compared his leadership to Jesus Christ's and referred to Jesus as "my commander in chief" (Lindholm and Zúquete 2010, 33). In 1999 he asserted: "true love for other human beings is measured by whether you can die for others; and here we are ready to die for others" (Torres 2009, 230). His prophetic words of following the example of Jesus, who gave his life to liberate his people, were dramatically manifested when Chávez compared his agony with cancer with the passion of Christ. During a religious service broadcast by television during Holy Week in 2012, he prayed out loud:

> Give me life. […] Christ give me your crown of thorns. Give it to me that I bleed. Give me your cross. […] Give me life because I still need to do things for this people and motherland. Do not take me. Give me your cross, your thorns, your blood. I will carry them but give me life. Christ my Lord. Amen.
>
> DE LA TORRE 2019, 14

His followers erected Chávez into a saint-like figure with the power to heal. In 1999, an elderly woman grabbed him by the arm to beg, "Chávez help me, my son has paralysis". A crying young man stopped him outside the door of Caracas Cathedral and told him, "Chávez help me, I have two sons that are dying of hunger and I do not want to become a delinquent, save me from this inferno" (Torres 2009, 229). After his death, his handpicked successor Nicolás

Maduro attempted to consecrate Chávez into a secular saint. Chávez was buried in a newly built shrine, a pantheon that "symbolizes the renaissance of the homeland and the immeasurable life of the Eternal Commandant". His coffin has the inscription "Supreme Commander of the Bolivarian Revolution". Above his sarcophagus in the centre there is a portrait of Bolívar the Father with images of Chávez his Son on its right and left sides (González Trejo 2017, 139–141).

Donald Trump triumphed in two mythical and almost religious arenas of American capitalism: the business world and mass entertainment. From the beginning of his 2016 presidential campaign, he referred to his own extraordinariness. "We need a truly great leader now. We need a leader that wrote *The art of the deal.* [...] We need somebody that can take the brand of the United States and make it great again." Billionaire Donald Trump flaunted his wealth; his name became a brand for skyscrapers, hotels, golf courses, casinos, steaks, and other commodities; he owned the Miss Universe franchise; and with the TV show *The Apprentice* that he hosted for fourteen seasons, he became a media celebrity. People at his rallies told ethnographer Arlie Hochschild (2016, 226) that they were amazed to "be in the presence of such a man".

3.3 *Mass Meetings and the Charisma of Rhetoric*

Weber (1978, 1130) wrote that stump speeches prioritize rhetoric over content and are "purely emotional". Rhetoric "has the same meaning as the street parades and festivals: to imbue the masses with the notion of the party's power and confidence in victory and, above all, to convince them of the leader's charismatic qualifications". Weber also differentiated between scientific and political speeches, "the enterprise of the prophet is closer to that of the popular leader (*demagogos*) or the political publicist than that of the teacher" (1978, 445).

Mass meetings are the arenas in which the leader is recognized and acclaimed by followers. These are the sites for "the recognition on the part of those subject to authority which is decisive for the validity of charisma" (Weber 1978, 242). With the repetition of songs, slogans and banners, mass meetings aim to create political identities or to at least differentiate the in-group from the out-group. In these meetings the people validate the authority of the leader and create horizontal links of belonging to the populist camp against a series of enemies. For example, in the 1940s Colombian leader Jorge Gaitán closed all his rallies by shouting "*Pueblo!*" ("People!"), and the crowds responded with, "Against the oligarchy!" (Braun 1985, 103).

Despite innovative uses of television to create media spectacles and social media like Twitter, Trump's 2016 and 2020 campaigns made ample use of mass rallies. He claimed to be "the only man without a guitar that can fill a stadium" (Wolff 2021, 201). His rallies resembled sport events where people had fun in tailgate parties, with a one-man show. Trump danced, cracked jokes, insulted rivals, and used violence to mark frontiers between his people and the out-groups and to arouse passions of anger. He often said, "Isn't this more fun than a regular boring rally?"

Love is the link between leader and followers. Jean Marie Le Pen presented himself as the "patriot of love," and the Front National as a community of love. Donald Trump loved "the poorly educated" – understood as those who work with their hands and produce tangible things (Berezin 2017). Hugo Chávez always talked about how much he loved his people. In the 2009 campaign to change the constitution with a referendum to allow for his permanent re-election, the following reasons were given to vote for Chávez's proposals: "because Chávez loves us, and we have to repay his love; because Chávez loves us and will not harm us; because Chávez and we are one" (Torres 2009, 231).

The triad of victimhood, resentment, and redemption characterize populist narratives (Pappas 2019, 114). Chávez's people, for example, were the victims of neoliberal political parties that gave priority to the dictates of the IMF over the well-being of their citizens. He politicized feelings or resentment to the oligarchy, empire, traditional politicians, and the bourgeois media. Whereas political neoliberal elites and their cronies became the symbols of oppression, he was transformed into the redeemer of the people.

3.4 *The Body of the Leader*

Weber (1978, 1112) wrote that charismatic leaders are "bearers of specific gifts of the body and mind that were considered 'supernatural' (in the sense that not everybody could have access to them)". The leaders claim their superiority because of naturally endowed powers, revolutionary ideas, or the capacity to become the centre of the social order. It seems that Hugo Chávez never slept during his long presidential tenure. He called advisors and ministers at any time of the night, started his days very early and finished late at night, claiming that he was always working to liberate the people. He created a new political ideology, socialism of the twenty-first century, and aimed to export it to Latin America and worldwide.

The body of the leader is omnipresent. The sociologist Juan José Sebreli (2008) explained that for seven years Eva Perón was everywhere. Her face was on thousands of billboards in streets, the state radio broadcasted her speeches daily, and she had a prominent role in the weekly news reels shown in all Argentinean movie theatres. In the same way, Hugo Chávez and Rafael Correa in Ecuador put their images and slogans in visible spots along highways and cities. They used mandatory TV and radio messages to constantly broadcast their images and to make their bodies seen in newspapers, on television, and on social media, as they were constantly on Twitter and Facebook. They had weekly television and radio shows where Chávez talked for about six hours, and Correa for about two and a half. Similarly, Donald Trump's image was everywhere. Pundits constantly discussed and analyzed his latest tweet. The obsessive needs of television for politics as entertainment met with the compulsive need of the populist to become a permanent feature of citizens' everyday lives.

The body of the leader is a site of antagonistic confrontation. Latin American societies that overvalue white skin tones were polarized by discussions about the colour of skin and the non-white features of some populist leaders. White and elite Venezuelans were repelled by Chávez's body, and especially by the visibility of his poor and non-white supporters. They called Chávez a monkey and made fun of his supporters' poor dental health. Evo Morales's *chompa* (sweater) and hairstyle were discussed in the Bolivian media as not fit for a head of state. Similarly, the Philippine middle class focused on Joseph Estrada's persona as the subject of an entire class of "Erap jokes" having to do with his alleged dim-wittedness, his infidelities, and his inarticulacy (Garrido 2017, 655). As in a play of mirror images, followers viewed favourably what elites considered to be affronts and denigrations of decent society. Hillary Clinton's remark that Trump's supporters were a "basket of deplorables" backfired and emboldened the millionaire's base of support.

The leader offers his body to be touched by followers. Estrada, Trump, Chávez, Correa, and Morales constantly toured their nations and met, talked, and were touched by common people. Populists like Trump and Berlusconi bragged about their hyper-masculinities. They claimed superiority by their successes in the business world and in "conquering" women. Joseph Estrada used his cinematographic roles as a Robin Hood-like character to claim to be the benefactor of the poor. Fernando Collor used his success in the world of sports. Juan Perón, Jean Marie Le Pen, and Hugo Chávez presented themselves as brilliant military men who sacrificed their careers for their nations.

The image most populist leaders share is their claim to be the fathers of their homelands. Getulio Vargas claimed to be "the father of the poor", while Lázaro Cárdenas was "Tata [Father] Lázaro". During his campaigns, Trump represented the image of a good father and surrounded himself with his children. Once in office, he named his daughter and son-in-law political advisers with almost unrestricted access to the White House. This millionaire patriarch promised to gather under his wise tutelage all of those who uncritically accepted his guidance. The father metaphor "turns citizens into permanent children. It turns a politician into someone who understands the interests of citizens – even when they do not – and who may punish wayward children who fail to recognize their wisdom" (Kampwirth 2010, 12). The job of a father never ends, and populists from Perón to Chávez and Morales attempted to stay in power indefinitely.

Female populist leaders, different from men, must "grapple with their own gender in ways that no male politician has to do" (Casullo 2019, 65). If she chooses the image as "a mother and wife, she can be deemed as too soft; if she tries to leverage her good looks, she might be considered unserious or frivolous; finally, if she chooses not to use a gendered appeal, she is going to be deemed as cold, unapproachable, and shrill" (ibid., 66). Sarah Palin and Cristina Kirchner combined images of the tough woman and strong politician with glamorous femininity.

3.5 *Populist Identities*

Weber (1978, 1116) argued that charisma revolutionizes people from within. Populist identities generated by charismatic movements could transform the attitudes and world views of followers, or at least of the intimate circle of close supporters that Eatwell (2002) calls coterie charisma. To be a Peronist, a Chavista, a militant of the Front National, or a Trumpist means to have a vision of politics and society in which all conflicts are dramatized as antagonistic confrontations between two camps. Peronist and Chavista identities lasted over time because these movements institutionalized charisma into parties and organizations of civil society. The longevity of populist parties is explained by organization and institutionalization (Heinisch and Mazzoleni 2016).

Populist organizations foster identities, a sense of community, and sometime give a purpose and even a mission to followers. Jean-Marie Le Pen argued that the militants of the Front National were the "true liberators of France" whose mission is to enlighten and unite those who are in the darkness (Zúquete 2007, 43). Since its founding, the militants of the Front National have seen "themselves as the only ones who have not deserted the people, only they have remained faithful to the mystical nation" (Lindholm and Zúquete 2010, 75). The Front and later the Rassemblement National organized rituals to build a community of militant believers. These include the yearly tribute to Joan of Arc, the celebration of the colours of France, summer schools, and mass rallies and feasts. These rituals reinforce feelings of belonging. For its activists their party is a community of patriots who are under siege by the enemies of the fatherland. They play key roles in mobilizing the vote and spreading the party's ideology. Their duty is not only to convince but to convert. Jean-Marie Le Pen asserted that the militant "has to recruit others who in turn recruit others in order to make a snowball that will end up to be the majority" (Zúquete 2007, 104).

Chávez used nationalists and religious symbols to portray the people of Venezuela as a community of patriots with the mission to liberate the motherland. "Let's be like Christ, let's be like Bolívar, let's get rid of everything, of any personal ambition, and let's give everything for this revolution, for this people, for this love, for this hope" (quoted in Zúquete 2008, 106). Lucia Michelutti (2017, 241) coined the term "mini-Chávez" to describe how local leaders of Chavista organizations "replicated and routinized Chávez's charisma by performing his divine kinship repertoire (made up of words and government programs) at the local level". Mini-Chávezes were at the front of a Bolivarian civil society whose members saw themselves as his sons and daughters, a moral community with the duty to support the revolution and perpetuate his legacy. "In his last public appearance, on December 8, 2012, Chávez told the crowd, 'We are all Chávez'" (Michelutti 2017, 244).

4 Leadership under Audience Democracies

Populism emerged in Europe and the United States in the nineteenth century, but populists first achieved power in Latin America in the 1930s and 1940s.[2] They created personalists parties and even when leaders attempted to create ideologies like Perón's *justicialismo*, the whims of the leader had priority over concrete projects or proposals.

In most of the West until the 1970s ideological mass parties were predominant. These parties had "a mass base which contributes to the functioning of the party both financially and with its political militancy; a large and permanent bureaucracy; a highly hierarchical and centralized organizational structure; a capillary territorial presence [...] and an explicit and persistent ideological orientation" (Gerbaudo 2019, 31). Bernard Manin argued that when the mass parties entered in crises the nature of political representation changed. He coined the term "audience democracy" to make sense of these changes. Under audience democracy there is a personalization of representation as the leader uses television to seek direct links with electors, personalities have priority over platforms, and "media experts take the place of party activists and party bureaucrats" (Manin 1997, 220). The metaphors of stage and audience better account for this new type of democratic representation.

2 See Álvarez Junco (2002) on Spain and Hofstadter (1955) on the United States.

Two types of audience parties have emerged. The first is the neoliberal television party that resembles a media or marketing company. Full-time bureaucrats and party militants were replaced by experts in media marketing and communication that appeal to voters as depoliticized consumers. The telegenic qualities of a leader take priority over platforms or ideologies. An example of neoliberal television parties is Silvio Berlusconi, the media mogul who dominated Italian politics and served as prime minister in 1994, 2001–2006, and 2008–2011.

As a reaction to these transformations, citizens demanded increasing direct participation without mediation. Digital parties like the Five Star Movement and Podemos adopted the platform logic of social media to seek the direct participation of citizens. Despite their promises to use technology to increase participation, digital parties recur to plebiscitary democracy, as members ratify the decision of the leadership (see Biancalana's chapter). In the absence of mediations provided by bureaucrats and militants, the leader becomes the embodiment of the party.

Under audience democracy most politicians, including light populists, personalize politics and occasionally use populist tropes. Full-blown populists perform populism to a different degree when they act as if it is their mission to redeem their people. Because their goals are colossal, they do not feel constrained by institutions and norms. Full-blown populists like Chávez or Trump have a sense of urgency to overhaul the existing order to create a new one to liberate the people. Populist leadership is based on embodiment and identification where the leader is the only voice and the projection of the ideals of followers. Hence populist leaders act as the only authorized mouth of the authentic people who trust and even adore their leader. Yet, their leadership must be validated and recognized in elections that in theory could be lost.

Institutions often tame wannabe full populists. The leaders of Podemos, for example, gave up their more ambitious proposals inspired by left Latin American populist experiences of convening a constitutional assembly to "re-found" all political institutions. In contrast, when the political institutions were in crises in Venezuela and Ecuador, Chávez and Correa constantly confronted and manufactured enemies, enacted new constitutions to concentrate power into their hands, used elections to marginalize traditional elites, and inserted cronies into the justice system and other institutions of accountability.

5 Conclusions

Engaging classical and contemporary theorists, this chapter reconstructed the role of the leader in different conceptual approaches to populism. It agrees with approaches that consider that a strong and/or charismatic leader helps to move populists from the margins to the centre of politics and to get to power. The chapter follows Weber to analyze populist leadership as a social process. Populist leaders have missions. They are linked to religious or secular national myths. They use mass meetings and the media to build identities polarizing society into friend and enemy. The body of the leader becomes an object of confrontation or identification. Populists imagine the people to be a homogeneous body, yet, unlike fascists (who abolish elections), populists claim legitimacy by winning challenges that they portray as gargantuan battles between the forces of oppression and redemption. Under populism, elections are used to renew the emotional, rational, and mystical bonds between the leader and the citizens. Followers and opponents give different meanings to a leader. For example, for the Fox News crowd Trump

> is a hero with the *business nous* to solve problems and the *cojones* to cut through the usual way politicians speak and "say it like it is"; for the online Make America Great Again crowd, he's an A-grade troll who has an unassailable ability to stir up and torment liberals; for the alt-right, he's a coded white nationalist; while in terms of his opponents, for MSNBC viewers, he's arguably the greatest threat the American republican project has ever faced, and for the online left, he's a symbol of the decline of America and a proto-fascist.
>
> OSTIGUY AND MOFFITT 2021, 65

This chapter illustrates that leadership is a social relation, and that all leaders but especially those who put their personality ahead of platforms and parties need to be recognized as such. Writing on charisma, Weber (1978, 1114) annotated: "[T]he holder may lose his charisma, he may feel 'forsaken by his God' as Jesus did on the cross, it may appear to his followers that 'his powers have left him'." In order not to feel abandoned by their electors, leaders constantly measure their popularity with opinion polls and focus groups. They know that their approval is volatile and they must constantly prove and perform their leadership in order to be accepted by their electors. The fluctuations of their popularity and the fact that electors are not passive observers that delegate power after an election, increases uncertainty and reinforces the attempts of leaders to be perceived as exceptional figures, and even to try to manufacture their charisma. Yet not all leaders succeed, and electors do not always recognize their leadership and even less their charisma.

The chapter shows that not all strong leaders are charismatic. MacGregor Burns (1978, 37) differentiated strong leaders who command authority and obedience from other types of transforming leader who, similar to charismatic leaders, have a transubstantiating effect on the leader and the led. Not all charismatic leaders are populists. José Figueres, for example, who was president of Costa Rica on three occasions (1948–1949, 1953–1958, and 1970–1974) created autonomous institutions and did not build a personalist party (Roniger 2019). Barack Obama, while charismatic, did not put himself ahead of constitutional procedures or norms, nor did he transform rivals into enemies.

The notion of charisma is not the anathema of organization, and only those populists who built organizations that lasted over time have been able to enter the succession of leaders. The Peronist Party and the Front National, which became the Rassemblement National, successfully changed leaders. When populists did not build organizations in civil society nor political parties, their movement disappeared when the leader passed away. Velasquismo ceased to exist after the death of their caudillo, José María Velasco Ibarra, who was president of Ecuador five times (1934–1935, 1944–1946, 1952–1956, 1960–1961, and 1968–1972).

The chapter also illustrates that not all populists are the same. Right- and left-wingers differ in how they construct the people and its enemies using ethnic or class categories (see Roberts's contribution to this volume) and on whether they promise more democracy or a return to an imaginary past of law and order. Light populists often reinvigorate democracy by raising issues that other politicians ignore, or by politicizing apathetic or disengaged citizens while accepting existing constitutional norms and procedures. Full-blown populists like Hugo Chávez, Juan Perón, Donald Trump, or Rafael Correa performed populism to delegitimize existing democratic institutions, norms, and procedures with the aim of building a different type of political system. Institutions, supranational institutions, and political cultures could tame wannabe full-blown populists as illustrated by the examples of Pablo Iglesias of Podemos and Alexis Tsipras of Syriza, which eventually became part of the establishment. Even though Trump attacked the legitimacy of democratic institutions, he was unable to destroy them.

When institutions are weak, polarization prevails, and leaders can prove their charisma in office by solving acute crises. They perform and act as full-blown populists constantly manufacturing enemies, polarizing society, and claiming that they only they can redeem their nations. Consequently, they delegitimize constitutional norms and procedures, transform politics into confrontations between two antagonistic camps, politicize all social interactions, and build up themselves into a leader who is a redeemer. Their rivals respond by polarizing society into the struggle between two antagonistic camps, and in the name of democracy they often try to remove populists – even by using military coups, as in Venezuela in 2002, Thailand in 2006 and 2014, Turkey in 2016, and Bolivia in 2019 (de la Torre and Srisa-Nga 2021, 120–127).

As long as elections determine who gets to wield power legitimately, populist hybrid regimes remain in the democratic camp. Yet under these regimes power is concentrated in the presidency, institutions of horizontal and social accountability are weakened (see Peruzzotti's chapter in this book), democratic rivals become enemies, and democratic conviviality is replaced by struggles between over-politicized and over-polarized citizens. Populist hybrid regimes could evolve into dictatorships or democracy might be reinstated, but the historical legacy of populists in power is one of polarization and democratic erosion.

References

Álvarez Junco, J. (2002) *The emergence of mass politics in Spain: Populist demagoguery and republican culture, 1890–1910*. Sussex: Sussex Academic Press.

Barr, R. (2019) Populism as a political strategy. In: de la Torre, C. (ed.) *The Routledge international handbook of global populism*. London-New York: Routledge, 44–57.

Berezin, M. (2017) On the construction sites of history: Where did Donald Trump come from? *American Journal of Cultural Sociology*, *5*(3), 322–337.

Braun, H. (1985) *The assassination of Gaitán: Public life and urban violence in Colombia*. Madison: University of Wisconsin Press.

Burbano de Lara, F. (2019) Populist waves in Latin America: Continuities, waves, and ruptures. In: de la Torre, C. (ed.) *The Routledge international handbook of global populism*. London-New York: Routledge, 435–451.

Casullo, M. E. (2019) How to become a leader: Identifying global repertoires for populist leadership. In: Stengel, F.A., MacDonald, D.B. and Nabers, D. (eds.) *Populism and world politics: Exploring inter- and transnational dimensions*, Cham: Palgrave, 55–73.

de la Torre, C. (1993) *La seducción velasquista*. Quito: FLACSO and Libri-Mundi.

de la Torre, C. (2019) Global populism: Histories, trajectories, problems, and challenges. In: de la Torre, C. (ed.) *The Routledge international handbook of global populism*. London-New York: Routledge, 1–29.

de la Torre, C. (2021) Charisma in Latin American politics. In: Zúquete, J. P. (ed.) *The Routledge international handbook of charisma*, London-New York: Routledge, 115–127.

de la Torre, C. and Srisa-Nga, T. (2021) *Global populisms*. London-New York: Routledge.

Eatwell, R. (2002) Charisma? The cases of Jean Marie Le Pen and Vladimir Zhirinovsky. *Totalitarian Movements and Political Religion, 3*(3), 1–23.

Garrido, M. (2017) Why the poor support populism: The politics of sincerity in Metro Manila. *American Journal of Sociology, 123*(3), 647–685.

Gerbaudo, P. (2019) *The digital party: Political organization and online democracy*. London: Pluto Press.

Germani, G. (1971) La integración de las masas a la vida política y el totalitarismo. In: Germani, G. *Política y Sociedad en una Época de Transición*. Buenos Aires: Editorial Paidós, 310–337.

Germani, G. (1978) *Authoritarianism, fascism, and national populism*. New Brunswick: Transaction Press.

Gerth, H. (1940) The Nazi party: Its leadership and composition. *American Journal of* Sociology, *45*(4), 517–541.

González Trejo, M. (2017) *Pueblo y democracia en el populismo venezolano*. PhD diss., Universidad Autónoma de Madrid.

Grint, K. (2014) Social constructionist analysis. In: Rhodes, R. A. W. and 't Hart, P. (eds.) *The Oxford handbook of political leadership*. Oxford: Oxford University Press, 240–252.

Heinisch, R. and Mazzoleni, O. (2016) *Understanding populist party organization: The radical right in Western Europe*. London: Palgrave.

Hochschild, A. (2016) *Strangers in their own land: A journey to the heart of our political divide*. New York: The New Press.

Hofstadter, R. (1955) *The age of reform*. New York: Alfred Knopf.

Kampwirth, K. (2010) Introduction. In: Kampwirth, K. (ed.) *Gender and populism in Latin America: Passionate politics*. University Park: University of Pennsylvania Press, 1–24.

Laclau, E. (1977) *Politics and ideology in Marxist theory*. London: Verso.

Laclau, E. (2005) *On populist reason*. London: Verso.

Lindholm, C. and Zúquete, P. (2010) *The struggle for the world: Liberation movements for the 21st century*. Stanford: Stanford University Press.

MacGregor Burns, G. (1978) *Leadership*. New York: Open Road Integrated Media.

Manin, B. (1997) *The principles of representative government*. Cambridge: Cambridge University Press.

Michelutti, L. (2017) We are all Chávez: Charisma as an embodied experience. *Latin American Perspectives, 44*(1), 232–250.

Moffitt, B. (2016) *The global rise of populism: Performance, political style, representation*. Stanford: Stanford University Press.

Mudde, C. (2004) The populist zeitgeist. *Government and Opposition*, 3(4), 541–563.

Mudde, C. and Rovira Kaltwasser, C. (2012) *Populism in Europe and the Americas*. Cambridge: Cambridge University Press.

Murmis, M. and Portantiero, J. C. (1971) *Estudios sobre los orígenes del peronismo*. Buenos Aires: Siglo XXI.

Ostiguy, P. (2017) Populism: A socio-cultural approach. In: Rovira Kaltwasser, C., Taggart, P., Ochoia Espejo, P. and Ostiguy, P. (eds.) *The Oxford handbook of populism*. Oxford: Oxford University Press, 73–97.

Ostiguy, P. and Moffitt, B. (2021) Who would identify with an "empty signifier"? The relational, performative approach to populism. In: Ostiguy, P., Panizza, F. and Moffitt, B. (eds.) *Populism in global perspective: A performative and discursive approach*. London-New York: Routledge, 47–73.

Panizza, F. (2013) What do we mean when we talk about populism? In: de la Torre, C. and Arnson, C. J. (eds.) *Latin American populism in the twenty-first century*. Baltimore-Washington, DC: The Johns Hopkins University Press and The Woodrow Wilson Centre Press, 85–117.

Pappas, T. S. (2019) *Populism and liberal democracy: A comparative and theoretical analysis*. Oxford: Oxford University Press.

Parsons, T. (1942a) Max Weber and the contemporary political crisis: The sociological analysis of power and authority structures. *The Review of Politics*, *4*(1), 61–76.

Parsons, T. (1942b) Some sociological aspects of the fascist movements. *Social Forces*, *21*(2), 138–147.

Parsons, T. (1955) Social strains in America. In: Bell, D. (ed.) *The new American right*. New York: Criterion Books, 117–141.

Roniger, L. (2019) The missing piece in global populism: The role populism played in Central America. In: de la Torre, C. (ed.) *The Routledge international handbook of global populism*. London-New York: Routledge, 451–467.

Sebreli, J. (2008) *Comediantes y mártires. Ensayos contra los mitos*. Buenos Aires: Editorial Debate.

Torres, A. (2009) *La herencia de la tribu: Del mito de la Independencia a la Revolución Bolivariana*. Caracas: Editorial ALFA.

Urbinati, N. (2019) *Me the people: How populism transforms democracy*. Cambridge, MA: Harvard University Press.

Weber, M. (1978) *Economy and society*. Berkeley: University of California Press.

Weyland, K. (2001) Clarifying a contested concept: Populism in the study of Latin American politics. *Comparative Politics*, *34*(1), 1–22.

Weyland, K. (2017) Populism: A political strategic approach. In: Rovira Kaltwasser, C., Taggart, P., Ochoia Espejo, P. and Ostiguy, P. (eds.) *The Oxford handbook of populism*. Oxford: Oxford University Press, 48–73.

Wolff, M. (2021) *Landslide: The final days of the Trump presidency*. New York: Henry Holt and Company.

Zúquete, J. P. (2007) *Missionary politics in contemporary Europe*. Syracuse: Syracuse University Press.

Zúquete, J. P. (2008) The missionary politics of Hugo Chavez. *Latin American Politics and Society*, *50*(1), 91–122.

CHAPTER 9

Labelling Parties as Populist? A Critical Appraisal and an Alternative Approach

Oscar Mazzoleni

1 Introduction

Despite the endless discussions over what populism is and how "best" to define it, the reason for labelling some parties as populist (and the way in which it is done) has not been the focus of in-depth reflection. The lack of attention to these conceptual issues reflects not only the marginal role of the debate regarding concept formation in social and political science but also the weak connections between the literature on populism and scholarship regarding party politics. However, the controversies about the definition of populism make it possible to open up the debate and tackle broader theoretical issues connected to concept formation (Outhwaite 1983; Sartori 1984; Gerring 1999; Goertz 2005). Addressing the issue of selecting and labelling populist parties can contribute to an epistemological, analytical, and normative discussion of how political phenomena should broadly be framed.

In pursuing three main goals, this chapter seeks to contribute to this debate. Firstly, it discusses the dominant approaches through which the so-called "populist parties" are selected and labelled. These approaches tend to conflate populism with party-based populism and legitimize the idea that selecting populist parties does not require an analytical definition of what a "populist party" is. Usually, populist parties are selected according to a definition of populism, along with a generic opinion by "observers", "scholars", or other actors who regard those parties as populist. This is the "circularity" paradox that Cas Mudde underlined some years ago: "We have to decide on the basis of which post facto criteria we should use to define the various parties, while we need a priori criteria to select the parties that we want to define" (2007, 12–13). Recently, a new methodological approach has attempted to overcome the circularity paradox, although it tends to remain essentialist as it neglects the observer's impact on the definition of populism and has a rather simplistic view of what a party is.

Secondly, the chapter tries to bridge the notion of populism with party politics literature by disentangling them from each other. Although there is a huge

 | DOI:10.1163/9789004679016_011

amount of literature on populist parties, what precisely a "populist party" is often remains unclear. While we know a lot about the *explanans* (e.g. its electoral basis), the *explanandum* is only occasionally tackled. Unfortunately, one of the characteristics that some academic publications share with journalism is the lack of a precise definition of concepts, for example, once "populist parties" are labelled as such (Mudde 1996, 226). A systematic analysis of recent publications in political science demonstrates that the prevalent use of the label populism – and, in particular, the populist party – does not go along with a precise definition of the concept of populism (Hunger and Paxton 2021, 11).

The reason for this odd situation is that scholars tend to blur the distinction between the concept of populism, on which there is an astonishing amount of literature, and party-based populism. In this chapter, we will argue that the definition of populism as such is not enough to define political parties conventionally labelled as populist. Our contribution will also show the relevance and the shortcomings of the recent literature seeking to define populist parties with quantitative methodologies. Despite their advances, these attempts do not consider the complexity of party organization but instead regard political parties as a unitary phenomenon.

Finally, this contribution allows an alternative, Max Weber-inspired approach of defining, selecting, and labelling parties. With this approach, we consider the multidimensionality of both populism and political parties. The crucial epistemological point is to abandon, in Weber's words, the "naturalistic prejudice" according to which concept reflects reality. Instead, concepts and theories should be considered as ideal types (i.e. approximate attempts to capture the complexity of reality). This means the multiple facets of political parties are not necessarily consistent with an overarching label of "populist party".

The chapter is organized as follows. The first section will examine the difficulty of coping with the tension between academic labelling and party self-labelling. Next, we will focus on the problem of concept reification, which is tied to the prevalent essentialist approach in populist party labelling. In the third section, we will highlight how the belief that academic work is untethered from the social and political environment has analytical and normative consequences for party labelling. In the fourth section, we consider how the dominant approaches of populist party labelling go along with a simplistic conception of political parties as a unitary entity. And in the final section, we will try to present an alternative approach to party-based populism based on Weber's ideal type by disentangling the notions of definition, selection, and labelling.

2 Between Labelling and Self-labelling

In the current literature on populism, the most controversial issue is how the concept of populism should be defined. And yet, the link between populism and party politics has rarely been discussed. According to Kenneth Roberts, "the study of populism and political parties has often been conducted along separate tracks that occasionally connect but never truly intertwine and enrich each other as they might, or more importantly, should" (2017, 287).

There are many reasons to explain the relative lack of interest in populist scholarship in political parties. The first relates to the various definitions of populism. Generally speaking, the populist scholarship interested in the content and form of messages, discourses, or performance (e.g. Moffitt 2016) tends to avoid the association with parties, as the focus is less on the characteristics of the actors and more on the message they spread. When it comes to an actor, however, the emphasis is more on the leaders than their parties. Scholars who conceive populism as an ideology tend to be concerned with a political party as a collective actor. Nevertheless, until recently, the literature focused on populist ideology has been interested more in studying electoral success or the impact of parties on the party system and government (e.g. Mudde 2007; Akkerman, De Lange and Rooduijn 2016; Inglehart and Norris 2019) and less in verifying how and to what extent political parties are populist.

The second important reason for the weak connections between populism and party politics research is that academics' selection and labelling of parties as populist do not reflect the labels the parties give to themselves. Parties presented as populist by scholars do not correspond to the official label of the party, nor to its manifesto. Perhaps the only exception is the People's Party in the United States in the late nineteenth century (e.g. Kazin 1995). Consequently, in Europe, Latin America, and the US, there is no agreement on either the choice of a label or the theoretical criteria that would justify calling a contemporary party "populist".

Of course, the multitude of definitions of concepts in social and political science is usual, and party populist labelling also reflects ongoing debates and controversies about the classification of political parties in general. A relevant issue relates to the categorization of parties within ideological families and the criteria that could permit including parties within a bounded party "family". When parties provide a relatively clear ideological supply, party classification is based on the name of the party, its statutes, and its manifesto. As Mair and Mudde argue (1998, 220), "the party itself is the best judge of its own ideological identity and that it will have reflected this identity in the name or label under which it chooses to contest elections". Of course, this kind of approach to party classification fits very well when it corresponds to the parties' ideological self-belonging and name (e.g. socialist, liberal, communist, or Christian democratic formations in Western Europe in the second part of the twentieth century, which corresponds to specific ideological families of parties).

However, the party's name is not always helpful, and difficulties arise if the different taxonomic criteria do not fit each other; for instance, this happens when the origins, ideology, transnational linkage, and policy orientation do not create a consistent configuration. In Western Europe, before the 1950s, there were some relevant cases where the link was less clear or rather contrasting. The most famous case is the National Socialist Party in Germany in the 1930s. However, in the past few decades, some "relevant" parties (according to Sartori's definition) characterizing West European party systems have also upended traditional party families, as in the cases of Forza Italia, led by former Prime Minister Silvio Berlusconi in Italy, and République en Marche headed by President Emmanuel Macron in France.

This difficulty to connect different taxonomic criteria also produces some ambivalences, including shortcomings about the so-called "populist parties". While party families in the party politics literature are usually tied to an ideological background (e.g. Mair and Mudde 1998), ideology is far from being the only criterion used to define populist parties. Cas Mudde (2004), who supports the definition of populism as a "thin-ideology", also seems sceptical about the idea of a specific European "populist family". It would be possible to recognize some consistency within the "populist radical right-wing parties" family in some regions (e.g. Jungar and Jupskås 2014) but not "populist parties" as such. At the same time, the "populist parties" label remains widespread in the literature, although often without a theoretical discussion on what precisely "populist" parties are (Hunger and Paxton 2021).

3 Essentialist Conceptualization

In current political science, there are two prevailing justifications for labelling a party as "populist": on the one hand, a supposed "public" or "expert" consensus and, on the other hand, scholars' supposedly rational assessment of the "nature" of the party. In both cases, scholars do not engage with clear and transparent empirical selection and labelling processes based on theoretical assumptions and hypotheses to discuss and analyze whether (or to what extent) a particular party is populist, not populist, or only partially populist. Widespread opinions or the "nature" of the party itself seems sufficient to select and label a "populist party" as such.

Shortcomings are connected not only to operationalization (e.g. biases in the selection of experts) but also to concept formation, that is, epistemological issues. As Meijers and Zaslove (2020, 378) point out, the most important stream of literature devoted to populist parties is based on a dichotomic classificatory perspective inspired by Giovanni Sartori's (1984) conceptualization. In fact, the dominant approach in populist party labelling tends to adopt a naturalist or essentialist conceptualization (Fuchs 2001; Bevir and Kedar 2008).

First of all, it implies a *reification* effect of party labelling as populist. The rigid opposition between "populist" and "non-populist" parties stipulates that some parties are "essentially" populist. According to essentialism, populist parties are characterized by core or stable features conceptually defining them as such, and these traits are independent of context: "[W]e do need, ultimately, 'universal' categories – concepts which are applicable to any time and place" (Sartori 1970, 1035). Essentialism implies that meanings and actions are not historically and geographically specific; consequently, a single minimal definition of populism is supposed to travel without worries among time and space, thereby allowing comparative analysis across regions and continents. In this regard, a reflection on the possibility that the significance of some aspects of populism varies across contexts – e.g. the meaning of the "people" and the "elites", but also the role of the leader (see de la Torre and Srisa-nga 2022) – is seen as a problem for the universal validity of the concept. Likewise, essentialist approaches do not care about the variation and contingent features of the party organization as they assume its nature is somewhat stable (e.g. based on an overarching ideological background), while party change is seen as evolutionary and following precise rules or steps. However, labelling parties as "populist" with this perspective risks neglecting the situatedness of the populist grievances expressed and performed by parties and, consequently, the changing meaning and relevance of populism across localities, regions, and countries.

Essentialism poses but does not fix the problem of the "border", that is, the distinction between the "true" populist party and a not really "populist" party. This is an epistemological and normative but also an empirical issue. In the context of populist protests growing and becoming widespread across a shifting party system, attempts to distinguish between populist and mainstream parties become rather tricky (e.g. Akkerman, De Lange and Rooduijn 2016; Blokker and Anselmi 2020; Weyland 2021). If we take these traits into account, it seems difficult to empirically substantiate why some parties are populist while others are definitively not (at all) populist. The problem is also linked to the fact that populism is not just a concept defined by the academic community, but is part of the world that scholars are supposed to study objectively.

4 Where Does the Populist Label Come From?

Essentialism implies that political actors and the public do not participate in the construction of the object of the analysis. It is assumed that the scholar does not contribute to the definition of observed reality. However, it is not enough to say that scholars are independent or refuse a prescriptive approach to escaping social and political influences, especially once scholars use a controversial notion such as populism.

However, party populist labelling is not just an academic activity. The notion of populism is widespread in the public sphere and the media. Scholars who adopt an essentialist approach to party populist labelling treat themselves as independent observers and pretend that their social or political roots do not influence their academic work, while the latter does not perform the political reality. This perspective implicitly views academia as a separate and autonomous world relative to the public controversies and political struggles. However, the role of the observer is crucial in social and political science and concept building (Collier and Adcock 1999).

On the one hand, what happens in the public sphere influences scholars, including those who believe in "value-free" science. The issue becomes particularly challenging when academic labels adopt a language that serves as a point of reference and makes sense in a universe that goes well beyond the scientific field and extends to the political realm and the media. As shown by a growing body of literature, populism is also a political and media weapon. Given its global success in recent years, populism has been "hyped" by journalism and in party competition (Glynos and Mondon 2019). Recent studies show that labelling a party as populist represents a strong rhetoric resource able to undermine party competitors (Brown and Mondon 2021; Casiraghi 2021). Media broadcasts also used to adopt "populism" to target oppositional or anti-establishment parties, thereby boosting the legitimacy of mainstream parties (Brown and Mondon 2021). Academic labelling is at risk of being instrumentalized by the media and in election campaigns. However, scholars rarely recognize the necessity of comparing their own definition of populism and populism as a public label, for instance, as the latter might influence how this label is utilized in the academic sphere.

On the other hand, because of the public visibility of academic knowledge, scholars also participate in public debates and the construction of party labelling. They contribute to performing the public perception of the party, that is, confirming its political "legitimacy" or "illegitimacy". When identifying some parties as "populist", scholars play a role in constructing parties' public image (Dean and Maiguashca 2020). Thus, when scholars label parties as "populist", they tend to avoid any normative and performative issue related to labelling them as such (but see Stavrakakis 2017; De Cleen, Glynos and Mondon 2018). However, tough academic scholarship is nowadays virtually globalized and scholars always work in a specific cultural, political, and linguistic context (Goodin and Tilly 2006).

Of course, not every scholar shares the belief in value-free science and considers it problematic to be involved in political struggles. The normative connotation of populism and its public use is not necessarily evaluated as a "danger". Some scholars engage in militant approaches to populism and, accordingly, identify some parties as populist because of what they deem to be "demagogues", "anti-democrats", or opponents of a fragile representative democracy. Militant approaches shape at least two opposing camps. While scholars argue that populism is a threat to democracy and emphasize the populist component of radical right or extreme parties, others consider populism to be an emancipatory claim at the grassroots level and tend to connect the concept of populism to egalitarian and progressive parties while leaving out exclusionary far-right parties. Why not, if we accept that political science should be militant or policy oriented? However, not all scholars accept being part of the public struggle around populism or being a supporter or opponent of some "populist" parties. More broadly, the lack of normative awareness and a clear analytical definition of what a political party is reduces the heuristic strength of populist labelling.

5 Party Complexity

The separation between the study of populism and political parties has at least three consequences: the tendency to conflate populism with party-based populism, the reduction of the party to its ideology or discourse, and the conception that designates parties as homogenous. Because the issue of the party as an organization is rarely taken up,[1] once the party is labelled as populist, the question of what the party is remains a theoretical reflection. Reductionism can be seen as a conventionalist or pragmatic approach. This is a result of some routines in political research in party ideology (e.g. in the Manifesto Project), which assumes the party's official discourse or ideology – for instance, spread by the national leader and usually based on electoral manifestos – is implicitly

1 For an exception, see Heinisch and Mazzoleni (2016); Albertazzi and Van Kessel (2021).

shared by all of its members. Those perspectives have relevant consequences for party populist labelling.

Populist scholarship – especially from the western part of the European continent – has been largely interested in studying party-based populism and often avoided the mainstream legacies of party studies by adopting a simplistic (and rather non-realist) conception of political parties. One of the oldest issues in party politics literature is what political parties are in general and how they are peculiar concerning factions or associations, with a focus on their "functions" as political socialization, elite recruitment, and electoral competition. However, scholars in the sub-field of party politics have started to recognize that relevant political parties are heterogeneous in terms of organization, networking, (national and local) leadership, activism, sympathizers, and voters. As usual in democratic regimes in different regions of the world, enduring political parties are moulded by internal diversity – for instance, between parties in public office, the party's central office, and the party on the ground, as well as informal networks (Levitsky 2001; 2003; Katz and Mair 2002; Hellmann 2011). Moreover, to some degree, parties are shaped by intra-party factionalism and characterized by variations in their constituencies (Janda 1980; Boucek 2009).

Parties with massive numbers of followers have social and territorial roots and shape party systems, parliaments, and governments, and their ideological stances cannot reduce their official supply. For decades, scholarship has focused on Western European democracies that were used to adopting an evolutionary party model approach and, to the same extent, avoided the relevance of the context. Moreover, recent trends in party politics literature tend to underscore the limitations of the dominant evolutionary models' approach, clearly showing how the general criteria of classification are inadequate to frame the current party complexity across liberal democracies in Western countries and beyond (Scarrow 2014; Mazzoleni and Heinisch 2023). While there is a tension between attempts to develop an overarching classification of parties based on models or ideologies, there has been a growing awareness that each party and their intra-party dynamics are peculiar, also with regard to the strong advances that have been made in data collection (e.g. Döring and Regel 2019).

Longstanding political parties might refer to a virtually singular political ideology (or, better, a doctrine), but how the ideological claims are expressed is a matter of empirical research. As there are many reasons to engage with a party and different interests in doing politics (e.g. grassroots activism and party elites), how and to what extent political parties share "populism" (discourse, ideology, etc.) should not be taken for granted. To capture party ideology, should we consider the manifesto or the speeches of the leader or the party's MPs? There is more and more interest in classifying parties as populist with a quantitative perspective based on manifestos and speeches by leaders (e.g. Hawkins 2009; Meijers and Zaslove 2020; Di Cocco and Monechi 2022). The strength of this literature lies in overcoming one of the main shortcomings of the current literature, namely the "circularity paradox", since they include all parties and adopt a gradation approach. However, other problems arise. Is it possible to classify a party as populist based on two or three texts? When the results of a big data comparative analysis appear counter-intuitive and clearly contradict significant streams of literature – for instance, deeming Sweden Democrats, Farage and Beppe Grillo as non-populist (Hawkins and Castanho Silva 2018) – what should we conclude? And, finally, this literature assumes that parties are unitary entities and, therefore, overlooks the possibility of a multifaceted phenomenon.

6 An Alternative Approach

How do scholars fix the challenges of party selection and labelling? Because of the lack of congruence between academic labelling and part self-labelling, scholarship is usually embedded in a "circular paradox", which it tries to fix by reifying the concept and avoiding the role of the observers in performing party labelling, the situatedness of any political reality, and the normative issues related to labelling. Classifying and labelling a party as populist is far from a simple analytical or pragmatic act.

Against an essentialist and naturalist approach, one alternative is a relational perspective based on a Weberian ideal type. Weber argues against what he calls "naturalistic prejudice", that is, the belief that theoretical constructs can portray the "true" content and essence of historical and political reality (1949, 94). This is precisely what essentialist approaches hope to find out. Within those approaches, the main concern is to find a good definition of the concept based on operational or instrumental criteria, including the detection of anomalies, the lists of shared attributes, and new parties supposed to be classified into the populist "family". Instead, in a relational approach, populism turns into contingent outcomes and multifaceted accomplishments. Whether a party "is" populist is not a good question; the question should be whom it exists for, when, to what extent, and under which conditions.

Bridging a relation perspective with Weber's legacy implies, above all, an ideal-typical definition of populism and, accordingly, a distinctive attention of situational contingencies and complexities. This approach assumes parties as associations with ideological supply but is also shaped by different organizational patterns with factional logics and characterized by individuals and groups with different interests and strategies and, consequently, different styles of communication. Thus, in the intellectual process that scholars use to classify political parties as populist, we can analytically distinguish four moments: defining populism, defining the party, selecting the party, and labelling the party:

1. *Defining populism* as an ideal type implies developing it as a theoretical construct that is approximate and "cannot be found empirically anywhere in reality" (Weber 1949, 90). An ideal-type is a guide for constructing hypotheses. Populism (e.g. as an ideological stance, a discourse, a style, etc.) should be distinct from party-based populism. An ideal-typical definition of populism can be more or less "minimalist", "hybrid", or "focus-oriented". The well-known minimalist definition is, of course, the ideological one, and "hybrid" is a combination of different definitions available in the literature, while "focus-oriented" definitions address populism in connection with dimensions such as economics or culture. The question here is not to define the "good" definition irrespective of time and space but to develop it with clarity and consistency (Gerring 1999) in maintaining it as provisional and focused on specific aspects of the reality.
2. *Defining the party.* The second step aimed at labelling a party as "populist" has to take into account the definition of the political party as such or, more precisely, with an ideal-typical definition of a political party. To take party complexity seriously, scholars might assume that the "populist party" concept does not necessarily correspond to empirical reality. Thus, an ideal-typical party-based populist perspective can fruitfully deal with party politics literature. For instance, inspired by Kurt Weyland's strategic conceptualization (2001), a populist party could ideally be defined as a charismatic party, that is, the leader-centred party organization highlighted by the seminal contribution of Angelo Panebianco (1988). At the same time, as a guide for empirical research, an ideal type approach deals with concrete parties that are heterogeneous in terms of their organization, networking, (national and local) leadership, activism, sympathizers, and voters. Definitions of populism in the scholarship embrace discursive and ideological components, and organizational dimensions are also part of the debate, although the reflections and results emanating from party politics scholarship rarely contribute to populist literature.
3. *Selecting the party*. This marks a specific moment when single parties are (tentatively) identified. Based on ideal-typical features, the selection should be done according to quantitative and qualitative data and by critically considering party complexity. Scholars face a choice: on the one

hand, selecting parties that parts of international or national opinion consider somewhat "populist" or, on the other hand, adopting a systemic approach that looks at a party system and finds to what extent populist traits are more or less shared by single parties (e.g. Jagers and Walgrave 2007). To some extent, this second option offers a way to fix the circularity paradox. Moreover, where populist stances are supposed to be widespread across parties, the second strategy seems to be a logical solution from an empirical point of view as well.

4. *Labelling the party* is the third moment when the selected party can be classified as populist or a party with populist components. Within the context of the growing public and political use of populism as a signifier (i.e. as a political weapon), a thoughtful perspective should be developed – also in connection with the so-called "non-populist parties" with which "populist parties" are confronted. Here we assume that scientific language is not distinct from the public labelling in which political and media actors are the main players. However, using an ideal-typical definition of populism and populist parties, we provisionally clarify our point of view over reality. It seems better not to label single political parties but rather facets of the political party as "populist". Given the changing intra-party diversity, populist ideology, discourse, and style are not necessarily shared by all the party components. Consequently, the "populist party" label should be provisionally adopted and confirmed by its ideal-typical definition and how the latter is embodied by the party among its different components.

7 A Conceptual Approximation

What are the advantages of an ideal-typical approach? First of all, it contrasts the belief that there is a kind of "essence" in populist parties. Populism as a party label is a relational construct influenced by the political and media environment, as well as the definition adopted by different "schools" of scholarship. Recognizing this fact allows scholars to develop a critical self-reflection about their own role in performing stigmatization or valourization of political parties in relation to political struggles. These struggles are always – at least in part – academic struggles. Words and language are not simply a means of communication but are inherent to political struggles and strategies. The public categorization of political actors as populists plays a role in the symbolic construction of political reality and, consequently, of the political parties (Edelman 1977, 23–41).

An ideal-typical approach might be useful to classify not only oppositional parties but also parties in contexts where populist discourse or style is not purely a matter of oppositional or fringe parties, and the populist label can be used as a weapon in the public sphere. This is also the case where mainstream parties are ideologically amorphous and have an ever-changing profile beyond traditional ideologies and styles of communication, and the so-called "populist parties" achieve strong institutional success, as is currently the case in Europe and elsewhere. An ideal-typical approach favours a gradational analysis. An increasing amount of research has noted that populism is also shared by mainstream parties that adopt populist aspects, even if they are rarely labelled as populist (e.g. Rodi 2018). An ideal-typical approach that assumes that reality virtually never corresponds to the concept is also an advantage for the gradational approach, although current versions, including those using "automatic" methodologies, provide reductionist wisdom of political parties. (e.g. Di Cocco and Monechi 2022).

There is another advantage to an ideal-typical approach that relates to the definition of populist and its analytical use. Many scholars are worried that there is not a consensus over a single and universal definition; consequently, the concept of populism is seen as problematic. With a concept of populism as an ideal type, each definition is taken as provisional and as approximate with respect to the complex. The plurality of the definition of populism is an opportunity for understanding different facets of reality. The definitions of populism are not mutually exclusive (e.g. Ernst et al. 2019; Bobba and Seddone 2022).

8 Conclusion

The primary aim of this chapter was to focus on the limits of the current scholarship approaches in political science that label parties as "populist". While the current controversies over populism usually focus on what this notion means and how it is adopted in empirical analysis, this chapter discussed an issue rarely considered in academic literature, namely why and how some parties are labelled as "populist". The question might appear irrelevant to empirical research, as the usual mainstream approaches tend to avoid complicated discussions about the selection of a party and justifying the way it is labelled. Of course, political scientists are usually interested in analyzing the rise, success, and consequences of so-called populist parties. In the past few decades, some specific parties – in particular, in Western European countries – have become points of reference, and scholars recognize them as a research opportunity precisely because they have been labelled as "populist parties". The advantage of avoiding labelling as an issue is to avoid anomalies that enhance populism as an academic sub-field.

However, the question as to whether some parties should be labelled as populist is crucial for analytical, epistemological, and normative reasons. The so-called "populist parties" never used to adopt the label of "populist" in their statutes (and rarely in public discourse) to categorize themselves. Moreover, scholars struggle to resolve the circularity paradox, namely that the selection of parties is based on a criterion that is not yet precisely defined. Mainstream strategies tend to legitimize an a priori populist party selection by avoiding any empirical verification in terms of selection and labelling.

These issues raise normative concerns. Often the scholarship is not aware that the label of "populist party" is part of a political struggle. By producing and disseminating this discourse, scholars participate in a labelling process that is also a polemical weapon, especially when dealing with parties associated with current "hot button" issues that heighten dramatization in politics and the media. While contributing to the public labelling of the party, scholars tend to confirm or challenge its political legitimacy or its image as a "public enemy" (Edelman 1988, 66–69). Although it is difficult to hypothesize a unilateral causal relation between scientific and sociopolitical worlds, the scientific labelling of political parties clearly depends on the universe of meaning and representation shaped by public actors, including party leaders and journalists.

To deal with these shortcomings, the chapter illustrated a critical approach based on three features: Firstly, it distinguished populism from party-based populism, as the latter should consider the peculiar complexity of parties in terms of their intra-party dynamics, their relationship with the party system and government, and variations in time and space. From this point of view, populist scholarship has to take party-based populist analysis seriously and look beyond a reified wisdom of parties as homogenous entities.

Secondly, this alternative approach implies a provisional selection of "populist parties" through a relational approach based on ideal types and inspired by a Weberian perspective. This means that discourse, ideology, and style are seen as crucial to party selection, depending on how the party ideal type is defined. Only with an empirical investigation would it be possible to know how and to what extent each party corresponds to this ideal type. The notion of populism cannot travel in time and space without considering the contextual dimensions shaping its meaning and relevance. If the "populist" description of a party is not verified and becomes a taken-for-granted selected object, it limits the capacity to understand the phenomenon.

The act of selecting some parties as "populist" should be taken as an issue and not an assumption. Selecting a particular party does not necessarily imply it is labelled as a "populist party", since parties that are not populist also have populist strategies, discourses, styles, and/or ideologies. While it is difficult to assume that a party is either "populist" or not without empirical analysis, it is also unlikely that all components of the party are consistent with the populist discourse or ideology. By assuming populism and parties as ideal types within a relational approach, populism defines one or more components of a single party rather than a notion embracing the party as a whole.

The approach presented in this chapter aims to contribute to a new research agenda that can boost populist scholarship and connect with recent streams in party politics literature concerned with party complexity. This also makes it possible to connect the debate in social and political sciences on concept formation, in particular with relational and constructivist approaches to concepts and theories pointing to a changing and complex reality.

References

Akkerman, T., De Lange, S. L. and Rooduijn, M. (eds.) (2016) *Radical right-wing populist parties in Western Europe*. London-New York: Routledge.

Albertazzi, D. and Kessel, S. (2021). Right-Wing Populist Party Organisation Across Europe: The Survival of the Mass-Party? Conclusion to the Thematic Issue, *Politics and Governance*, 9 (4), 365–370.

Bevir, M. and Kedar, A. (2008) Concept formation in political science: An anti-naturalist critique of qualitative methodology. *Perspectives on Politics*, 6(3), 503–517.

Blokker, P. and Anselmi, M. (2020) *Multiple populisms: Italy as democracy's mirror*. London-New York: Routledge.

Bobba, G. and Seddone, A. (2022) Between the ideological and communicative approaches: Hard and soft populism in France and Italy. *Representation*, *58*(1), 49–66.

Boucek, F. (2009) Rethinking factionalism: Typologies, intra-party dynamics and three faces of factionalism. *Party Politics*, *15*(4), 455–485.

Brown, K. and Mondon, A. (2021) Populism, the media, and the mainstreaming of the far right: *The Guardian*'s coverage of populism as a case study. *Politics*, *41*(3), 279–295.

Casiraghi, M. C. (2021) "You're a populist! No, you are a populist!": The rhetorical analysis of a popular insult in the United Kingdom, 1970–2018. *The British Journal of Politics and International Relations*, *23*(4), 555–575.

Collier, D. and Adcock, R. (1999) Democracy and dichotomies: A pragmatic approach to choices about concepts. *Annual Review of Political Science*, *2*, 537–565.

Dean, J. and Maiguashca, B. (2020) Did somebody say populism? Towards a renewal and reorientation of populism studies. *Journal of Political Ideologies*, *25*(1), 11–27.

De Cleen, B., Glynos, J. and Mondon, A. (2018) Critical research on populism: Nine rules of engagement. *Organization, 25*(5), 649–661.

de la Torre, C. and Srisa-nga T. (2022) *Global populism*. London-New York: Routledge.

Di Cocco, J. and Monechi, B. (2022) How populist are parties? Measuring degrees of populism in party manifestos using supervised machine learning. *Political Analysis, 30*(3), 311–327.

Döring, H. and Regel, S. (2019) Party facts: A database of political parties worldwide. *Party Politics, 25*(2), 97–109.

Edelman, M. (1977) *Political language: Words that succeed and policies that fail*. New York: Academic Press.

Edelman, M. (1988) *Constructing the political spectacle*. Chicago: University of Chicago Press.

Ernst, N., Blassnig, S., Engesser, S., Büchel, F. and Esser, F. (2019) Populists prefer social media over talk shows: An analysis of populist messages and stylistic elements across six countries. *Social Media + Society, 5*(1).

Fuchs, S. (2001) *Against essentialism: A theory of society and culture*. Cambridge, MA: Harvard University Press.

Gerring, J. (1999) What makes a concept good? A criterial framework for understanding concept formation in the social sciences. *Polity, 31*(3), 357–393.

Glynos, J. and Mondon, A. (2019) The political logic of populist hype: The case of right-wing populism's "meteoric rise" and its relation to the status quo. In: Cossarini, P. and Vallespin, F. (eds.) *Populism and passions*. London-New York: Routledge, 82–101.

Goertz, G. (2005) *Social science concepts: A user's guide*. Princeton: Princeton University Press.

Hawkins, K. A. (2009) Is Chávez populist? Measuring populist discourse in comparative perspective. *Comparative Political Studies, 42*(8), 1040–1067.

Hawkins, K. A. and Castanho Silva, B. (2018) Textual analysis: Big data approaches. In: Hawkins, K. A., Carlin, R. E., Littvay, L. and Rovira Kaltwasser, C. (eds.) *The ideational approach to populism: Concept, theory, and analysis*. London-New York: Routledge, 27–47.

Heinisch, R. and Mazzoleni, O. (2016) *Understanding populist party organisation: The radical right in Western Europe*. London: Palgrave.

Hellmann, O. (2011) *Political parties and electoral strategy: The development of party organization in East Asia*. New York. Palgrave Macmillan.

Hunger, S. and Paxton, F. (2021) What's in a buzzword? A systematic review of the state of populism research in political science. *Political Science Research and Methods*, online first.

Inglehart, R. and Norris, P. (2019) *Cultural backlash: Trump, Brexit, and authoritarian populism*. Cambridge: Cambridge University Press.

Jagers, J. and Walgrave, S. (2007) Populism as political communication style: An empirical study of political parties' discourse in Belgium. *European Journal of Political Research*, *46*(3), 319–345.

Janda, K. (1980) A comparative analysis of party organization: The United States, Europe, and the World. In: Crotty, W. (eds.) *The party symbol: Readings on political parties*. San Francisco: W. H. Freeman, 339–348.

Jungar, A.-C. and Jupskås, A. R. (2014) Populist radical right parties in the Nordic region: A new and distinct party family? *Scandinavian Political Studies*, *37*(3), 215–238.

Katz, R. S. and Mair, P. (2002) The ascendancy of the party in public office: Party organizational change in twentieth-century democracies. In: Gunther, R., Montero, J. R. and Linz, J. J. (eds.) *Political parties: Old concepts and new challenges*. Oxford: Oxford University Press, 113–135.

Kazin, M. (1995) *The populist persuasion*. Ithaca: Cornell University Press.

Levitsky, S. (2001) An "organised disorganisation": Informal organisation and the persistence of local party structures in Argentine Peronism. *Journal of Latin American Studies*, *33*(1), 29–66.

Levitsky, S. (2003) *Transforming labor-based parties in Latin America: Argentine Peronism in a comparative perspective*. Cambridge: Cambridge University Press.

Mair, P. and Mudde, C. (1998) The party family and its study. *Annual Review of Political Science*, *1*(1), 211–229.

Mazzoleni, O. and Heinisch, R. (2023) Party change beyond the classical models? The role of agency, context, and democracy. In: Carter, N., Keith, D., Sindre, G. and Vasilopoulou, S. (eds.) *The Routledge handbook of political parties*. London-New York: Routledge, 10–25.

Meijers, M. J. and Zaslove, A. (2020) Measuring populism in political parties: Appraisal of a new approach. *Comparative Political Studies*, *54*(2), 372–407.

Moffitt, B. (2016) The global rise of populism: Performance, political style, and representation. Redwood: Stanford University Press.

Mudde, C. (1996) The war of the words: The defining of the extreme right party family, *West European Politics*, 19(2), 225–248.

Mudde, C. (2004) The Populist Zeitgeist, *Government and Opposition*, 39(4), 541–563.

Mudde, C. (2007) *Populist radical right parties in Europe*. Cambridge: Cambridge University Press.

Outhwaite, W. (1983) *Concept formation in social science*. London-New York: Routledge.

Panebianco (1988) *Political parties: Organization and power. Cambridge:* Cambridge University Press.

Roberts, K. (2017) Populism and party politics In: Rovira Kaltwasser, C., Taggart, P., Ochoia Espejo, P. and Ostiguy, P. (eds.) *The Oxford handbook of populism*. Oxford: Oxford University Press, 387–304.

Rodi, P. (2018) Populist political communication going mainstream? The influence of populist parties on the discursive strategies of mainstream centre-left political parties in Western Europe. In: Diamond, P. (ed.) *The crisis of globalisation: Democracy, capitalism and inequality in the industrialised world.* London: Bloomsbury, 53–72.

Sartori, G. (1970) Concept misformation in comparative politics. *The American Political Science Review, 64*(4), 1033–1053.

Sartori, G. (ed.) (1984) *Social science concepts: A systematic analysis.* Beverly Hills: Sage.

Scarrow, S. (2014) *Beyond party members: Changing approaches to partisan mobilization.* Oxford: Oxford University Press.

Stavrakakis, Y. (2017) How did "populism" become a pejorative concept? And why is this important today? A genealogy of double hermeneutics. POPULISMUS working paper, no. 6.

Weber, M. (1949) *The methodology of social sciences.* Glencoe: Free Press.

Weyland, K. (2001) Clarifying a contested concept: Populism in the study of Latin American politics. *Comparative Politics, 34*(1), 1–22.

Weyland, K. (2021) How populism corrodes Latin American parties. *Journal of Democracy, 32*(4), 42–55.

Index

Printed in the United States
by Baker & Taylor Publisher Services